"A CLOSER WALK–
The Chad Clark Story"

by

Charee Clark

"A Closer Walk"
The Chad Clark Story

ISBN: 978-0-9837334-3-0

http://www.entrywaypublishing.com

For information contact:
VicToria Freudiger, Editor-in-Chief
And Publishing Director
editorshepherd@gmail.com
972-517-6513
Linda T. Phillips, Cover Designer

Printed in the United States of America

"A CLOSER WALK
The Chad Clark Story"

Dedication by Charee Clark

As you will learn within the text of "the Chad Clark Story," my eldest son, Chad was involved in a horrific accident. His accident happened on my Grandmother, Gladys McCrossen's birthday – July 29. The year was 2007 and it is my belief my Grandma was one of Chad's guardian angels at the time of the accident. She has been his guardian ever since and therefore I would like to dedicate this book in the memory of my Grandmother, Gladys McCrossen.

Thank you Grandma, for teaching me the true meaning of love, and for showing me how precious my children really are in God's eyes. Thank you also for taking me to church when I was little and for you and Grandpa always making sure you knew I believed in God.

My Grandfather, Harold and Grandmother, Gladys were married for 50 years. Harold died on May 7, 1985 just

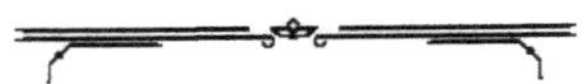

three months before my husband, Scott and I were married. I remember my Grandfather telling me when he met Scott that "he was the one!" Gladys died on May 16, 2000. I believe that when two people are married to each other that long, that when one passes, the other one dies of a broken heart and I believe that's what my Grandmother finally died of. Their anniversary was May 1st.

Grandma got to see all of my children before she passed. Though she was able to spend time with them, Grandpa never did get a chance to see any of my children. My heart aches for that because I know he would have been so proud of how Scott and I raised them with strictness and love. And I believe with my whole heart that Grandpa Harold would have been very proud of how we handled Chad's motorcycle accident. Both of my grandparents would have loved how we turned to God instead of turning away, and that's all because of how he spent so much time in my life telling me about God and his love for me.

To Kayla, my little 'punkin head'. I want to say I am so proud to be your Mom! You have made me so proud. You have been there to help your father and me whenever we needed you and along the way, you have never complained. I am so sorry for the times you needed me and I couldn't be there for you. You have been there for your brother when he needed you most. *Yes*, even though you told me not to bring Chad home from the hospital if he was a brother you have become such a huge part of him

getting to where he is today. I wish you a lifetime of love and happiness. No child has made their parents any prouder than how proud you have made dada and me. We love you so much!

To Chad, you are my hero! You my son are the true definition of a hero! There are no words I could ever try to even think of to explain this long journey you have taken us all on. I know now why I chose the name Chad for you because it means 'God's warrior'. I am so proud of your determination to fight this fight; not just to fight but to win! You are a huge influence and a great example to your siblings. I know this long journey with me has been long and hard, but out of all the kids, you were the one I knew could come through and fight all the trials and turmoil you have been through since your accident. It has been an honor not a chore to care for you and help you. For as long as I live, I will never forget what we have all shared together as a journey. It has been special to share the moments - good and bad - that we shared together! I love you 'my Chatters'!

To Kaitlyn, you are the definition of everything good in my life. You have been glued to my side from the day you were born, and I beamed with pride as I

watched you become independent without me, as you had no choice when your brother's accident happened. As a young girl, you learned how to cook and clean and do the laundry. As a young teen, you were there to care and hold

Kaycee and Noah when we couldn't. Now, you have grown to be a fine beautiful young women and all of our trials have served to make you stronger. I love you 'Christine', keep being who you are, the kind, carefree and forgiving woman we know and love today.

To Kaycee, you are everything and more my little 'Roni'. You, sweet daughter are the child that parents could ask for. I know I tease you about being Chad's partner in crime, but I am so glad and thankful that you two are close. I prayed and worked so hard to keep all of you kids close and loving toward one another and it has paid off immensely. The thing I am most proud of in you is your faith in God. Remember, you are so strong and you are well liked in this world by many. Also, you are strong and stubborn. You are the spitting image of me, so sorry little girl. You have helped me carry my faith through in this storm more than you even know! I am so sorry your two times you were on Queens Court in high school that Daddy and I weren't there 100% for you, but you gotta know if this hadn't happened with Chad you would have been #1, right at the top! WE are so, so proud of you! I love you with my whole heart and then some! You keep going my 'little Shamrock baby!'

To Noah, or 'Fip', as you like to call yourself, I am so sorry your childhood got ripped away from you. I went in to the hospital with Chad one evening when you were a small child and when we came home you were bigger than me! Where did the time go? I am so very proud that you also kept your faith. I am so proud that you took over Chad's jobs such as getting in the wood for the wood burner, and doing his chores around our home to help our family out, such as changing the oil and brakes etc… on our vehicles. Thank you for helping to pick Chad up when he fell, and doing all the things you do to help me care for him. You will always be my 'little Harold'. Now I know the reason I called you that when you were little; I thought at the time it was because you looked like the Harold character in *Harold And The Purple Crayon*. However, you are so much like your Great-Grandfather who had the kindest heart and a love for the Lord, and that's just how you are today.

Because of you, a piece of my Grandpa will always be with me and he would have been so proud of you also! I am so sorry I couldn't be there for all your classroom parties in elementary schools. It hurts me more than you know to have to of missed that. You were my last little one and I did all those things with the other four and you got left out because of this horrible accident. And I am so, so sorry.

At last, to my wonderful, amazing husband Scott, I love you and cannot believe you and I have lived a life where our son had to bear such a horrific accident. And it is so hard to believe this happened to us. We never planned for this and this is not how our married life was first envisioned by us…

but, the events and all we have endured have only made our marriage stronger. A good many marriages fall apart in a time like this...however, our marriage didn't fall apart. Everything we have gone through served to bring the two of us closer. You were my rock and I thank God every day that you were there for me. Thank you for praying with me to save our son. Thank you for your hard work in providing for us and for the love and support you give each and every one of us. I believe with my whole heart that God is healing our boy, and he will walk again someday. Thank you for putting up with me and my grumpiness and all of the time I put into writing this book. I know that you will join me in praying that we hope that "Chad's Story" – this book - helps many people; but it helps just that one person, that would make the work worth every bit of my effort. It breaks my heart to see you struggle with feeling guilty about doing things with Noah outside knowing Chad is watching you, and I know you feel guilty about making Chad go get wood with you that day before his accident when he didn't want to, but my love, you have to let that guilt go. It's not your fault. And I hold no anger or hate toward you for letting Chad have that motorcycle. I know you love our boy and that you and Chad are really close. I'm sad to see your pain knowing that the two of you used to do everything together and that you miss those times. But God is so in control, and he loves you more than you could ever imagine. You have taught our children so much! Each one of us is so blessed to have you in our lives. You have been the best dad and husband a person could ask for; so, I say thank you and I wouldn't have wanted a different life and I wouldn't trade one thing or do anything different and I am proud to be your wife! The best is yet to come! I promise you that!

The Scott Clark Family
Chad, Charee, Scott, Kayla, Kaitlyn, Kaycee and Noah
and the family pet, Bear

Table of Contents

“A CLOSER WALK–
The Chad Clark Story”

Chapter One – Accidents Do Happen

On July 29, 2007, my world, as I had known it, crashed to the ground and life, as I knew it, was about to change forever.

It was a typical Sunday afternoon; we had gone to church, as always on Sunday mornings. On all of our minds that day was the fact that my oldest son, Chad's mind had been set on purchasing a new motorcycle. Not able to discard the idea of buying a new bike, and out of a particular excitement, he bought it Thursday before his accident. He had been working in our family business extra long hours all summer long so that if an opportunity arose he could take care of his own 'wants'.

Our life and especially Chad's life, however, was forever changed on July 29th. Though I can still see his face all full of pride, just beaming from ear to ear while he stood showing the family his new *ride*! Who would have ever thought such happiness could turn into such a horrible disaster. I would have never in a million years believed our circumstances would, or even could, have turned out like they did.

~

The following Saturday morning of that same week, Chad and my husband, Scott had gone to get Chad certified and get the endorsement on his license. These two did everything together and this was just one more thing added to their list of adventures for that day. Everything seemed fine. As they walked into the door, huge smiles on both of their faces told me things were indeed perfect! My husband, Scott and Chad were going on and on about what happened and each of them shared the news that Chad had passed his tests! Oh, the joy they had! Me too, even though I was like every other typical mother worried about the motorcycle and all the possibilities of someone getting hurt. Like they were going to listen to me, after all, I was just another worrywart and a female to boot!

Then Sunday came and so did Chad's motorcycle accident. If only we had just known that the very next day would bring about a change in Chad's life and ours as well. Little did I know that God had been preparing me for all that I was about to endure on this day.

Chad who had bugged my husband and me to ride this new motorcycle to church that morning, pulled out of the parking lot before us. As I looked up to his face, which was full of pride about his new purchase, a feeling came over me and fear set in right away. Right there in the church parking lot and suddenly, without thinking, I said to the rest of my family in our van, "You guys, this is an accident waiting to happen and when it does, it's going to be bad!"

Of course my husband and son just looked at me wondering how I could say such a terrible thing on a day that they were so excited about the bike. I was shocked myself because I have no idea still to this day where that statement came from. But I am sure now that it was my heavenly Father preparing me for my newly changed life. Little did I know that within five hours of my making that statement that it would be *my* words that would come true? Can you imagine ever saying something so horrible and then seeing it come true? That's what it was like for me. I felt it was just all a dream.

~

After learning about my son's accident, I for the very first time in my whole life doubted God's love for me. The horrific events caused me to doubt if God really was punishing me for something I had done in the past. I never in my whole life felt such pain and hopelessness as I did that day. Moreover, I also wondered why such a loving God as the one I had learned about and trusted in could be so cruel and mean and want to hurt me so much.

We all had lunch after church, as usual. Then Noah, my youngest son, Chad and Scott all went to get wood as they usually did for the cold winter we would have ahead. My girls, Kaitlyn and Kaycee and I had gone to visit a friend who had just been blessed with a new baby, and all was well! I thanked God as I saw this precious baby and was remembering the times when my children were just new like this, hours old! By the way, I need to share that has been the greatest gifts I ever received from God, my precious babies! Well, besides Him giving so freely of His only begotten Son to die on that cross for my sins. There is nothing like the smell of a brand new baby!

৵-৵

On the day of the accident, we were visiting my friend who had just given birth to a baby. We were walking out of the same hospital that they were bringing Chad into for care and we walked past the ambulance with Chad in it not even knowing it was him in there.

After our visit with my friend, while walking out of the hospital, I saw an ambulance across the street pulling into the emergency entrance. I said a prayer as I always do when I see things like this, praying that the person whom they had just rushed into the emergency room would be okay. I had always told my children when they were little that they should pray right away for the person in an ambulance. We had talked about remembering to say a prayer if we saw a car accident or house fire. I told them to say a prayer of blessing on the person's behalf, especially when they don't even know you are praying for them. That in itself is the greatest gift you could give a person. Little did I know that I was for one, practicing what I preached and two, I was praying for the life of a son I had given life to!

My girls and I not knowing who the accident victim was went on home. We were having such a great time on the ride home, discussing how cute the baby we had seen in the hospital had been. I was even teasing them about me having another child. They hated that, the thought of me having yet another baby to add to the five we already had! Then, I remember the conversation turning more serious, we were talking about people dying and going to heaven and what heaven must look like, who would be there, and of course they again teased me telling me that there would be in heaven a book store and a place for all the stray animals I always took in. And once again, we talked about us praying even more for the ambulance we had just prayed for and...well; we talked about if that person was going to die! Little did I also know that this particular time I was praying for my own son, the one I had given life to. He had been the one inside that ambulance!

৵-৵

When we reached our home, it was a nice day and everything was calm and still; what a beautiful day! I remember coming up from the basement with a load of laundry, saying 'hi' to my husband who was home watching television.

{The Clark's long stairway leading to second floor}

I remember thinking to myself that this would be a nice afternoon to just spend time doing nothing with him and watching television all day. To me, doing nothing all day meant that I had to do something even if it meant doing the laundry! As I passed the kitchen, my cell phone rang. The number in the screen was not familiar so I thought about not answering it and letting it go to voicemail. You have to understand that just days before I had just gotten a newly refurbished phone and didn't realize it was someone else's phone before mine. Therefore, I was getting odd calls for different people the day before, so I was really leery about answering the call. My heart sank and I suddenly felt sick. Somehow though, something within me told me that I had to take this particular call. So I did. This is how the conversation went:

"Mrs. Clark?"

"Yes." My voice trembled.

"Yes, ma'am. This is Christy, a nurse from Covenant Cooper."

"Yes, hello. How can I help you?" I asked.

"Are you Chad Clarks' mother?"

My heart was already sliding to my feet, "Yes," my answer came in a whisper surrounded with fear.

"Your son has been in a motorcycle accident and we need you to come to the hospital right away, can you do that?"

"Yes, of course we can come. His father and I will be there right away. What...?"

The nurse cut me off with her next question, "How long will it take you to get here?"

"Well, we only live about 15 or 20 minutes away." My mind was already zooming with the details of what I needed to do next. I must grab Scott quickly. We have to hurry...oh my God!"

"Okay, but could you please hurry?"

I hung the phone up and walked into the room where Scott was still watching television. He listened while I explained the conversation that I had experienced on the telephone. Watching the fear quickly appear on his face, I explained what had just taken place. I remember the look on his face to this day; my husband looked a little like I had felt. We both felt disgusted to think that our boy had hurt himself on that motorcycle!

Scott and I got ready to go and hurriedly walked out the door. We didn't want to be angry, but Chad's history thus far had been of him being a little dare devil and doing things like climbing too far in large trees. Often he'd take it close enough that it would look like he was just about to fall out! He was always getting cut or scrapped by pocket knives. It was ordinary for us to see him with banged up knees from riding and jumping off his bike, you know... typical boy things!

As we left the house, I told the rest of my children, who were out playing basketball by then, that their brother, Chad had been involved in an accident and to please pray for him and for the overall circumstance. Even more seriously, I instructed them to call my oldest daughter, Kayla, at work and tell her to come home right away, so they could be cared for and talked to in case of confusion, etc. I also remember telling them that I needed all my children with me. Looking back on everything now, it must have clearly been God who was preparing me....again, because we had no idea how badly hurt Chad had been. Too, why would I have called Kayla home from work if it were just a broken arm or leg? But back then of course one would not think of such things!

Plus, I was so very grateful she and Anthony were not yet married and she still lived at home. Another grace provided by God. Scott and I do not know what all we would have done without our oldest daughter's help. True faith teaches you that God places people exactly where they should be at the time they need to be there.

Chapter Two – Caring about Chad's Safety

Wow! Those were my first thoughts. Chad had broken an arm, or leg. Never in my wildest dreams did I ever think it could be anything worse than that. In fact, I found myself getting a little upset with Chad because I knew if he had a broken arm or leg how this was going to be hard. After all, it was still summer and he was such a dare devil. Chad was the type of teen that he most likely would not be still long enough to allow whatever was broken to mend.

You see, Chad had taken every safety course. He had driven every known type of vehicle: four wheelers, snowmobiles, tractors, motorcycles, go-karts, mini-bikes; you name it, he had driven them all. And I have to say he was pretty good and responsible about driving the different vehicles. He would have had to have been pretty good to make Scott feel comfortable enough with him to go get his endorsement on his license, which made me feel better about letting our son have a motorcycle.

{Chad riding a Go-Kart ----- Chad on motorcycle up North}

As we were driving toward Covenant Cooper Hospital in Saginaw, Michigan, on such a wonderful perfect day, I felt the urge to call my father-in-law, Aveary. I knew he would pray for Chad and direct my steps as to what we all needed to do next. That was one thing my father-in-law always was good at and I knew he would come through, anytime I asked him to pray...Aveary would do so with no questions asked. And he prayed faithfully, which was a big thing that I always tried to instill in my kids. If you tell someone you are going to pray for them or something along those lines, then you better make sure you pray! And then be prepared if you asked someone how they are doing...you better be ready for them to complain to you and you better listen or else don't ask!

As I made that call to Aveary, I broke down and knew it was bad. I thought for a minute, *come on girl, get it together, after all, you don't even know yet how bad the accident had been!* Something inside my gut as soon as I told my father-in-law about Chad's accident made me feel so sick to my stomach. It was like someone had just punched me in the gut. Even as I told him I could clearly hear in Aveary's voice his concern. And for those of you who don't know me and my history with my father-in-law, I always called him because he was always close by and would be calm and tell me what to do. He is very good under pressure and I thank God for that! Aveary had been so good and calm when my youngest daughter, Kaycee, cut her ring finger off in the bedroom door when she was just nine months old. Because of his and Scott's quick thinking, Kaycee was able to keep her finger! My father-in-law assured me that he would meet us at the hospital.

When we arrived at the hospital, the Chaplin met us. She asked us to have a seat in this private room, and said a team of doctors would come to talk to us. All I remember is asking over and over again, "Where is our son? Is he alive? When can we see him?"

The answer my husband and I kept getting from the staff was, "The doctors will be here to talk with you, please just wait."

Something just didn't seem right. I felt like we were in a dream or a place faraway. I understand now that that was shock setting in. We were watching the words come out of the staff member's mouths, but couldn't really understand what they were saying to us. It was like I was having a bad dream and was waiting to wake up. And I compare it to one of those scenes you see on television or a funny cartoon where you see the words coming out of people's mouths and everything is in slow motion? That's the way it was for us! You know it's like when they show in television, the clock and the hands on the clock just keep going by fast as the hours go by? This too was how everything seemed at that moment. And if there were people coming in and out of the hospital we didn't notice, but I am thankful to the people who came to pray and be with us. If you are one of those people reading this book and I haven't thanked you yet – well, I want to thank you now! "Thank you from the bottom of my heart!"

As we waited, our pastor, Mark Karls, showed up and prayed with us. Several friends and family members arrived, including my mom and step-dad, Jan and Ron Whalen. Next to arrive were my in-laws, Aveary and Becky Clark, Bill and Margaret Cornish from church; and our next-door neighbors, Sam and Tina Hernandez. Of course our children had come by then. I just remember everyone kept praying and holding hands. There was so much love in that little tiny room; you could feel it I swear. I really thought although it was scary, there was a lot of love and I was always a believer that love could cure anything at anytime.

{Aveary and Becky Clark with Chad on Graduation Day}

We all just sat and waited and waited, you know how when you watch a movie in slow motion? That's really what it was like. The more we sat, the more scared everyone became. The more friends and family were praying, the more tears everyone was shedding. Plus, the longer we stayed in that little room, the more staff stared at us with their long faces. They looked like they had so much compassion on us. New arrivals wondered why everyone was showing so much compassion toward the family and friends gathered by Chad's side. At this time, we had not been told even how bad the accident really was or even any details of our son's condition.

Finally, a doctor came out and explained that Chad had been the victim of a hit-and-run accident. With a very worried voice, he explained that our son's condition was very serious. He had been working on Chad all this time because Chad kept crashing and they could not get him stabilized. So by now, we realized that's what was taking the doctors so long to come and talk to us. Our hearts sank once again. And again, we were just watching the doctor's mouth move not actually hearing and comprehending what he was saying to us. Imagine hearing the words every parent dreads; this was especially hard since we had originally thought it might be just a broken arm or leg! My goodness, this was not what we were expecting at all!

At the time when the doctor first came out to meet us, he looked so tired and sad. I really honestly thought he was going to tell us they were not able to save Chad. There are no words at all that can describe how scared I was. I did not want to hear such words. This physician looked like the doctors you see on television medical shows where they come out and tell the family members that they were sorry and they did all they could do but they couldn't save the person. That is honestly what I expected to hear. So, imagine if you will how surprised I was when they told us all the problems that Chad had.

Now, imagine a mother getting anxious because her son had developed all these problems but still he may have a chance to live, *even if it meant he would never walk again*, or so they told us. For a second, I really thought somewhere in the back of my mind how sick I was to think that our son might never walk again...truth is we were not even certain if Chad was going to live at this time. I mean right then and there I thought I was a good candidate for the mental ward! Isn't it funny how you think those kinds of things when a crisis like this comes up?

I just kept contemplating so many things. My mind continued going back to when I arrived home from the hospital earlier that day and I was asking Scott where Chad was. At the time I learned Chad had finished getting the wood at the house...and he had asked hid dad if it was alright if he took the new motorcycle down to the barber's so he could get a haircut. Chad always kept his haircut nicely and looked so handsome! It was on the way home from there that Chad had been struck by the car. Actually, to tell you the truth, I had to smile when Scott told me he was getting a haircut. Even though he kept himself well-groomed, I thought to myself, *there must be a new girl*. It also occurred to me that he was going to get an award at church or something. Who knows...kind of silly, but then you had to know my *Chadders*!

Also I remember the *look* on my husband's face. Scott was always so full of pride for our children. Each of them worked so hard for the family and was always polite. Now here was his oldest son becoming a man with his first new wheels and was willing to be responsible. Scott knew that Chad cared about his appearance and even instead of us nagging Chad to get a haircut, Chad himself was being responsible with his own appearance! I remember saying to myself as I sat down to fold the laundry, "life sure is good and it doesn't get any better than this!"

Now come on; my children are far from perfect and they are each far from being angels. Humbly, I will be the very first one to admit that! Still, I believe that God just gives His children that inner peace and He gives His children that pat on the back, which says, *thus far you are doing a great job*! And besides, I know my loving husband and I were blessed. There had always been an infinite amount of compliments about our kids because they had never been in trouble with the law. Scott and I had been given compliments left and right when we were in church. Friends, family and church members told each of us about how well our kids would sit patiently and how helpful our children had been through the years. We received compliments about how respectful they had been while in school and Sunday school both. As parents, we were miraculously given children that parents all over the world dream of having.

Like all parents, we would ask ourselves if all these well-wishers had been talking about the same kids...our children. Because we sure had our fights and fits around home here, but maybe it's true what they say, that children are always better behaved when they are away from home and in someone else's care. Anyway, I thank God my children are being respectful to this world and the people in this world. Scott and I are grateful that God guided us along the way and are certain that all the credit does indeed not belong solely to us, as man and wife, much less as their parents.

> *"Train a child in the way he should go, and when he is old, he will not turn from it."*
>
> Proverbs 22:6

Chapter Three – Learning the Details

Our meeting with the doctors was grim. The doctor explained that Chad had crushed lungs, broken ribs, a broken hip, a broken back, broken collar bone, broken scapula, shattered right wrist, and worst of all, a spinal cord injury. Hearing all these things at once caused us to wonder at the time what was left on his body that wasn't broken! I realize now that there were actually quite a few bones that he had not broken, but sitting there listening to a doctor give you a list of broken parts on one person's body, you start to think that his insides were completely broken, that nothing was intact like it should be. Your mind starts to put all the different combinations together, none of which were good. The doctor then explained to us that it was in God's hands and that Chad would probably not make it and to even worry about a spinal cord injury and the ability to walk again was the least of our problems right now! Chad's crushed lungs were our immediate concern; his lungs were filling up with fluid and he had a lot of internal bleeding. We had the next 12 hours to see how it would turn out. I couldn't believe what I was hearing!

Almost immediately I began to think, "This just could not be! Everything was fine this morning when I woke up, and in less than eight hours our world had shattered and was literally falling apart!"

Sadly, the news just continued to get worse. Chad had been in an accident, they couldn't stabilize him, and now the doctors believed they couldn't do anything else. They expected him to die. In just those few short hours, everything had changed. What were we going to do? And that's when I really started to learn what our next hours would be like, and what the future might be like if Chad weren't in it anymore. I was so sick to my stomach and really felt like I could vomit. And...this is going to seem over rated...but I swear I could smell death in that hospital that day. It's a smell one cannot describe, and here we were with the worst because it doesn't get any worse than this! I watched and listened to the hospital staff just going in and out of Chad's room talking in terms as they were just waiting for him to die and take his final breath. It sickens me to think that that is how they were feeling about my son! What would they be doing if this was their son and I was the one talking like this in front of them? This too is where I learned I needed to be a forgiving person, after all, this staff dealt with these types of medical traumas day after day with thousands of people dying all the time. I bet they have seen in some of their careers.

Here are some glimpses at how our world looked during this time:

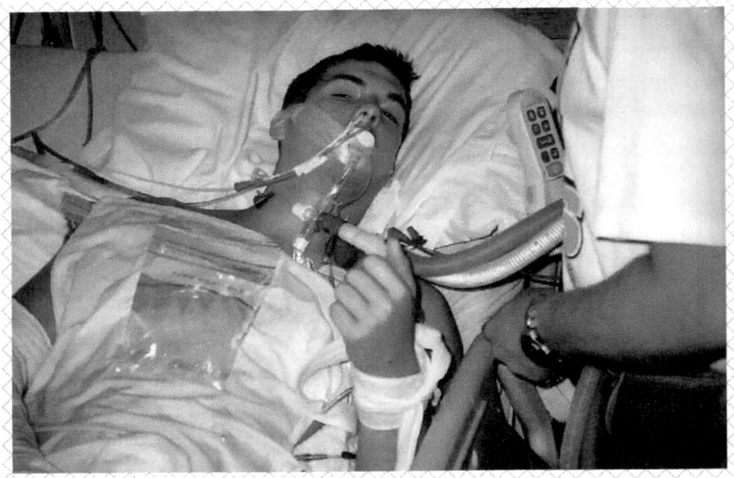

{Chad trying to tell Scott he is in pain}

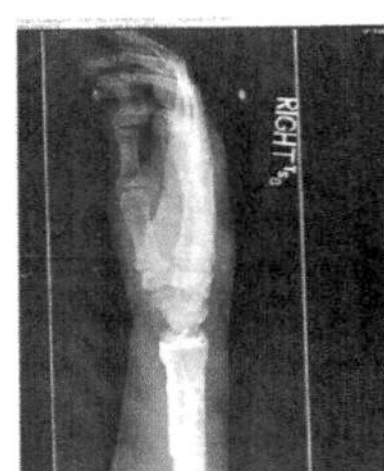

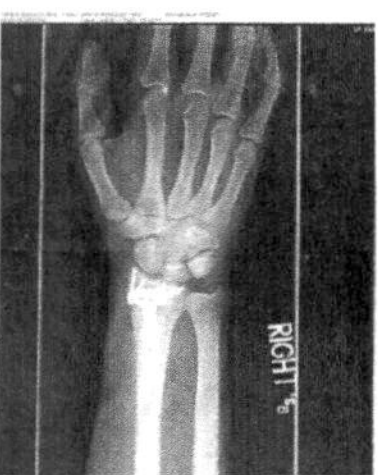

{X-Ray #1 Chad's shattered right wrist with plates and screws}
{X-Ray #2 – A view of shattered right wrist with pins and screws}

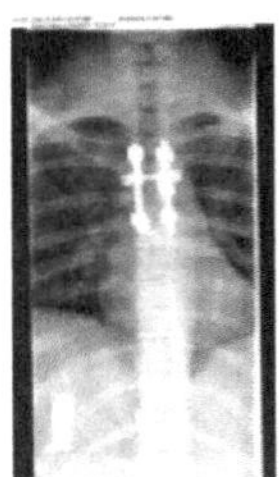

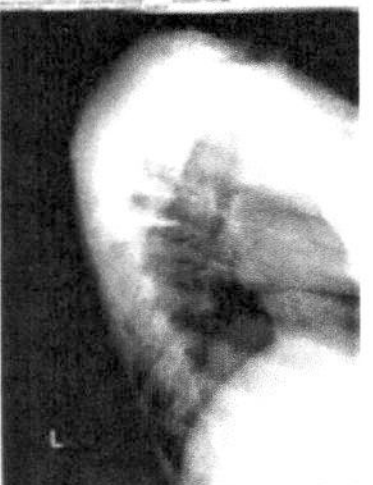

{X-Ray #3 – Plates and screws in Chad's broken back}
{X-Ray #4 – Collapsed lung}

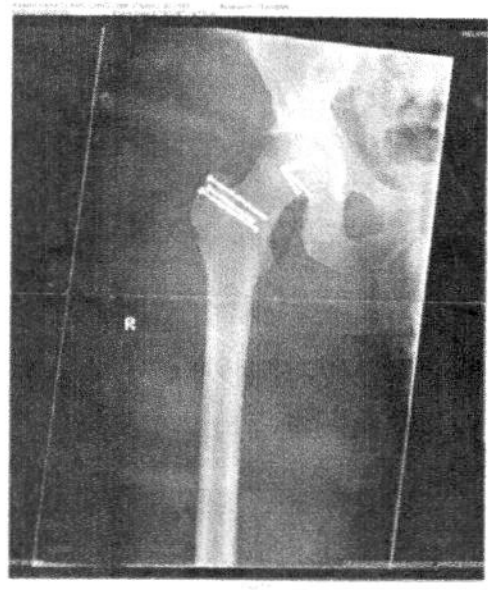

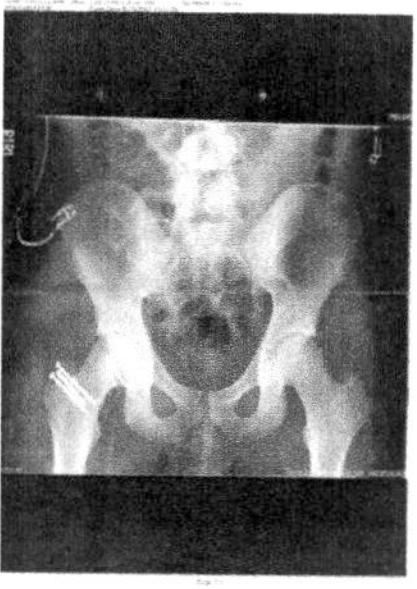

{X-Ray #5 – Screws and pins in shattered right hip}
{X-Ray #6 – Close-ups of Chad's shattered right hip}

We were finally allowed to go see Chad. As we entered the room, it was every mother's nightmare: my son was lying there on a table, his blood-stained clothes cut and torn off his body lying all around the room. There were tubes all over his body, running in every direction to every possible pump and bag. As I went up to him, I told him I loved him and that he needed to talk to God inside his head. I told him he was going to be alright and that God was watching over him and not to ever forget that.

{Chad after they put him in a self-induced coma for three weeks}

With a tear rolling down his cheek, Chad said he was sorry over and over again, and that he loved me. I said no matter what, he should just lie still like they told him and talk to God. No one could ever know the horror of seeing that in that ER room unless you walked in our shoes!

The hardest thing besides telling my son that he could not walk was telling him then he was going to be okay, I didn't know it for sure, I was praying and trusting God he would, but maybe God had another plan for Chad. One thing I knew was that it wasn't about what we wanted...it was about God and the plans he had for us. I didn't want to lie to Chad, but then how do you tell your son the doctors told us he wasn't going to make it?

Tears stream down my cheeks as I write this to you thinking about the events, feelings and emotions during that time. It's a hurt like you cannot believe. But in the back of my mind, I just knew God's love for me and for Chad. And the thought kept going through my mind that God loved me so much he gave me his ONLY son to die on that cross for my sins so that I could go to heaven one day! Now if that isn't love I don't know what is! Still to this day, my dad asks me over and over again, how God could be so mean to allow Chad to go through this. I think that this giving of His son thing didn't really hit me until this happened to my son. Everything began sinking in and it was at this very moment, I started to have a closer walk with God, a walk so pure and so, so special that nobody or anything could come between God and me.

The truth for me then came clear. I knew...I just knew all that I am sharing and about to share with you in this book needed to be shared with God's children. It's all true, I told myself as I prayed about writing this book that I would not tell a lie or over exaggerate on anything and no matter what the hurts were or no matter what conflicts arose, that after people read this book I was going to speak from my heart and tell the truth. I hope and pray I don't step on anyone's toes or hurt anyone in any way; that's not my intent in writing this book at all. My full intent is to show my fellow sisters and brothers about God's love for each and every one of us and the lessons I have learned with this horrible tragedy. And I am not looking to get rich off this book and my goal is if sharing Chad's story – our story – helps just one person who reads it then it has all been worth it to me.

Chapter Four – If Only We Knew

So much had happened to Chad and in such a short period of time that our family with all of its members (and that's a lot of people) began going in circles. We had never experienced life in the way that we were being forced to and certainly not before this trauma came our way. But with all these new feelings about death and emotions running through me, this was so, so different. I had been there to see all my grandparents pass away and I had close friends who lost parents and both Scott and I had been exposed to going to numerous funerals. Once even, I had been there watching as a little boy I used to sit with died at nine months of age from crib death. While growing up it just seemed that death was just another part of life to me...you know...the natural type existence that one goes through in this life here on earth. But no one can compare or prepare you when it's your kid lying there dying and there isn't anything you can do! I carried and gave life to that young man lying on that table.

{Great Grandma Gladys and Chad at 2 weeks old}

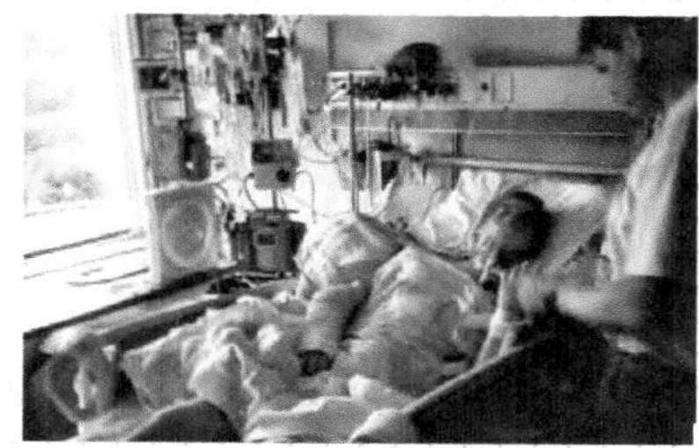

{Chad trying to ask Scott if he hurt anyone in the accident}

My son was now fighting for his life, gasping for every breath. Each time I tried to communicate with him it seemed he was trying to tell me how sorry he was that he had messed up. Can you imagine how sad it was for me to realize that my son, Chad was trying to tell me that he was sorry about how I felt? Though with him being in so much pain...well it prevented him from being able to communicate normally with us. Everything he tried to say to me was compromised by his current health conditions and he just kept trying to tell me how much he did love me. This we could see. Love from the face of a child with all the love in his heart being communicated to us, his family was awesome...and at the same time, it was so sad.

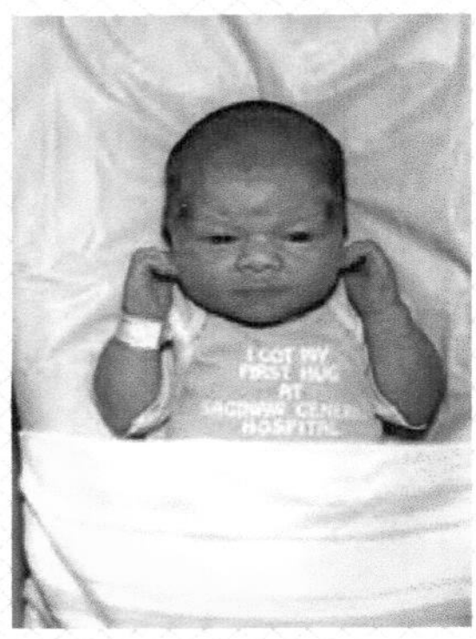

During the time that I gave birth to my oldest son, I remember having a hard time during my labor that day. The cord was twisted all around Chad's neck when he came out and bounced into the world. I teased him about coming out all blue. He's heard how he came out with his fists up in the air and in his newborn baby photos they took in the hospital he had his fists up like he was showing everyone he was indeed a fighter! And once again, God oversaw everything, and Chad was fine; there were no complications and we went home the very next day from the hospital! Lord, how I wish that were true with this situation.

> *Brothers, we do not want you to be ignorant about those who fall asleep, or to grieve like the rest of men, who have no hope. We believe that Jesus died and rose again and so we believe that God will bring with Jesus those*

who have fallen asleep in him. According to the Lord's own word, we tell you that we who are still alive, who are left 'til the coming of the Lord, will certainly not precede those who have fallen asleep. For the Lord himself will come down from heaven, with a loud command, with a loud voice of the arch angel and with the trumpet call of God, and the dead in Christ will rise first.

After that, we who are still alive and are left will be caught up together with them in the clouds to meet the Lord in the air. And so we will be with the Lord forever. Therefore encourage each other with these words.

Thessalonians 4 13:18

And this, my friends, is where I really felt God's presence! No one is ever going to tell me he doesn't exist because no words can describe to you what I felt then and there in that moment. I swear I heard a voice that said, "Kneel, pray and be faithful. I am in control. I will bring you through this. Trust in me, for I gave him life. No one knows but I, I am the Alpha, the Omega, and I will bring him through!"

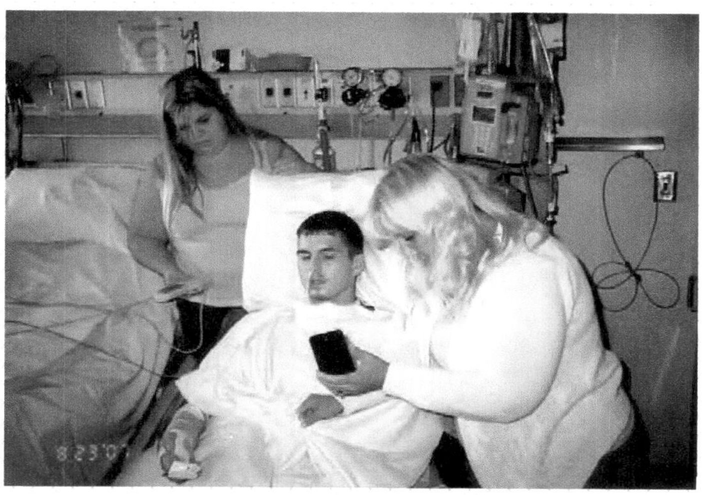

{Kayla watching as Mom (Charee) records meds for Chad}

Reactions toward us from friends, family and strangers were so different from moment to moment. Not everyone is going to react the same way and most react out of what has already been their experience in the past. So, it is with this in mind that I share this with you – something which I have never shared before with anyone due to the fact that I had already lost some of my friends because they didn't know what to say to me now that there was a chance that Chad might die. Some could not handle the circumstances, so they simply stayed away and waited. The other reason these times were thrust upon me in particular, and really I can only speak for me personally – was that it felt like it was my time to be quiet, my time to be still, which is why I tell you that my favorite verse in the Bible is "Be still and KNOW that I am God!"

Things got 'real' as they say. It was either I was going to believe and trust in God to see this trauma through and God was going to spare Chad's life or He wasn't. The choice of how I could behave and the level of my own belief system was mine, and it was a choice only I could make for myself and all by myself!

~

My next few days, few weeks, few months and now years have been spent with my heart crushed, broken in half. A good bit of my time has been spent thinking I was going to have to say goodbye to my son. I spent time thinking and trying to hang on every word he said to me, trying to remember how he sounded when he said it and I was in fear I would never hear his voice again. Of course as with any normal parent, I was thinking about how unfair all this was. His father and I had also been thinking about how very hard it was because Chad was so young. After all, he had just graduated from high school only five short weeks earlier! And now what? Is this how it was all going to end? It just couldn't be! But if it was...and I had a choice to make...

> *Discipline your son, and he will give you peace; he will bring delight to your soul.*
>
> Proverbs 29:17

Back at the hospital during the first days and as the hours went by, we asked Chad's doctor what he would do if this was his son. The physician in charge of Chad's charts and health told us that if Chad had any possible edge up on medical breakthroughs, we should fly him to University of Michigan (U of M). My father-in-law and the doctors got on the phones and starting making the arrangements to get Chad moved to U of M in Ann Arbor. We were told that the helicopter here in Saginaw would not try to fly Chad until he was stable. In addition to that, both of the helicopters were busy with other traffic accidents and so unbelievably, Chad was at the bottom of that list. At the hospital we were at, the staff said that Chad showed no signs of being able to pull through and they were not going to take the risk at all and fly him all the way to Ann Arbor Michigan. Finally, and I know it was but by the pure grace of God, the staff at U of M said they would pick Chad up because there was no time to waste.

Once again I had prayed and God had answered my prayers. So I continued to pray. I prayed more often and more intently than I have ever done in my entire life up to this point! The worst part for me was to see with mine own eyes my son's pain; to realize that this was not a dream but was actually our new sense or reality. It was all so sad and heartbreaking; hearing my son say over and over again how sorry he was. This broke my heart because we could not communicate in a normal way...I thought, *For what? He got hit; he didn't do anyone else any harm*.

~

I found out way later on, after several weeks in the Intensive Care Unit, that Chad felt guilty about all the stress he had put me through. He told me that he remembered the look on my face and the worry in my eyes that night before he lost consciousness. He also said to us that he was mad because he made us cry, especially his father. Never in my whole life did I ever expect to be in this situation listening to my child tell us such things. And how could we reply? What were we to say really? Were we to say to our son, "It doesn't matter, Chad, because your time is short now."

Or should we leave him with the impression that we were hurt to see him like this so be mad that he made us cry not knowing if these were the last words or the last conversation we would ever have with him? But then my mind was thinking of twenty different things all at once knowing time was short or so they said. Of course we weren't mad; the accident wasn't his fault, and it was only a motorcycle, what was important was right now, the time we still had left. But then from my point of view something kept telling me to pray, just pray. On the other hand, I wanted to spend every second of the time we had together with Chad. But I had to trust that while I was praying for my son's life God was indeed watching over him as I pleaded to God.

It was right after midnight that the U of M Life Flight Team came and took our son. Aveary and Scott went ahead to meet Chad as soon as the helicopter had landed. My mother-in-law, Becky, waited with me for quite a long time for the flight crew to plan out how they were going to transfer Chad and what their course of action would be if he began taking a turn for the worse on the flight over to Ann Arbor. They were afraid that once they were in the air, the medical team there wouldn't be able to do anything.

{University of Michigan's helicopter that transported Chad}

One of my memories was of my looking around wondering where my mother had gone. I questioned where she was. It seemed to me that everyone had just given up and left...everyone but my in-laws. I was hurt. I felt people who did that did not care if Chad was going to die. In my mind, I wondered if they even wanted to be there when he did pass. Then my mind came back to this mess at hand. Who and/or what was going to get my son over to U of M right now so that his life could be saved?

Chapter Five – God Really Does Send Angels

I remember God sending me another angel named Jeff; who was the pilot for the helicopter that took Chad to where God could save his life. Jeff was so honest and pure in talking to me. He introduced his crew and explained to me what they were going to be doing. I just kept talking to God in my head because I couldn't focus on anything people were telling me. I recall Jeff telling me he was also praying for Chad and he would do anything in his power to save Chad's life!

The pilot said he had a son Chad's age and that he would want his son treated the same way. Jeff asked me if I believed in God and as I shook my head, 'yes'. He kissed my forehead and said, "That's all we need, ma'am."

See, that's why I know that God had His hand in this from the very beginning! To this day I can see Jeff pulling Chad over to me while standing in the hall and letting me kiss him *goodbye*, we also prayed over Chad and call me crazy...still, I swear to you all, as Jeff wheeled Chad away there was a glow all around them, not a really bright light, but a special glow that was so silverfish-white that it just made me believe that this was a glimpse of heaven's light! And Jeff's smile and his assurance was something I will cherish the rest of my life! I remember thinking *if only my Mother could see this! I believe she would have felt the presence of my Grandmother in this life, if only she would have been there.* It was like this was my Grandmother smiling her smile to us saying *she had this, no worries!*

For those who doubt me, I know it sounds crazy but it happened, and so many people tell me I was in shock. Others have said to us that a person's body and mind plays tricks on them. Nevertheless, that was not it, and I can't explain it other than to tell you from my heart that it was all pure and true. I knew that I knew that I saw the glow over the pilot and my son; and no one was going to tell me different. And today I believe that's as close to heaven as I will ever get here on this earth.

~

David, Scott's brother stepped up to the plate and stayed in Chad's room with him so I could talk to Jeff and his crew. It was then and there that I saw another miracle. I had never seen David in that position before. He was listening and talking to the staff and keeping track of what they did to Chad.

The crew finally prepared for take off and we said goodbye to Chad. Jeff had stopped and told me one more time he promised to take good care of Chad, he said he would meet us in Ann Arbor and to stop and get some coffee. He wanted us to at least drink along the way. Then he asked his crew to step aside one last time so I could kiss Chad goodbye. I didn't know if I was kissing him *goodbye* for the last time ever or if it was just goodbye knowing I would see him again in Ann Arbor. Of course, I prayed that it would not be the last time I kissed my son.

I remember looking into my children's eyes because Jeff had gone to get them so they also could say goodbye to their brother. Noah was so scared, and my girls were crying. Kayla just held me and told me it would be alright and that I had so much faith. I had taught them to have so much faith and now I had to do what I had taught them to do. Wow, another blessing from God! I felt so proud and so sad and scared at that moment! I really did because I knew how scared I was seeing Chad like he was and hearing he was probably going to die. As a parent, I can't imagine what that was like for my children who were so young and so unexposed to this, to bear such a load at this time! Poor little Noah and Kaycee were so very young, seeing all that blood and the clothes with all that blood on the floor of the hospital room, and hearing Chad was going to die and not be with us anymore. And for Kayla and Kaitlyn also viewing Chad like that, to see a person who was their brother with a face so swollen it didn't even look like the brother they had known and loved! And how they were going to be the ones to take the younger two home to cope with the questions they were going to ask, to hold them in my place while they cried with fear and sadness! Little did I know that my little ones cried themselves to sleep that night while I was away. That shattered my heart when I learned about this later. And to have to have my two older girls who I was sure were in shock too...handle this and explain when they themselves didn't know the answers to any of their questions.

❧-❧

That first night was one of the toughest in a long trail of many long, hard nights. I was shocked because I thought my mom or some other relative would have offered to stay the night with our children. So much happened so fast and there just never seemed enough time to think of everything when needed. I remember thinking I was a horrible mom because I hadn't thought ahead of time to ask someone to stay with the kids. Scott and I did not ask anyone to stay at the hospital with us to do this until they took Chad on the flight.

When a mom has so much added stress, thinking and reacting often get compromised. In fact, I believe a good mother thinks of her children. A loving parent puts her children first...and proper parenting consists of a mother that would make sure her children would have that care. And, for me, as a mom, I believed that if I needed to be away from my children, that there would be food and clean clothes for them; that all of my children would be able to get their essential needs met. In my heart it became a feeling that if I didn't think of all these things first then maybe I deserved for God to take Chad from me. I thought, if this was the type of Mom I was then maybe I was not even truly prepared for parenting my other children's needs at night; and especially while they were horrified like this with their brother's needing so much care. In reality too, if Chad would have died the night of his accident, no one would have been there to tell them the horrific news. At any rate, then maybe that's why it felt like God was punishing me and wanted to take Chad from us. After all, I have learned from this accident that God only gives you blessings if you really try to live a Godly life and live for him. If you're not going to cherish the blessing He gives you and really change or try to change to live a Godly life as He asks us to do, then why should He keep blessing you? If you are going to keep going and not try to change then you don't deserve anything from Him at all.

ঌ-ও

The helicopter took off and we all watched Chad just disappear into the clouds. And it was right at that moment I swear I felt the hand of God wrap around me as if to say He was right there in that moment with us. I still, to this day, cannot explain that feeling and I have only felt that feeling once in my life. But it was good, peaceful, so warm, how I long for that touch again!

David had made sure we made it to the car. He hugged us and told Becky and I to drive careful and to call him when we knew something. It was the first time that David had ever told me he loved me. And I remember thinking that Chad's situation and our situation as a family in general must really be bad because everything was so different and people were acting so very different. And yet there was all this unclaimed love that was just there; no one had claimed it. It was like all the bad things had gone away and no matter how bad this accident was, love still stood there.

This horrific event had proven another thing to me; although I had been married into Scott's family for 22 years now, I always felt a part of me just was never really accepted as I longed it would be. I always felt that they judged me because of my upbringing and my home life. I felt although all of these years that no matter how much I did things for them or how good I had been to them it was just never was good enough. Maybe this was the love I felt I could finally claim with them. You see, it was Scott's family after all who stayed with Chad – with us. They were there. My brother-in-law whom I always thought just put up with me, stepped up to the plate. He told me did love me. My mother-in-law drove me to Ann Arbor. God can do so much if you just trust Him and seek Him and the amazing part is that He can do all this in the midst of a storm as this accident was with Chad.

Becky, my mother-in-law drove me to Ann Arbor as I said, and it was a long drive. As I looked at my children who were watching their brother take off in the copter – it never dawned on me what they were thinking or what their feelings were. I left the three little ones in Kayla's care, not really giving them a second thought, all my focus was on saving Chad's life. I didn't realize that I wouldn't see them until nearly two weeks later. And believe me it was two LONG weeks!

Chapter Six – Making it Through the Night

At the hospital in Ann Arbor, we met Scott and his father, Aveary. The staff told us Chad had pulled through the flight. They were trying to keep him stable because he had crashed twice in the flight over. They said they were waiting to take him to surgery, but had to wait for him to get stronger.

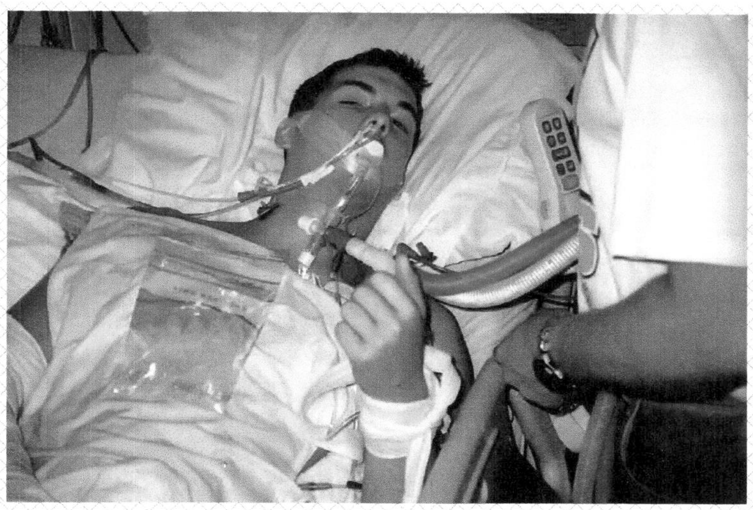

{Chad Clark holding on for dear life}

Later that night, the hospital staff gave us warm blankets and talked to us about being in shock and what to expect. They also tried to get us to eat something. I kept looking at Scott's face and it was so sad. So much hurt had filled that face. He looked so lost. And so he and I waited; and we waited; and waited. In a little tiny room they kept us in, right there in the Emergency Room, we stayed together just the four of us – parents and grandparents, alone with our thoughts, fears, hope and prayers.

Morning came! The night, now past, felt so very short. We found ourselves praising God for Chad making it through the night! I knew Chad was a fighter like his mother. I knew he would make it; I mean he did have that DeShone blood running through him; didn't he? I thanked God and I tried to focus on what was to happen next. It seemed like such a huge mountain to climb just to have him make it through the night, but we did it; or at least we had conquered one night. If we could just make it just one more night and then just one more night, that's what my thoughts were at that time.

The next days were a blur, as all I seem to be able to remember was the staff telling us Chad needed multiple and extensive surgeries. Also the doctors explained that Chad was too weak to have them. They kept re-emphasizing how crucial the surgeries were in order to save his life. I remember being too tired to think and knowing that if I signed those papers allowing them to operate on him, if anything happened...well, you see, it felt as though I held my son's life in my hands.

Because of this, I looked to Aveary every time before signing. He would nod his head and I would sign. And I have to be honest, I got real sick of them telling us although it was critical for Chad to have these surgeries to live, it was also critical enough that he could also die while having the surgeries performed!

So I felt like screaming at them, (and quite frankly, who wouldn't?). "Then what's the point? Why do you want me to sign the stupid forms then?"

I knew right then and there that I was becoming this person I would later on down the road come to hate! My thoughts didn't seem normal to me. My reactions just didn't seem to be me at all; normally I would have never felt or thought those things!

> *Trust in the Lord with all your heart and lean not on your own understanding; in all your ways acknowledge him, and He will make your paths straight. Do not be wise in your own eyes; fear the Lord and shun evil. This will bring health to your body and nourishment to your bones.*
>
> Proverbs 3 5:8

Chad had three surgeries and each time the hospital staff and/or the doctors would tell me to kiss him *goodbye*. They would assure me he was very weak, but I was doing the right thing. It was like saying goodbye three times. Imagine how difficult that was. And the wait while he was in surgery was unbearable, not knowing if Chad was going to come out of it or not. He looked so white and pale, so thin, so bruised and swollen up, and all these tubes and wires all over his body made him look so helpless. Then there were more bandages. Still, he survived each of the surgeries – he had made it! Then and there I knew God was with him and we were going to pull through this someway, somehow.

My confusion came from not knowing why God was being so good to me because I had prayed at times with a lot of anger. I would tell God how I hated him for allowing this to happen to us and how angry I was.

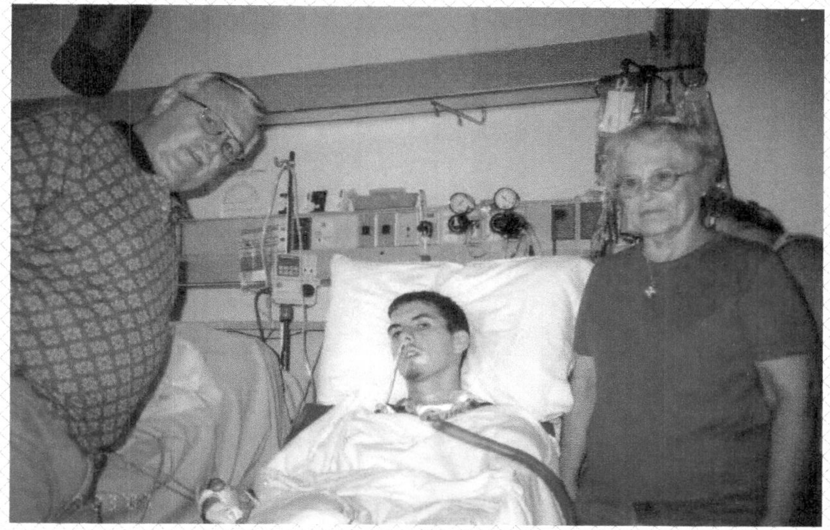

{Grandma (Jan) and Grandpa (Ron) Whalen}

Chapter Seven – The Longest 7-1/2 Weeks

Chad was admitted to the ICU unit for 7-1/2 weeks. Night and day we sat there, watching our son fight for his life. That was the longest 7-1/2 weeks of our lives. Day after day, night after night, we took turns sitting at his bedside, watching our son suffer through the pain. Pretty soon, the days and nights ran together. Weeks and months started to run together for us also.

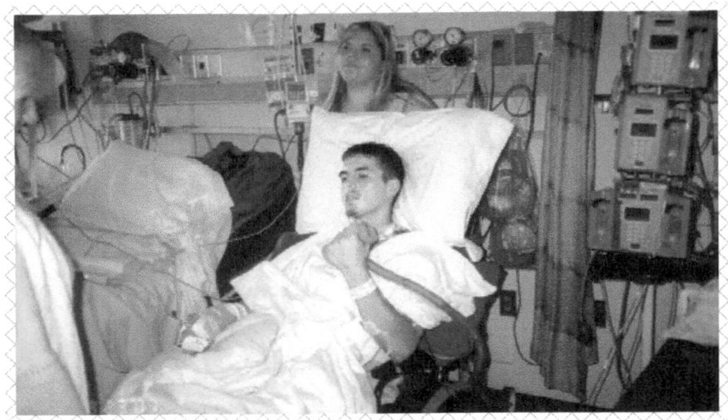

{Chad trying to take his trach out while Kayla listens while Mom gets him to stop}

While in the ICU, every day brought yet another set of new problems. Nothing ever seemed to go right or ever get better. I recall my mom coming to see us and when I saw her I cried and said, "Mom, I just can't do this anymore; I am so tired!" She just held onto me and said, "Yes, you can!"

I was so drained for a while there I thought maybe it would be best if God would just take him. Yes, I know that is a horrible thought for a mother to have, but I was way past the point of being exhausted and way past the point of being able to even think clearly anymore. And Scott was just so consumed with guilt; I couldn't possibly think of piling any more stuff on him.

One day we had a visitor walk into Chad's room. As Scott and I looked up, Scott was sure he knew this man, but couldn't place him – probably because we were too exhausted to think. The man came over to us and as he approached, he had this certain glow about him that both my husband and I were able to recognize. As the visitor came closer to hug us, Scott recognized him as being one of Scott's good customers. He handed Scott his house key and said he had a mother-in-law suite built onto his home and we could use it for as long as we needed. The house was only twenty minutes away from the hospital. Was that God watching out for us, or what? Our luck seemed to be changing.

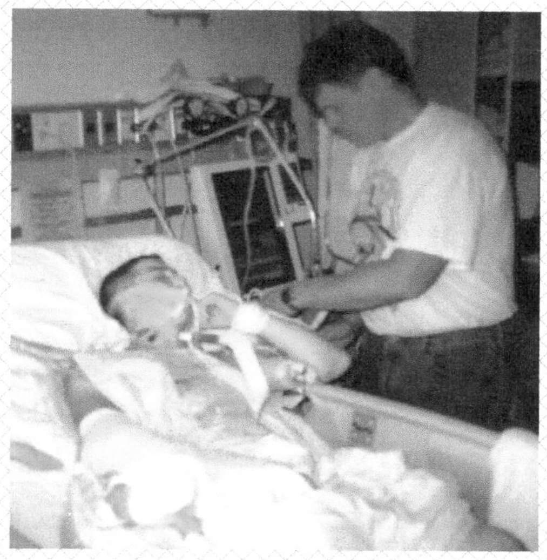

{Dad (Scott) suctioning out Chad's trach so he can breathe better}

Bottom line for us was that we still had no money. We were sleeping on chairs in Chad's hospital room taking turns watching him while the other one slept in waiting rooms all over the hospital. This had become our new life. But how wonderful it would be for us to have the kids come on the weekend and have a house to stay in where we could try to be a family again at least just for a weekend or so. Praise God for bringing him to us!

I must also tell you that as Chad lay in surgery one day, we had another miracle happen that also changed our lives for the good. After the doctors took Chad to surgery, Scott and I sat in the lobby just weeping uncontrollably. *God is so good!* I mean not that we were weeping so much was the reason God was so good...it was that as we sat there, this woman walked by and I felt the urge to look up. As I did, I saw the profile of her face, which had a certain glow. She made eye contact with me and smiled.

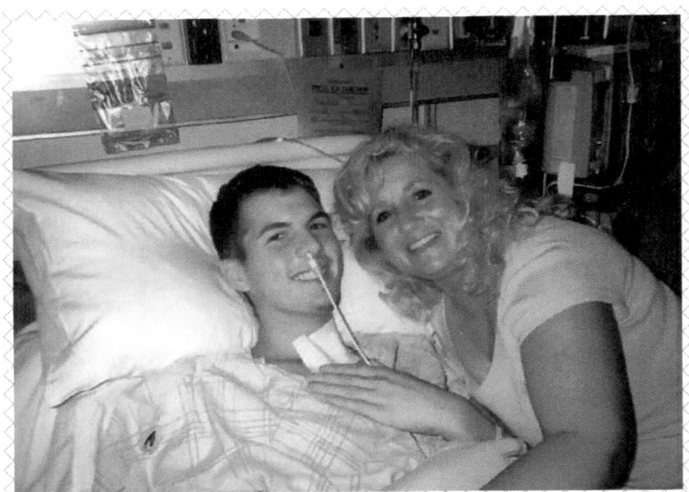

{After 7-1/2 long weeks, Chad's trach comes out! One happy Momma and Chad!}

I felt peace; it felt so nice for a change. I hadn't felt this calmness since the Sunday I was in church on the day of Chad's accident.

The young woman came back to us and knelt down on the floor in front of Scott and me. She was this very attractive black woman who showed she had a lot of dignity and respect. She said, "You don't know me, but God told me to come over here and tell you that you only have to have faith as small as a mustard seed, and if you believe it shall be."

As we exchanged stories, the young woman, Nyeesha, informed us that her husband was the victim of a drive-by shooting and that he was in the room right next to Chad. Actually, there was only a wall that separated Chad's head from her husband, Donta's head. That was God watching over both of our young men. Later on, we learned that she and Donta lived in Saginaw and that Donta's accident had happened the day before Chad's.

How good is God? He knew I needed support from my own hometown and He had sent Nyeesha. She was all alone, at least I had Scott. It's true what they say, that no matter how bad your situation is, if you look you can always find someone who is worse off than you. I also found out she had four children back in Saginaw. And her husband and sole mate was fighting for his life. And here this woman was consoling me and Scott. I couldn't believe it. She stayed with us until Chad came out of surgery the first time. It was nice because as we talked, we got our minds off the worry that was driving us insane. Nyeesha was bound and determined to meet Chad sometime within the next couple of days when he felt better. And I wanted to meet Donta.

ঌ-ৡ

It was while Chad was in the ICU, I had to stand outside the door and ask the staff to please not tell him he could not walk. We had made the decision that we would tell Chad after we prayed about it and the time was right. Days turned into months somehow. Finally the day did come when we explained to Chad the details of his medical condition. Actually we had put it off far too long and he had figured it out a long time before we told him. Because he couldn't talk and he was so heavily medicated we never thought that he would even think about whether or not he could feel his feet.

Sometime during the night he woke up and was unable to feel the lower part of his body. We never knew of this or even suspected it until quite some time later. He looked at me one day as I was putting lotion on his feet and motioned to come up by his head so he could try to spell to me. I will never forget the day he said/spelled to me, "Mom, I know I cannot walk because nothing works down there and I can't feel when they poke my feet with a needle to take my blood."

My son telling me this was just so shocking. I was so stunned I didn't know what to say. I said to God in my head, "Right now, Lord, put the words in my mouth as to what to say to this boy. I need you now more than ever."

Thank God that Scott had come back into Chad's room and he just knew that we were talking about Chad not being able to walk. And the funny thing was that I didn't even have to say anything, Scott took over and everything worked out perfectly. Scott just simply told Chad that his diagnosis was only the doctor's opinion and we just have to believe and trust in God. Chad seemed to accept that because of the miracle Chad witnessed with his cousin the summer before.

ঌ-ৡ

Kyle, our nephew, was in a swimming accident and broke his neck body surfing in Lake Michigan.

We all prayed for Kyle, and Chad was a big part of this as he and Kyle were always really close. Kyle broke his neck, and there was talk that he would not survive either or if he did he may not walk. However, thank God, Kyle made a full recovery and is fine today. He walks, and lives a normal life. Praise God. At any rate, Chad knew there was a good possibility that he too, might be able to walk again; but, that this would probably only happen by God's grace.

The one good thing that was so personal for our family that happened during Kyle's accident is the one night I got the late call that Kyle had been hurt. Of course the kids were coming into our bedroom asking who was on the phone and I told them all what had happened to Kyle. For the first time we as a family sat and all prayed together for Kyle. For the first time as a family we actually prayed together outside of church. I mean, I know it sounds crazy, we took our kids to church every Sunday from the time they were infants. They had been baptized, they were in events such as a children's choir that I directed, they were in youth groups, even were confirmed in their faith in front of the whole church, but we never prayed together. Well, we did pray at meals when we would eat dinner every night, but never did we at anytime pray for a specific need or for a friend or family member until that night. It was the most special experience that took place that night, to see their little heads bowed with hands folded, praying for their cousin Kyle to live and not have a broken neck. I remember each and every one of us going around the circle on our bed pleading our pleas to God.

When we were finished, they all went to their rooms and there was peace and a feeling of knowing we did something right. Scott and I knew that we had been good parents. Also we just knew we had been so blessed and had done something right in God's eyes!

I must confess Chad was very upset when he found he still wasn't walking after a good chunk of time had passed. I mean after all, it hadn't taken Kyle that long to recover. He was getting scared and more frustrated by the moment. We tried to tell him that his accident was much worse than Kyle's. For one thing, Chad had several broken bones and his lungs were crushed. But to Chad that didn't matter, all he knew was that if God healed Kyle, God would heal him also. I prayed so hard for Kyle all that night when we found out about his accident. When God had healed Kyle, I just knew He would heal Chad too. I was always taught that if you believed and were faithful to God, and you asked it in His name, it would be. And I really trusted and thought for sure that this is what would happen. So I kept telling Scott and the kids that God is so good, and that this would all work out. But I must confess, the time I spent alone with Chad when Scott left to go back to work, I thought to myself many, many times, *where in the world is God?*

I made such a fool out of myself telling Scott and the kids things would be alright, and it wasn't changing for Chad's condition. His condition was remaining critical and I wanted so much for my son to walk again. In fact, it had gotten worse; they all think I am crazy. I mean, after all, Kyle's healing had come sooner rather than later, and he was able to even walk in just a short time after he got hurt.

At this point and time I really felt God was punishing me for something. I found myself all alone because Scott had gone back to Saginaw to return to work. While I missed my family, home and even my pets, I knew this was the right place for Chad and I both to be. I didn't know how I was going to do this. Always I felt so scared and alone. On top of that, I was exhausted and never got any sleep. All of the alarms would constantly go off on the different machines that carried IVs and other medications into my son's body and the heart and oxygen monitors that they had on Chad were noisy as well.

Every day we would wake for a new day and I would find my son once again groaning in pain. During this period, each time I did go to sleep, I always had nightmares that Chad had died. It was terrible. There was no one there to relieve me. In addition to all that, my kids would call telling me of things at home that would make me sad and miss being at home with them. I knew they needed me, but so did Chad and that's a tough place to be in when you are a parent. I couldn't stand it. And then I learned that my poor husband would just go up the stairs to Chad's bedroom and sit in the middle of the floor and cry. I needed to be there to consol my husband who felt so much guilt for allowing Chad to get that motorcycle and go get a haircut that day. And then I would look at Chad with all these lines and machines. He was on so much medicine; it was making him turn into a whole different person. I just kept thinking all the time, "Is this right to do this to him? He is suffering so much." I could tell on the rare occasions when Chad would wake up and try to stay awake that he was so scared. They finally put him in an induced coma to rest just to be able to stay alive because he would get his heart racing and he needed just to be still and give his body a chance to heal.

God is our refuge and strength, an ever-present help in trouble.

Psalm 46:1

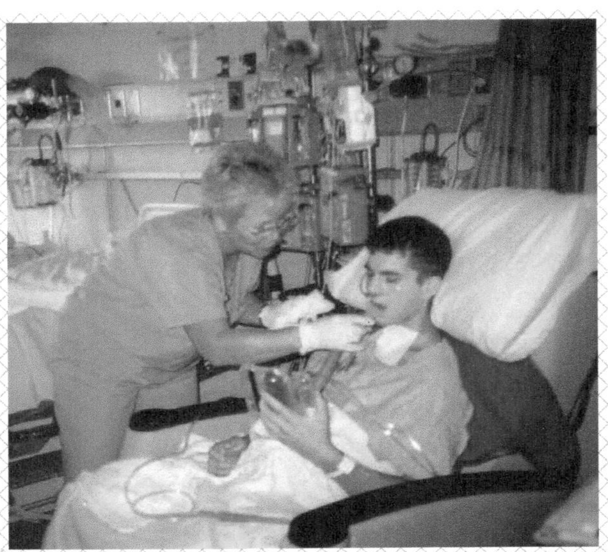

{Chad getting a breathing treatment}

Every night at 10:00 p.m. sharp, Chad would crash; which meant either his heart had stopped beating or he was lacking oxygen. The staff would rush into his room and start working on him; doing everything in their power to save my son. This in itself was another nightmare!

I felt as though I was all alone because I was there by myself watching them care for Chad. Every minute there – I was scared...to be alone if the worst was to happen and Chad were to die. The good news is every time something would happen, or this scare would occur, Chad would come back stronger.

At this point, my Kayla had come to Ann Arbor to try and give me a bit of relief. She would stay with Chad during the night and would come back in the late afternoon, after getting a few hours sleep, to keep me company and help with Chad.

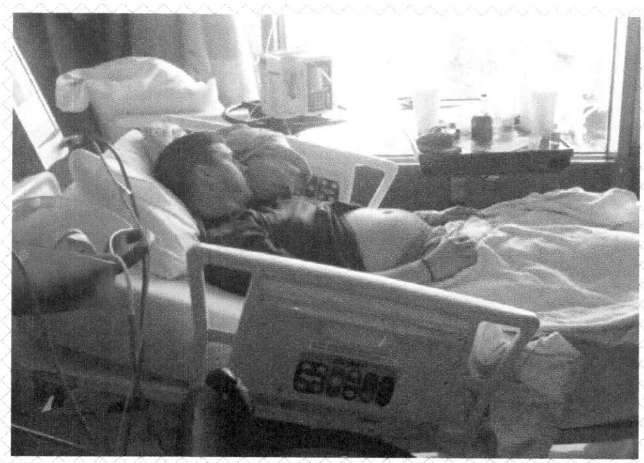

{Chad's extended abdomen from tubes in sides to drain out blood and fluids}

I really believe that there was a presence in Chad's room; a calming, peaceful presence. I don't know if anyone else felt this, but to me, as soon as you stepped foot into his room, the air even smelled different. At night, being there all alone by myself, watching him sleep, there was a radiance around his bed that made me feel at peace so that I was able to fall asleep. During the time I experienced this I wasn't scared at all. I recall thinking whatever this thing was, it was supposed to be there...so, it was okay to try to rest. The glow was incredible. Every time I would close my eyes, I would plead with God to send me a dream to show me Chad walking. See, I have this thing...if I have the same dream three times in a row, then things I've asked almost always come true and if not, then I know it was not meant to be. That's how it has been since I was a little girl. For a long, long time that dream never came; so, you can imagine how scared I was feeling. Sometimes, well a lot of times, I felt like Chad's situation for himself and for our family was going to be so hopeless.

> *So do not fear, for I am with you; do not be dismayed, for I am your God. I will strengthen you and help you; I will uphold you with my righteous hand.*
>
> Isaiah 41:10

Chapter Eight – The Meeting of Nyeesha and Donta

I remember Nyeesha, the wife of the gunshot victim, Donta Young, in the room next to Chad's. Frequently, she would visit us in Chad's room and share a lot with us saying that God was there with us. She and I became friends really fast and we spent a lot of time alone together. Nyeesha was there to support and help care for her husband, Donta...still, she was by herself and missed her kids, home and pets also back in Saginaw. We had so much in common.

July 28 gunfire claims victim

COREY MITCHELL
THE SAGINAW NEWS

In the 3½ weeks since a gunman's bullet lodged in her husband's spine, paralyzing him from the neck down, Nyesha Clark-Young said Saginaw police detectives haven't contacted her or even returned her phone calls.

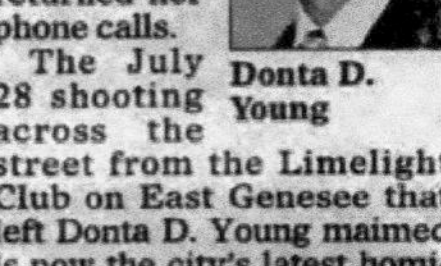

Donta D. Young

The July 28 shooting across the street from the Limelight Club on East Genesee that left Donta D. Young maimed is now the city's latest homicide.

Young, a noted mid-Michigan musician, community theater actor and father of four, died Wednesday night at the University of Michigan Hospital in Ann Arbor after complications from surgery.

PLEASE SEE YOUNG, A8 ▸

Young, Mr. Donta Depreist
Saginaw, Michigan

Family hour will take place at 10:00 a.m. on Saturday, September 1, 2007 at the Wolverine Baptist Convention Headquarters, 615 S. Jefferson Ave. with the funeral commencing at 11:00 a.m. Pastor Ron Frierson will officiate with interment in Forest Lawn Cemetery. Friends may call at the Browne's Mortuary, 441 N. Jefferson Ave. on Friday from 2:00 until 8:00 p.m.

Mr. Donta Depreist Young, beloved husband, father, son, grandson and friend, walked into his marvelous light August 22, 2007. Donta was a rising star; an accomplished actor, gospel rapper, model, poet, community activist and most importantly, a King's Kid. He was a member of New Covenant Christian Center Church and also attended Agape. Donta leaves to cherish his memory his wife, Nyesha Clark-Young; four children, Nia Young, Tayah Young, Kahlil Clark and Imani Clark; his mother, Carol Young and his father, Thomas Carter (Brenda Martin); grandparent, Ollie Reid; eight sisters, Quatisha, Daketa and Brittney Crowley, Patricia McNeal, Lavette Gist, Aneisha McDaniel, Veronica Gibbs and Jacqueshia Watkins; four brothers, Mychael Young, Barnard Adams, Derrick (Shawn) Martin, Adrian (Christy) Esters; four aunts, Delores (James) Wright, Frances Reid, Pennie Quinn and Ann Gibson; Dwight (Parlee) Ealy and Ephraim Carter; a special cousin, Tony Young; a host of nieces, nephews, cousins, many other relatives and friends, including special friends Ahmad, Patrick, Kardell Tangela, Dena, Ken, Detr and Von.

Browne's Mortuary
441 N. Jefferson Ave.
(989) 754-0481
brownesmortuary.com

One evening, as I was coming back from the hospital chapel, I passed by Nyeesha's husband, Donta's room and he was looking up at the ceiling just staring at it. I felt the nudge from God to go in his room and talk to him. Though I was hesitant to follow through with this thought, I have found out from past experiences that whenever I think God is trying to get me to do something and I disobey, the end result is so terrible; that if I would have just listened and obeyed in the first place, I could have avoided all of the negative side effects. Having thought it through, I said out loud, "Okay, God, I am going in there!" I walked over to Donta. I didn't think he knew I was there because he couldn't see me. This young man had on a collar like Chad...one like most spinal cord patients wore the first couple of days after an accident to stabilize their neck and spinal cord. But Donta knew I was there; he motioned with a small movement of his hand for me to come closer. He couldn't talk of course because he was also intibated like Chad. However, he was able to blink his eyes in response to people.

I said, "Donta, you don't know me, but I am Chad's Mom. My son's next door to you," motioning to Chad's room. He blinked his comprehension. I told him that Nyeesha and he had a lot of faith that I only wish Scott and I had, and I told him about his wife meeting us in the lobby. He blinked to tell me he already knew; that Nyeesha had told him all about it. We, or rather I, talked for a while, telling him about stories about Chad and how Nyeesha had become my rock. Donta listened while I shared how I had learned from Nyeesha about how he had given everything he had to get this building and start a drama program to help troubled kids in downtown Saginaw where he lived. What an amazing couple these two were! And so full of faith. I also told him how I knew Nyeesha's maiden name was Clark also, just like our last name.

Finally I told him I was going to go because he needed some rest and I didn't want to keep him up. He motioned with his hand for me to stay and started blinking. I sensed that he wanted me to stay and hold his hand for a little while until he fell asleep. I didn't mind because I knew Chad was still in his coma and I really had no way of knowing if he knew I was there by his side or not.

Nyeesha was always bringing me messages from her beloved Donta. His messages were packed full of hope for Chad. She would consistently tell me, 'Donta is looking out for Chad'. And in fact, I remember Nyeesha telling me almost every day that Donta said God told him that Chad was going to come out of this thing. I didn't feel so alone then. Nyeesha understood what it felt like to feel the fear.

Several times Donta crashed late at night. I remember there was this one time when Donta crashed while Nyeesha was visiting Chad. The staff went running into Donta's room and I asked her, "Shouldn't you be in there with Donta?"

She replied, "God is there that's all he needs right now. He will be fine, wait and see." And she was so right! Oh, how I wished I had Nyeesha's strong faith! I longed to be that close to God; to be able to not worry and just *let go and let God*. That has become one of my new sayings that I have found to comfort me since dealing with Chad's accident.

Then one night, early in the wee hours of the morning, the time came when Donta had crashed again. This time, he didn't come back. He went to be with God. He had died during surgery to repair a hole in his lung. Right where the bullet had pierced his lung, where no one could see it in the CAT scan, he had developed several blood clots. These blood clots had broken loose and were going through his body. One finally made it up to Donta's chest cavity and into his heart. He went to be with the Lord. I remember thinking that it was possible for Chad to be next.

~

There were only eight rooms in this particular ICU. As time passed, the unit got emptier, as we lost patients. I felt so hopeless that I cried out to God and told Him that I couldn't take it anymore. I begged God to take Chad next. To some this may seem unthinkable, I'm sure.

You see, as the mother of Chad and seeing him there so powerless and so unable to communicate his thoughts and needs - just made me feel so sad for him and I just could not believe he might possibly live forever this way. It was thoughts like this that were so pressing on my heart.

Chad had just graduated from high school in June with a welding career. He had planned a full life. Knowing this and seeing him in his coma and like I say, so powerless, I began to be unable to bear the thought that he would end up like this for a long lifetime. This whole burden (his and mine) caused me from time to time to think that Chad might be better off if he passed like Donta had.

Another burden was that I knew if and when Chad came out of his coma, that someone would need to tell him that he would never walk again...most likely, since I was closest to him and I was his Mom, that it would be my job to explain his health conditions. I pleaded with God, begging Him to let me be the one in the wheelchair; that I would do anything if He would just wake me up from the hellish nightmare. And then seeing the pain Nyeesha was going through, it seemed there was no hope whatsoever in sight. People kept telling me that it would get better, time would heal. I just kept thinking to myself, "Easy for you to say, you all get to go on with your lives. It's not your son that is suffering; it's not your life that is going to change forever.

> *The Lord is my light and my salvation—whom shall I fear? The Lord is the strong hold of my life—of whom shall I be afraid.*
>
> Psalm 27:1

Scott came home to return back to work with his dad, Averay, in the family business. Scott wanted to be there with us and I can only imagine what it was like for him to know he had to be away from me and Chad knowing that at any time his son could die because at this point Chad was still not out of the woods. Kayla had come to replace Aveary during the night so I could leave at night. This enabled me to return to the house where we were staying that Scott's customer had offered us...thankfully, I could try to get a good night's sleep not having to hear alarms. It was great to be able to sleep in a bed instead of chairs or in the hospital lobby.

Scott would call and check up on us and Chad condition several times throughout the day and evenings. He was there by phone to help me make medical decisions. Scott desperately wanted to be there with us in person instead of by phone, but at this time we were so behind on bills that he had no choice. We had been away from home for over two months at this point!

It was also at this time that Chad's specialists were trying to get Scott and I to plan for the worst and start making funeral arrangements, Such as if we were going to have his body transported back home, donations of Chad's organs, you name it, all the bad stuff we were not going to discuss at that time. So we did what any parents would do; the two of us got on our hands and knees at the hospital chapel when Scott came up to visit. The two of us, as parents, and as husband and wife, gave our boy to God. Whatever God wanted to do, we trusted him.

Scott and I even discussed what and how to tell our other children about Chad's injuries, or God forbid how in the world we could even begin to explain to them if God were to take Chad home. We couldn't get the two younger ones, Kaycee and Noah, to stop crying as it was! Even though we said to each other we were giving Chad's life or death to God, we contemplated whether we should look into where the cemetery plot was that I had won at some church function years ago and if we could purchase additional plots for the rest of our family. Now that this happened to Chad, we realized it could happen to another member of our family...perhaps even one of the younger ones. Of course this helped us to see that we wanted all of us to be buried together.

Imagine what I was thinking in my mind at this time. Here I was the mom thinking about not having her son by her side anymore. Flashes of images showing Chad lying on the hospital bed apologizing over and over again to me.

This next part is so terrible but it's the truth: I imagined Chad lying in his casket and then suddenly my mind leapt to his body decaying in the ground with worms and maggots eating away at it. This was such a terrible image that I never did tell anyone else in my family about it. This is something that they are learning from me now as they read my story. Such horrible images like this haunt me to this day.

Thank goodness that we received yet another blessing from God – the knowledge that we are only earthly flesh and that the soul goes to heaven immediately. That body of flesh in the ground would no longer contain the Chad that I know and love, he would be with God long before the decay of the body.

❧-❧

Our family had become quite close with Donta's family. Donta's dad, Doug, was also a great man of faith. He talked to Scott a lot and made sure Scott kept his faith. In fact, the night Donta went in for his surgery to repair his lung, Doug and I stayed up and talked while Donta was in surgery. The doctor came into the lobby where we were waiting to hear how the surgery went. I could not believe my ears with what I heard Doug say next!

We learned that the doctor wanted to talk to Doug by himself, and Doug said, "No, she is family and I want her to be here with me for whatever you have to say." I felt really proud inside and so very thankful to God because He had granted me an addition to my own family. I believe that Doug didn't want to be alone when he heard whatever the doctor was about to tell him; heck, I wouldn't have either. And suddenly the doctor broke into tears and said that Donta did not make it. You see, all the doctors and nurses get to be really close with the ICU patients because, like I shared earlier, there are only eight rooms in the whole wing. This doctor had also taken messages to Chad from Donta when I was sleeping, or gone, or whatever. It was certain that this doctor could see how worried I became thinking Chad could possibly be next. He began assuring me that Chad would be okay because they had already placed what they call a green filter in Chad during one of his three surgeries to prevent this. That was God working because I do not at all recall ever signing for this filter to be placed in my son's body, but it ended up saving his life because Chad did develop a blood clot later on in his right leg.

Then there was a time after Nyeesha left to go back home to have Donta's funeral and to be with her kids. I found myself all alone once more and feeling more terrified than ever. *How could this be happening to me? What next,* I thought. I thought we were pretty good parents. I was also upset because I couldn't be home with the rest of my children. Here I was at the hospital caring for my son, as any parent would want to be, but it felt horrible not to be able to help them sort out their feelings. It was only natural that I wanted to help talk to them to see how they felt about their brother's condition. I couldn't console them as they were having nightmares themselves. Much more than this, I was missing, my loving husband, Scott. He was my rock throughout all this, and we were side by side from the very beginning of this nightmare. We made all the decisions together on Chad.

Suddenly I had to make all the decisions, and every time Scott and I talked on the phone, we would cry and then it made it worse because I couldn't be there to hug him. I would get calls from my kids asking me to come home because they missed me, and that they were scared. Their Daddy was always crying and alone upstairs in Chad's room.

ঌ-ঌ

Time goes on, as they say. Chad was getting better, but still so frail. He couldn't even keep his eyes open and yet they kept saying he was healing and surely getting better.

Nyeesha came back one last time to see me after the funeral for Donta. She came to give me the message of hope, as we cried together she told me that Donta is seeing Chad through this all still. He is pulling Chad through all this with God's help. That was so good to hear, I needed some words like this that I could cling to. Because all along, all the hope I had stored up had got taken away daily by the staff at U of M.

ঌ-ঌ

The day came when Chad finally moved out of the ICU unit. My daughter Kayla had taken my place in staying with Chad now so I could come home, because the kids were about to start school and Chad wasn't in any danger at this particular time. Plus, we had to prepare our house with a ramp, etc...so that our son could finally be released from the hospital to come home when he got better. That was one of the things that needed to be done or else the hospital would not release him. This was also hard for me.

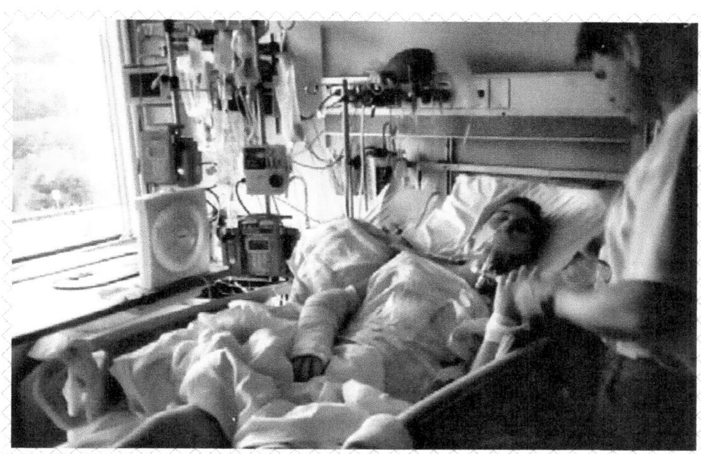

{So much equipment – Dad holding on to Chad for dear life}

But I am so proud of my daughter Kayla for taking on such a huge responsibility. She would call me all the time with updates and to discuss treatment plans with Scott and me. We would bring the kids with us on the weekends to visit Kayla and Chad. This was a struggle too because the kids had homework to do now that they were back in school but wanted to spend every second of the weekend with their brother and sister instead of focusing on their studies. Kayla and Chad had become close while she was learning how to take care of him at home. She would call me all the time to talk through the instructions being given her revolving around her brother's medical situations. We would go back on the weekends and stay with him until Sunday night to be with our family and to give Kayla a break.

This new schedule and all that fit in it was also a struggle, as homework had to be completed by the rest of our children and we all had a fear of leaving Chad again.

Chapter Nine -Preparing Our House

Thank goodness our house originated as an old farm house (still is in some small odd ways). In fact, when we first bought the property and moved into the house, we let all of the kids pick their own rooms. Shortly afterward and in doing this, Chad sat down in the middle of our long hallway upstairs and cried. Because this was supposed to be an exciting day for us all, I asked our son what in the world was causing him to cry...after all, we had even let them pick their own rooms. Chad looked up at me with big crocodile tears and said, "Mommy, this house has too many doors."

{The Clark's long hallway upstairs of their home}

I know that to a 7-year-old this may seem kind of scary but I couldn't believe this kid was actually crying about hallways! My first thoughts were when we bought the house my children got so excited because they now believed that they were in a park or something. Our house is surrounded by land...so much land for them to even be able to see the woods that they finally had a yard they could play in and even be able to make tree forts. We have open fields to run in and it truly is every child's dream. However, here Chad was thinking about how many doors this house contained. This too would soon change.

~

When I was little I loved the outdoors! I ate, played and took naps outside.

{Charee as a child playing with her pony}

Never did I care what the inside of our house had! So my reply to my cute little son was, "What in the world is wrong with you? Here we have this huge yard and all these woods with empty farm fields for you to play in and go explore every day, all day and now you are in this house crying about how many doors there are?" And yes, I said it with a smile and a laugh in my voice as I couldn't control it.

{Backyard view of Clark's home}

I further commented to him, "Chadwick, you are one silly little boy!" I remember he sat real still and thought for a minute. He then looked up at me with a huge smile and said, "Mommy, I want to tell you something."

"What's that?" I asked.

Chad replied, as he wiped the tears off his face, "I am going to like it here!" And with that he ran out the door and outside into our beautiful landscape! From that night on, Chad always said he saw a man sitting in the tree that was right outside his bedroom window! If you ask my son, to this day, he would say it was his true memory. Every night Chad saw this man with a hat sitting in the tree. Part of the memory was that he watched him smoking a pipe and smiling at him!

Later we talked to Chad about this. We all came to an agreement after many times of Scott and I checking several times a night for a couple of weeks that as long as this 'so called man' looked happy and Chad wasn't scared of him, we decided to leave it, as the vision must be an angel that God had sent to watch over Chad so he wouldn't be scared by us having so many doors! I liked to always think of it as if it were really true; it was my Grandpa McCrossen watching over his Great Grandson! Back to the house now....

~

Because the house was so old, a lot of the doorways in the house were already wide enough for Chad to get his wheelchair through the entry. Another issue that was on our side was that because the house was an 8-bedroom home, we had two extra rooms on the first floor; one of which was connected to a bathroom that had just a shower in it, but no tub. It would make it easier for Chad to get into the shower stall versus getting him into a bathtub.

Our countertops in the kitchen were within his reach, as were the stove and dishwasher; not that Chad would ever be using them to cook! Ha ha! The only appliance that had to be modified was the microwave, and that just required being brought down off a shelf and set on the countertop, this I knew Chad would use if anything to cook!

{The microwave brought down from shelf in Clark's kitchen so Chad could reach it}

Since our house was built in 1945...it had a very high foundation, which meant that the ramp that had to be built had to be 14 feet long! We never ever gave it a thought that when Chad came home from the hospital that we would have to have one of the hospital officials come and okay our house before Chad could be released. And I have to admit I was quite angry when the personnel staff member that the hospital sent out to look at our house said to us that it's a good thing our house was pretty much safe and ready for Chad to come home. I thought to myself, *so what if it weren't 'up to snuff'; does that mean they were not going to let us bring our own child home?*

> *I will lie down and sleep in peace, for you alone, O Lord, make me dwell in safety.*
>
> Psalm 4:8

So after we got the house pretty much in order and by 'in order', I mean you all need to know that the previous owner had rented this house out to college kids before we bought it and they basically ruined it. When we purchased the house the pipes were broken. Hence, there were at least three or four inches of water in the basement. The gutters and downspouts were in pretty bad shape, which makes all the sense in the world to the people we saw that were driving by our home probably complimenting us for repairing the house! It was most likely an old run down farm house and an eyesore to them, but to us, the 'Clark's new home' was our little piece of heaven. In fact both sets of our parents thought Scott and I were crazy for purchasing this house especially with all our little kids and then we were still talking about having more babies! But it was all part of God's plan!

Anyway, so I was starting to tell you all, that once the house was settled enough to move into, which really it wasn't by some people's standards – because we had bathrooms to redo and a kitchen to fix up...but, we... mostly me...wanted my children to have pets! Lots of pets! In fact Scott had promised me that if I agreed to buy this home with him I could have all the pets I wanted. Therefore, Kayla, who was eight at the time, raised and sold baby bunnies, which later helped her along with odd babysitting jobs to purchase her first car three months before her 16th birthday!

In addition to rabbits, we had chickens and ducks for fresh eggs every morning. My wonderful husband even went as far as to buy incubators to show our children how chickens lay eggs and see baby chickens and ducks hatch! With each new 'first' fall weather we ended up with dogs and kittens that got dropped off here because our place looked like the type of home you'd find a lot of animals. Besides, the people who dropped them off most likely saw our old dilapidated shed as perfect for stray pregnant cats that weren't wanted anymore. Believe it or not, at one time I had 16 cats! I found good homes for all of them. However, it was added work I didn't need with all these kids and this big house! And yes, I had always wanted a pet sheep, so once I got one and tamed her. Scott took her to someone and had her bred so we could have a little lamb. I wanted to teach my children how to bottle feed them. The help would come in handy because as a working mom, with an abundance of children...and now pets...I needed more hands. Help was needed, especially since my husband at that time was in the business was doing service calls for 10 to 16 hours a day...every day and leaving me to be a one parent team! But it was all worth it and you will hear no regrets from either Scott or me with all that!

{Hank & Bear (laying down) enjoying the floor & picket fence Chad made for Mom before his accident}

In fact I will tell you that we had made a decision while most of our friends were going places and getting new cars, I was still driving a van I had had for 13 years! We believed in staying home with our children and spending time together; those things weren't important to me or to Scott. We wanted our kids to have a home where at 5:30 p.m. we all ate dinner together as a family. Now, if that meant Scott was to come home from his long hour days just to go back again to work...he did just that!

Scott and I wanted our children to show pride in their home, to learn all the ways things work within the home. Hence, we taught them how to do repairs so they could save money and do this when they had homes of their own; which is why today, all of my girls know how to change the tires and oil in their own cars!

I love our home now. It just has that homey smell. In fact, one cannot explain what the smell is; especially when I make bread in our bread machine. With all of the candles I light, there is really...as they say...*no place like home*! The one thing that always brings my family together, like many other families, is food!

No matter what my kid's ages were during the years, they would come from wherever to see me when they smelled food (still do)! Every Sunday I make a huge dinner and we all come home from church to eat together. Yes, even Kayla and Anthony join us. It's like a family tradition now! I get all warm inside as I write this to you and can just smell those homemade rolls with their warm butter melting on them. All of us love the sweet smell of my deserts baking in the oven, and when I make roasts, you can smell the odor coming from the oven outside before you even open the door to come in!

Those are the times that one has to admit is just pure blessings from God; to be able to still do this all together even after Chad's accident. You know thinking back, I believe my true friends – Barb Hoffman, Patty Aklam and Barb Kelly, who really knew me realized that was important to Scott and I to have us all eat together. One day my dear friends made us a huge thanksgiving dinner so we could all eat together when we came home with Chad for the first time. They were so sincere, I remember meeting them in the driveway of our home and they had all this food in their hands and just the way our friends looked at me, I broke down and starting bawling; they were true angels. Our friends hugged me, shed some tears with us and gave us the food. They were so respectful; they never came in to see Chad even though they had been concerned, our friends allowed us our time alone being home together for the first time in months. Thank you my dear friends. And to this day, Patty writes me emails telling me what a great Mom

I am and how every night she prays for my family and for Chad to walk.

ॐ-ॐ

Now back to the house: so I had this old farm house that was now my dream home, and at times I told Scott our new home reminded me of that movie, "The Money Pit"; truly, that's what it seemed like; and yes, it still does!

We finally tore down the old shed and replaced it with a brand new steel pole barn, which was Chad's last huge project before his accident.

I love my home. I love my life and I have no regrets, and yes, it's so worth it and gives me a sense of accomplishment when people come over to either visit or do phone repairs, etc...even when professionals come to see Chad for whatever reason, they say this house is unbelievable. It seems as though people always want to come over because they feel at home, and they feel happy (at least that's what they say). Wish I could take the credit for that but the truth is, this is the Lord's home, and it's because "this is truly the house of the Lord, and those that dwell in it abide in him"!

Looking back, redoing the house was fun. I love to decorate and redo rooms. Plus, I find I am most happy when I garden or work in my home because it's where I really get the one on one time with God. This time brings my walk closer to Him each time we spend time together and it so amazes me that just when I think I can't get any closer with this great God of ours, I do!

I will end this chapter leaving you all with some odd thoughts. 'Yes', I did say this to Scott one day and I still to this day tell him from time to time, "We replaced our furnace with a wood stove to heat the house and we have said this is the house we will die at because neither one of us could ever do this to a house again and move."

Scott replied, "Instead of spending money on a funeral, let's just throw my body in the wood stove." You see, his wishes are when he goes to see God he wants to be cremated.

I said, "Just bury me out in the field!" I know to some of you, our statements seem somewhat morbid. Sorry if our attitude offends anyone, but you know when you work so hard at projects that take so long and the projects drag on because NOTHING in the house is just standard; well, you get my drift. An example would be if we needed to replace a door, our doors are seven foot tall! That's not standard, so everything has to be special ordered. If you're anything like me, when I get tired, I get silly; and often I laugh at things and say things; that's what happened with our 'funeral plans'. Maybe you find it not funny – for this, please forgive me – but I guess it's one of those *had to be there* moments to find the humor!

I know some of my readers might think that my house may be too elaborate and very large. However, let me tell you the truth, 'yes' – our home is huge. It's in fact, over 3,300 square feet, with a 2-car attached garage and a full basement.

{Clark household dining room}

Our dining room area is huge and we have a pretty good sized kitchen and living room. There are two full-size bathrooms, eight bedrooms, two of which are used for my in-home office and one that we used as Noah's nursery when he was an infant. Really I am not sure if in today's time if they'd classify the nursery as a bedroom instead because there is no closet in it. Since Kayla got married and moved out, we have a spare room for the first time ever since Noah took over Kayla's room. In our home we also have an enclosed porch or front room; maybe it's called a family room? I call it *my room* as it's my favorite room in the whole house. This is a room I redid myself. It was a porch where the previous owners stored potatoes and things from the harvest. A carpet was installed and it has windows all around with a nice view. I spend my quiet time in there, listening to God's creation, the birds, and the morning doves as they sing. I watch my five baby squirrels munch walnuts from our trees and while I am out there I can see through an old wooden door that has windows like a French door into the other rooms of the house. It's where I find and catch my breath and where sometimes I find the *real* me!

This house is certainly not to everyone's liking, a lot of people think if you have a huge house like this it should have chandeliers and fancy things. Nope, that's not *this* house. Instead you will see old doors and scratches in the woodwork. In fact, for outside lights to the driveway you have to open the back door and turn on the lights outside!

Behind the wanes coating there is coloring and writing by my kids; and each scratch in the woodwork and all of the old wooden windows have carvings that say, 'Noah' or 'Kaycee'. Honestly, we even have little feet or handprints in the new cement we have put here and there.

{Family room – aka – "Charee's Haven"}

Our home is simple and plain with open spaces. There are cracks in the walls from the house settling, but it's filled with love and a lot of great memories! And they are all mine. Nothing fancy, no fancy cars, no great landscaping, and there are lots of doors and windows! I know, I clean those windows! But this house is what God blessed us with and with all the repairs we have had to do, we praise His name still!

I hope you enjoyed the tour of the Clark Family Home...that suits us all wonderfully.

Chapter Ten - Help

Here is another miracle in Chad's story I must share with you! The teacher, Ann Riffle from Western who had mainly put the fundraiser together for Chad, which was held at Bay City Western High School, made some calls about the ramp and things that needed to be done for Chad to come home. We were so upset because we didn't know how we were going to get this ramp built. We had no money! Besides, there was no time left over after being with Chad all the time. I was really freaking out. Plus, we had to have the curb cut in front of our house that goes from the driveway up to the sidewalk so Chad could get onto the ramp.

Mrs. Riffle said, "Let me make some calls." She got a company to come over right away and trim the curb area, free of charge.

She called Scott with a number to *The United Way of Bay City* that would help with the ramp. Scott made the call and they said, "We would really like to help you but we have met our quota for this year. We can't build more ramps until next year!" So we all prayed and prayed and then took a chance and we called this man back again and told him our son could not come home if there was not a ramp. We also told him that we didn't know what else to do. The suggestion was made for us to call *The United Way in Saginaw*. So, of course, Scott called them. They said, "Well, we have the materials but no volunteers to put the ramp up." Then Bay City was called and they reported, "If you have the materials, we have the workers!" Amen, we got our miracle – the two organizations got together and planned everything to help us successfully achieve having a ramp for Chad.

Workers and helpers showed up on a Saturday and within four hours, we had a beautiful ramp that looked like a deck on the front of our house! This was all of God!

{Beautiful ramp United Way built for Chad}

I remember when they came we were leaving to go see Chad for the weekend. The man in charge said to Scott just show us where your garden hose is and go see your son and don't worry about anything! He was right. Everything worked out; we exceeded the expectations of the hospital staff and Chad was able to come home!

৵-৵

Chad worked really hard in therapy at U of M. While the staff was all pulling for him, they showed no signs of hope. We watched our once strong young son flop around on this mat like a fish. It was worse for Chad because even if he wanted to try he was too limited due to his broken hip, wrist and back; not to mention the broken ribs they later found out he had.

Week after week we went back to see him, and saw no improvements. I was beginning to lose all hope again. And for the first time ever, I thought I had made a huge mistake by working toward a goal of Chad needing a hip to walk. I was beginning to think maybe all the hospital officials were right. *This is Chad's new life like it or not,* I thought. And I was reflecting on all the times the staff would say to me, that they were just waiting for me to accept the fact that Chad would not walk again. It was even suggested that I just have a good cry. Huh? A good cry, that's all I had been doing every single day since the accident.

৵-৵

Life for Scott was so hard. He had a rough time especially watching Chad not be in control of his body. Daily, hourly, minute by minute, we fought back tears, and there were a lot of times Scott and I had to leave and go out so Chad wouldn't see us cry. Here again was another time when I prayed for God to just take Chad. This was really unbearable for any parent to see. It really was, and until you walk in our shoes, you might not ever fully understand.

You know you reach a point where you cry all you can cry, and you feel all the guilt you're going to feel. Nothing could make you feel worse or any guiltier than you already do. And along with all of this, we had to find it in our hearts to forgive that person who hit our son and left him for dead on the side of the road. I knew that's what the good Lord would have wanted from me, so I tried my best; and believe it or not, there were days I did feel as though I had forgiven the driver. I so wanted that person who hit Chad just to walk in our shoes and see what we were having to see for just one hour. That's all.

Here again, I kept telling God that I was doing what He wanted of me, couldn't He just give back a little to me?

Peace I leave with you; peace I give You.
I do not give to you as the world gives.
Do not let your hearts be troubled
and do not be afraid.

John 14:27

Chapter Eleven – Adventures Outside

The time came when Chad was able to go outside for the first time since his accident. This was in the early fall when all the leaves were changing. At this time, my son was so frail but I thought if only he could just smell the fresh fall air; or, if only he could simply see the sun maybe that would help.

For days, Chad fought going outside until I had to get tough with him, which was extremely hard for me to do. After all, this was the first time he had really been awake for any real amount of time in quite a while. And the last thing in the world I wanted to do as his Mother was to yell at my son.

My thoughts were so strong on this point because in the beginning, *he wasn't even going to live*, they said.

At the hospital courtyard where Chad could go outside there had been many times when we would see babies, toddlers, young kids pulling IV stands around with them – who were even trying to cure their cancer. I remember fighting back tears and thinking how blessed I was that Chad was born healthy. We were blessed that he made it to 18 years of his life with no problems.

Mott's Children's Hospital is connected to The University of Michigan. And I found out right then and there that no matter how bad this was for us; there is always someone out there who has it worse than we do. Chad had often asked me when we were alone, *why hadn't we let him die*. My response every time was, "Chad, it wasn't my choice. God had a greater purpose for your life."

So with that said, Chad and I decided we were going to fight the fight of him getting well no matter what. Days went by until the time came when Chad could finally come home. After being away from home for four months, and three different discharge dates, the day finally arrived.

Chad's Homecoming!

{Sibling Helpers}

One would think that we would all be so happy to have our son home with us again after all this, especially after it looked like he would never come home and be with us again. But the truth was that we were terrified! Neither Scott nor I knew how to take care of our son in his current condition! And that was hurtful just to admit. And little did we know another nightmare was about to unfold right before our eyes! *Yes*, it got worse!

Chad had only been home two weeks when he was taking a shower and because he couldn't feel the feeling in his feet, he had got second and third degree burns on his feet!

~

It started off as a typical day; we struggled to go through the necessary steps we needed in order to care for Chad. We placed him in the shower and left the bathroom door open in case he needed anything. Scott and I were trying to give him some privacy because he lacked a lot of that during all the months he spent in the hospital. Besides, what 18-year-old boy really wants his parents in the shower with him?

Chad was starting to feel his ab muscles work so in excitement, he yelled for us. Happy for his progress, Scott had instructed him to sit there and keep working his abs for a while.

Little did we know that because the nozzle to our showerhead was on the end of the hose that it was causing it to dangle across the top of Chad's feet and the scalding water was burning him. We had no way of knowing the water was as hot as it was.

My husband went into check on Chad and called for me to come and look at his feet. They were a funny color; you see, Scott is colorblind and therefore unable to determine that Chad's feet were getting burnt!

Scott came out of the bathroom and said, "Chad's feet look a funny color, it's like they are pink, I think."

I said, "Honey, they are getting burnt! And, yes, they are all pink!"

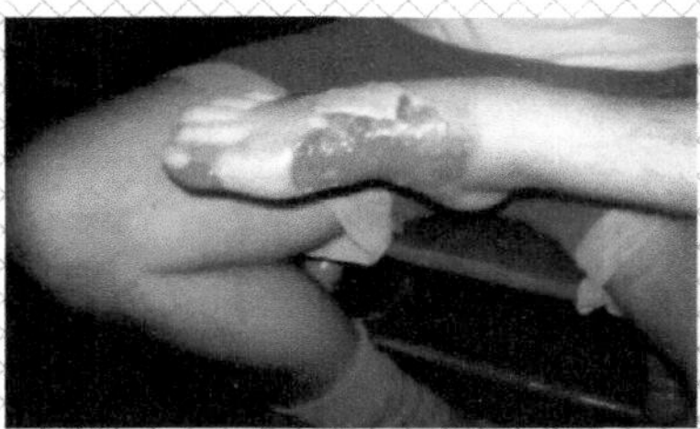

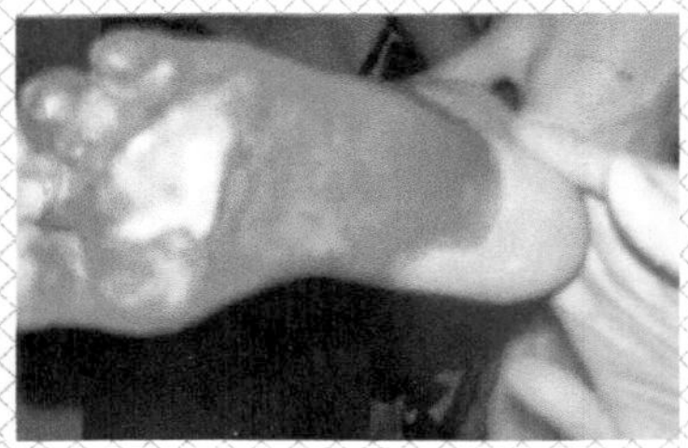

{Chad Clark's burnt feet}

Imagine how we felt, holding back tears, trying to get our son out of the shower to tend to his feet. I immediately stuck both feet in ice water, thinking this would be helpful. However, as soon as I did, the skin lifted right off the bones of the feet. Talk about a putrid smell, it smelled like burnt flesh! As soon as the skin lifted, huge blisters developed. Sadly, all the rest of my children were watching as this took place. It's bad enough for a parent to see, but when siblings who have never seen this before are right there looking and trying to help, that's another story.

❧-❧

So, back to the hospital we went. Only, this time, thank God, we went to one right here in Saginaw. We were told Chad had second and third degree burns, as I previously mentioned. The doctor there was really kind. He assured us that they see a lot of this with spinal cord patients because they have lost the sensations in their feet. It was nice to hear, but we really felt like parents who were failures. Consumed by guilt once again, I pled with God to spare us one last time; which, of course, He did.

They told us Chad would need to have fresh Band-Aids twice a day. Also they instructed us to wash his feet and then be sure to keep them dry so infection would not set in. I learned how to care for his feet and held back tears every time we looked at this poor boy's feet. It was absolutely horrible. The smell made me gag every time I had to change the Band-Aids!

During one of the washings, Chad looked up at me and said, "Mom, it's going to be okay; I can't feel it, remember?" This was one time I was so very thankful Chad could not feel his feet. No parent should ever have to do that to their child.

I pleaded with the doctor to please let Chad come home and I promised to do my very best to continue caring for my son's feet. I didn't want him to have to stay in the hospital again after only being home for two weeks. Besides, this was the eve before Thanksgiving! Knowing we had a lot to be thankful for thus far, I was bound and determined to have my family all together and at home, not in the hospital.

Long Days

Several days after Chad had made it home; I recall thinking that I just couldn't believe this was our new life. It just seemed I was in a dream and couldn't wake up. We struggled so with Chad; his body temperature would not regulate. This is a common thing with spinal cord patients. That kid would break out in a sweat when he ate! We had to learn how to dress him and how to lift him. Also, we had to be careful of broken bones mending, and learn how to bathe him. As one might guess, we even had to learn how to help our son go to the bathroom, and just when we were getting that down, in the first two weeks home, he burned his feet! Everything we got adjusted to, no longer existed because now we had burned feet that you couldn't bump! So a new routine had to be thought of and rehearsed.

This is when I thought, *where is God? Why me? Why Chad? Why, why, why?* It couldn't get any worse; even if he had died, which was very likely now if infection would have set into those feet. Each day seemed to get harder and harder and there was a moment that I thought it would just be better for us all if the unthinkable happened. I can truly tell you I was tested to the limit! But we managed all, but only with the help of God. Because once again we were told they had done all they could and it was all in God's hands once again. It was like having a newborn infant again; it really was.

Worrying was tough. I had to worry if anyone visited our son and they were sick with even a common cold – that Chad would get it. We feared he would catch an illness from cold air on his lungs that weren't even fully healed yet. Plus, it was hard on Scott and me both to deal with everyone's emotions, which were all over the place! Most nights we were not getting enough sleep. Oh, this all gave new meaning to the phrase for me, "hell on earth".

These were the days I fought back tears all day and had huge anger issues with the guy who hit Chad and left him there for dead. My faith was really tested and I began to learn what the meaning of God telling us, 'no matter what...we need to forgive one another for whatever they did'.

> *God is our refuge and strength, an ever present help in time of trouble.*
>
> Psalm 46:1

Visitors

The hardest part for us was seeing family members and friends treat us differently. They all meant well. But no one knows what to say to someone when something like this happens. And it was really hard trying to be strong, when someone had seen Chad for the first time since the accident. There were all kinds of reactions. Some people couldn't help it; they just broke down and cried. Chad handled it like a pro though. He kindly told them it was okay. Some people just looked or ran the other way because they simply didn't know what to say. I always just said a prayer for them. And when something like this happens, the old saying stands true, "You never really know who your friends are until something like this happens." I know that people really meant well, but I have to be honest, sometimes certain people drove me nuts! I got so sick of hearing "Chad will be fine!" Or "It will get better!" Or "At least he is here with you. He could have been killed and not be here at all!"

After a visit from a friend or a family member, I would rethink what they had said to Chad or to one of us. All I can say is that the words said to me after all the time we had spent away from home and how things had changed my family and my life, just made me wants to crawl out of my skin. No one knows until something like this happens to them. And just because I walked around trying to be positive and hold onto my faith and tried to keep a smile on my face doesn't mean those people were right!

Also, I had a lot of people who said that I made our new circumstances look easy, and that I could handle it because I was strong and had already endured a rough life due to my parents' divorce and my father's drinking. *Well*, I thought to myself, *then why do I deserve this and just because that happens to be true doesn't mean I was wonder woman.* On the flip side, I had a lot of people who assumed just because I had five children that I could handle one with special needs now. I tried to just think of their words as some sort of compliment and believe that those people only meant the best for me, but the truth was, this was all new to me, and it was hell! No kind words from anyone or tons of compliments were going to get me out of this and make me feel better. This was real hurt and hardship. And it wasn't going to just go away. And no one could console me.

I thought for sure I was being punished by God for something I had done, and the truth was at the time, I thought maybe God was punishing me for being a bad parent. I know now that that was not true, but at that time, it's what it seemed like to me. I know that God loved me more by allowing this to happen because out of all this, as I've said time and time again, came a lot of miracles I saw with my own eyes to show me that my God really does exist and that God never left me like He said He wouldn't and that Chad will be a walking miracle one day!

> *When you pass through the waters, I will be with you; and when you pass through the rivers they will not sweep over you. When you walk through fire, you not be burned; the flames will not set you ablaze.*
>
> Isaiah 43:2

Skin Graphs

Chad had surgery on December 22, 2008. Dr. Mitchell Farber did the skin graphs, which was done by them harvesting skin from Chad's right thigh. Everything went well; Chad ended up staying the night and I stayed with him. The next evening he came home.

Needless to say, Christmas was gloomy and we stayed home because it was very important for him not to bump his feet and mess up the skin grafts. People from our church were so kind. Some brought over gifts and some suggested we start a new family tradition. Various people offered to help us at church if we wanted to bring Chad to church. Actually that was my Christmas thing, for all my family to go to Christmas Eve services together. Our precious church family was even willing to rope off a section and post signs saying, 'be careful not to bump Chad's feet'. We opted to stay home though; I didn't want to change anything.

It was weeks and months of waiting, but the day came when the graphs took; healing had definitely taken its course and all of that was behind us. Even though the scars are still there to this day, they are fading, and it is a reminder of God's faithfulness, and a moment of pride that we can say we can overcome! *We shall conquer* is what I thought!

While waiting for the skin grafts to heal, Chad continued therapy at Covenant; it did slow down the process, but he was still able to continue. However, he was working on trunk control and he wasn't really working on anything that had to do with the feet. Due to the fact that Chad had been classified as a complete A, which means there was no hope for the feeling to ever return to the lower half of his torso, there were really no instructions to ever have him try to take steps and walk in his future.

Afterward, the weeks flew by; we had lots of miracles happen right in front of our own eyes. We had no idea what was to happen next. I went to each of Chad's therapy sessions with him, only to learn that every person that worked with Chad questioned why he was classified as a complete A. In fact all the therapists said that they didn't understand Chad's classification.

I prayed for God's help and strength, and as the days went by, Chad began to have sensations that would come and go, nothing that stayed, but nevertheless there was some feeling, and again, Chad was not walking, so we were trying to figure out how to try to get the classification changed on Chad's charts and paperwork. We just knew we were on the right track, but all the professional people we came in contact with just kept telling us that we weren't and that there is no hope. After a while it was pointless to even try.

Chapter Twelve – The Beginning

The winter before Chad's accident, I had taken a course to become a women's Christian counselor and did a book study for a book written by Joyce Meyer, called "Beauty for Ashes". If I would have known then that the class that I felt inspired by God to attend would do me more good than I ever realized, I would have never believed it. In fact the day after Chad's accident, I was supposed to pick up a key and preview my new office. These two events never took place. However, the following events did take place:

I met a woman there named Carolyn Maksimowitz. She was my teacher throughout this woman's study. Her wisdom and her pushing me to go further was what Carolyn felt God was telling her to do.

In my mind today it is possible that this was all part of God's plan in preparing me for the accident that was to take place the following July. Had I not taken this course I swear to you I would not have survived as well as I did. I would have totally lost all my faith and doubted God for being so cruel. Instead, I learned to trust and rely more on God and to give thanks for all He has done for me. Plus, I learned that this horrific ordeal was indeed a blessing from God.

One memory I have is of being in my darkest hour, calling Carolyn when we got Chad to Ann Arbor. We had gotten our son in his room, which would become his new home for the next 7 and 1/2 weeks. I asked her to pray for Chad, and she gave me the inner strength I needed once again. Carolyn also called my other teacher, Betty Rowe who said she had a vision from God and she saw Chad not walking but running through fields. To this day, Betty has never been wrong with her gifts from God and the visions she is able to see. And to be honest, I am so blessed with not one...but two...of the most spiritual God Mothers a girl could ever ask for. They have been so much support for me. I am not even sure if these two ladies know the depth of this reality.

My gratitude comes from being truly blessed to have friends such as Carolyn and Betty, who share my deep faith in the Lord to carry me through trials and tribulations. To this day, they pray for me all the time, and it's nothing for Carolyn to call me up out of the blue and ask me 'what's the matter'. Also, it is like them to say that the Lord dropped in their spirit the fact that I was struggling with something. *How cool is that?*

Carolyn and her wonderful husband, Carl have blessed us so much. I recall that we were too poor to be able to buy a mattress for our bed that we needed so badly because we were sleeping on 'nightmare' springs, and at that time all our extra money was going for Chad's medical needs, which our insurance wasn't covering. Exhaustion had set in on us from learning all of the details that went into his care.

Also Scott and I learned that this new care-giving we had to provide our son by picking him up and down, and just plain caring for him were tasks to learn. We also learned it would take all day to provide this type of care and well, just to acquire what little rest we did was difficult. Not to mention the springs were poking out of the mattress, causing a very uncomfortable sleep, as well.

One day, Carolyn called us after church and said they were going to bless somebody, (that's the way they always are, blessing others), and she said it might as well be you! Next thing I knew she had called a store and had given them her credit card number with a certain amount of money on it. Next, she told Scott and I to go pick out a mattress and box springs! I'm telling you, God is so good!

❧-❧

Another way I am blessed is that these two women, Betty and Carolyn are true friends and are helpful to me. When I am having a pity party for myself they tell me to stop feeling sorry for myself or for our family or even for Chad and to pick myself up and go on. They will tell me that there is no time for crying; we have Jesus' work to do! But when life gets unbearable for me, or for others, they are right there with an ear and hands to hold me as I cry. Plus they will even bring a big box of Kleenex! The truth is that a good friend tells you things that sometimes you don't want to hear, but you need to, and that's why I love these two ladies so much!

Prayer Partners

When we got home with Chad from Ann Arbor, Carolyn called to see if she could come and talk with me. Right away I said 'yes' because I needed her touch so desperately. Upon her visit, she asked me to go hear this doctor who gave up his title as surgeon to help people and he had tons of love for people! This man was truly a gift from God. He helped a young girl walk after seven years of her not being able to take a step. Later in my story, I will share more about this with you.

This gift from God was about to change my life, as well as the lives of some of those around me. This man's name was Dr. Andrew Sears. He had walked away from his profession because, as he put it, he was tired of "physicians giving dope, and taking away hope!" Dr. Sears meant he was tired of physicians telling people how long they had to live when really no one really knew. He was tired of the doctors sucking up any of the hope they had and giving out medicine instead of giving them love, along with the hope and will to fight. Dr. Sears is great for saying, "Everyone has the power to live; they just need the will."

Carolyn said if you just go see this man and hear him speak then you can make your own decision if you want him to treat Chad. And now here is the story with Dr. Sears that stunned us all.

I went to see this dear man speak at a church called *The Miracle Center*. Right away I thought the name of this church itself was enticing! I walked in and sat down, and then waited to hear Dr. Sears speak. I had no idea what this man from God even looked like. After a couple of worship songs this man from Uganda stood up to speak. His words were so overflowing with love and compassion. He told it like it was. I admired him so much and it caused me to wish that I could stand up for what I believed in. His words were so very powerful.

At the end of his speech, there was an altar call. We were witnessing that he was actually healing people, and I looked up at God and asked, "What do I do?"

I felt the urge to at least go down the aisle to meet this great man who would later treat my son. I walked up to him and said, "My name is Charee Clark. I am not here asking for healing for myself; I am asking it for my son."

To my surprise, this dear man of God, lifted his hands to the sky and with tears rolling down his face, he cried out in a loud voice," Father in heaven, I ask you to please heal Chad and get him out of that chair!" I knew right then and there this was another gift from God and he knew nothing about me or my son at all. After returning to my seat, I asked Carolyn if she had said anything at all to Dr. Sears about Chad, our names, his situation, etc. Our dear friend promised she had said nothing. To the contrary, she said he didn't even know we were coming.

After the service, Dr. Sears came up to meet me. He said, "Call my office and make an appointment." I listened while he said that he would love to meet Chad and work with him.

Chapter Thirteen – Meeting Dr. Sears

{Dr. Andrew Sears, Chad & Scott with new leg braces}

Well, I could not wait to take Chad to visit Dr. Sears. I really felt I was onto something and this was going to be bigger than life itself! The days would not go by fast enough for me before we would meet.

The day finally came when we were to go meet him. It was the very best day of my life since his accident. Dr. Sears gave us three hours of his time; no charge! From the very beginning he told us there was hope. I remember Dr. Sears asking Chad to look into the mirror and he made Chad see things that were in Chad's future. He pointed out that Chad had to forgive the person who had hit him and he needed to forgive himself. He also made Chad see the hope and convinced our son that he had a lot to still offer this world. Most of all he showed Chad once again to believe in God.

Dr. Sears assured us at the end of the meeting that Chad would receive the best treatment and that our son would one day walk again. He quoted verse after verse from the Bible where it said

God healed the lame. He said God allowed this to happen to our family for a reason. It wasn't anything to do with us being bad parents or God being mad at us and wanting to punish us at all. Dr. Sears said this was a gift from God and we should see it as a blessing. He said he was willing to treat Chad and looked at Scott and told Scott not to worry about money to pay for the services and that he would work with Chad one on one and Chad would get the best care ever.

{Dr. Sears counseling Chad}

Next, we discussed treatments, Scott said we had no money and that insurance would not cover the costs of these treatments because they were called integrated medicine, which had to do with the energies, a lot of faith and people would consider this to be weird. I remember the doctor putting his hand on Scott's shoulder and him saying, "Don't worry about the cost. Chad needs the best care and lots of love and hope and that's just what we are going to give him here."

Scott and I were so overjoyed all we could do was to thank him with tears streaming down our faces. This was the first doctor, who gave us back all the hope again, when everyone else kept slamming the doors on us and telling us we need to face reality, Chad would never walk again.

Like I said, I was so overjoyed when I prayed. Later that night I thanked God and I must admit I was unable to sleep. I myself thought this all sounded a little weird. But I was so desperate, I would try anything. I gave it to God and asked him to direct my steps and give me the strength to fight the good fight. And He did.

The Treatments

We started seeing Dr. Sears once a week. These visits were filled with how to do things at home to strengthen Chad up. One of the first things Dr. Sears did help build up Chad's self-esteem, and he made sure Chad felt loved. He made Chad have stronger faith and the doctor gave Chad the will power to begin this long battle he would be undergoing. Plus, Dr. Sears was also there for me. He became like a father figure to me. He told me how to massage Chad to get the muscles and nerves to start working again. This was all done with believe it or not, olive oil!

Dr. Sears helped our son get to a place where he was only taking three prescriptions a day instead of 17! Some of the meds Chad was taking were to stop leg spasms, which are what he needed to tell the nerves in his legs they were still alive. Later, Dr. Sears also took Chad off all depression medicine. It only made sense Chad was depressed, who wouldn't be? But he helped Chad work through the feelings that were causing him to feel depressed. This made all the difference in the world to our son and to us – the family.

> *Come to me, all you who are weary and I will give you rest.*
> *Take my yoke upon you and learn from me, for I am gentle*
> *and humble in heart, and you will find rest for your souls.*
> *For my yoke is easy and my burden is light.*
>
> Matthew 11:28-30

Therapy

{Al from Heartland Homecare working with Chad at home as Bear protects}

In late January 2009, Dr. Sears had decided that Chad needed in-home therapy.

{Al and Charee standing Chad up for the first time since accident – home therapy}

So, he wrote a prescription for Chad to work with Heartland and a set of leg braces were prescribed for Chad. I was involved in helping three days a week to stand Chad up and assist with physical therapy. What a job! Up until now - remember, leg braces were never thought of to help Chad, but Dr. Sears knew this had to be if Chad was ever going to walk again. These procedures were done for the next three months, and yes, things were coming alive again inside Chad's body.

Healing Begins

Dr. Sears had discovered that Chad still held a lot of anger inside that he needed to get out in order to heal completely. I knew this to be true and eventually this was going to come up some time in treatments.

I tried myself to hide my own anger issues on top of making excuses for Chad. You see, I was receiving the end of Chad's anger myself. There were days when he would punch me in the face, flip me off, yell and scream at me, pull my hair, and say lots of hurtful things. We were together 24 hours a day and 7 days a week. I knew he was frustrated, who wouldn't be. I tried to hide the bruises and make excuses, like I said. It was never a big deal because Chad felt bad after he had done such horrible things. Plus, he was so doped up before Dr. Sears took him off all those meds, I don't think he could have helped it if he tried.

After the meds were gone, he began to be a much better person and was quite a bit better behaved.

Dr. Sears recommended Chad talk to Faith, who worked with the energy within the body. She was the one person whom Chad found it hard to work with. All because she knew how Chad felt and made him talk about it. In fact, Chad said he never wanted to work with Faith again. Oh yes, Chad can be very stubborn but then again, so can I! Like it or not, this was working! In fact, Chad is presently working with Faith today. I call them 'two peas in a pod'. Yes, Chad still pushes Faith's buttons but thank God, she sees the good in our son. Thank God for Faith!

In talking to Faith, we discovered Chad held hurtful feelings with the person who hit him. He also was mad at himself. And this is where you need to know how the accident happened:

> *Bless those who persecute you; bless and do not curse. If it is possible, as far as it depends on you, live at peace with everyone. Do not take revenge, my friends but leave room for god's wrath; for it is written: "it is mine to avenge: I will repay" says the Lord.*
>
> Romans 12:14

Bio Feedback

{Colleen Rholoff & Chad}

Bio Feedback was started with Chad right away. We met Colleen Rholoff. She specialized in this machine. After doing Bio

Feedback treatments with Chad, we began to notice movements in his legs! I hadn't seen this at all since Chad's accident. This procedure that Colleen performed on him weekly was awesome. They would provide feedback for us to be able to see what levels Chad was at; like for example, his stress level and depression level. The machine would also provide feedback about Chad's anger that he carried. All of these feedback reports needed to be addressed for complete healing.

Chad Clark and his mother, Charee, feared Chad would never walk again after his motorcycle accident last July. (Courtesy Photo)

Doctor's faith helps teenager defy all odds

By JENNIFER HOEWE
The Township Times

Countless doctors agreed: Chad Clark would never walk again.

After a horrific motorcycle accident in July 2007, the 19-year-old suffered injuries leaving him paralyzed from the waist down. Seven weeks in an intensive care unit followed by rigorous physical therapy led specialists to believe Chad would remain permanently wheelchair bound.

"Medical science had given up on Chad," his mother, Charee Clark, said. "We were dedicated to finding someone who would quit saying no."

That someone was Dr. Andrew Sears. As medical director of The Living Well, 3190 Christy Way, Sears welcomed the distraught patient.

"The people I want to help are the ones the doctors have told, 'There's nothing we can do,'" Sears said.

But Chad's discouragement was twofold: a bleak prognosis coupled with extreme financial strain. His family's funds were running low since he lacked medical insurance at the time of the accident, and the initial hospital stay had accumulated an extensive bill. With little hope, Chad scheduled his first appointment with the optimistic doctor.

Sears willingly offered his services.

"Am I going to turn away a 19-year-old just because he can't pay?" Sears said, holding back tears. "I would rather be dead."

The Living Well provides uniquely therapeutic healing processes to its clients. Massage

See "FAITH" on Page 3

Dr. Andrew Sears helped Chad Clark regain feeling in his legs after being paralyzed from the waist down. Sears predicts Chad will walk again by August 15, though other doctors said it would never happen. (Photo by Jennifer Hoewe)

{Article in "The Township Times}

Colleen also saw Chad weekly for free. She prayed with Chad and taught him how to meditate. And along with this, she could use her computer to electronically zap the nerves that weren't working.

That was when Chad started regaining feeling every now and then in his lower body.

To some, all these different kinds of treatments may seem weird; I mean they were all strange to us also, but I was desperate and by this time, I had learned to listen and do what God said even if I didn't want to or thought people would think I had lost my mind, which many of them did! I also learned I would rather listen to God and do what he says than not to follow His instructions.

I let God take care of the rest; like what people thought about me or how I was going to pay for these treatments. I know that even if Chad is not walking as of yet that these things helped bring things alive again like the nerves in his body. Had I not met Dr. Sears, I am telling you, as sure as I sit here and write these words to you that Chad would not have received any help whatsoever, he would have not ever taken that first step because he was classified and was also considered as a patient that would never walk again. Before this time, we didn't really have anyone that was going to even do anything to work with him to make sure he could get the mindset to get better. We were told that to our face so many times!

Rain Drop Technique

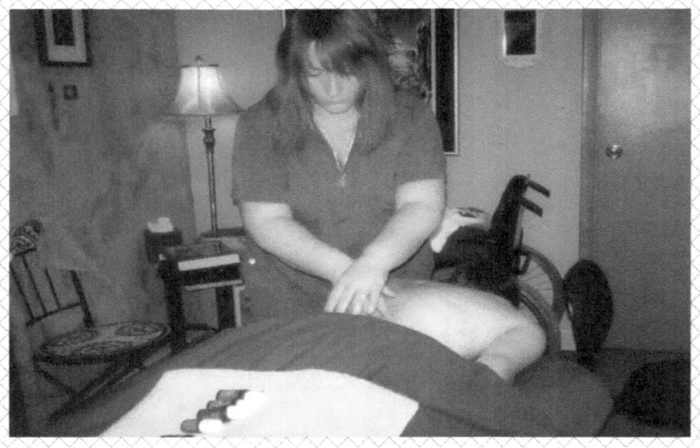

{Jill Burke and Chad}

Another type of treatment Chad was receiving at the same time was called the "Rain Drop Technique". This was massages given to Chad using oils that were blessed and all pure. The young lady who did these massages for Chad was named Jill Burke. And this was a treatment Chad looked forward to because it made him feel so good. What the idea was with the massages is to make everything start working again after laying dormant in Chad's body all the time he had been recovering from the accident. I have video I shot of Chad's feet moving as Jill would massage! This again was only the work of God!

Acupuncture

Jon Poit was in charge of making sure Chad received the acupuncture treatments. He also was a blessing to know and have work on Chad.

I must admit, both Chad and I thought this was going to be weird. But what did we have to lose? You see, Chad was afraid of needles from having so many stuck in him in the hospital.

He finally said to me, "Mom, after everything I have been through, what is a little needle?"

I said, "Not little needles, several little needles!"

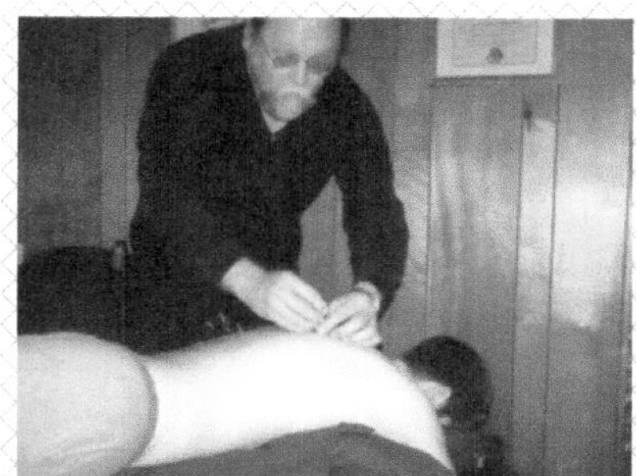

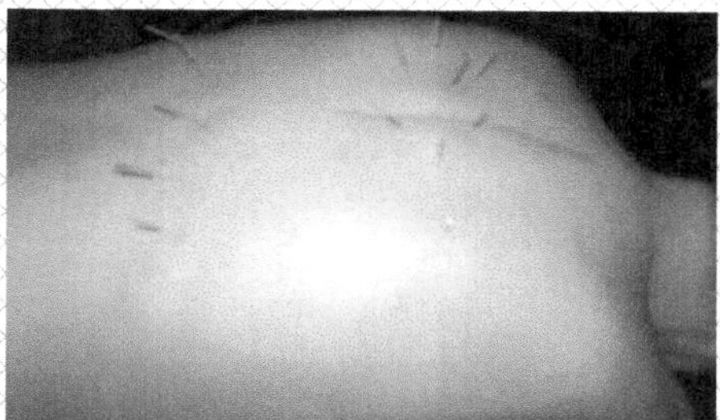

{Jon Poit and Chad – acupuncture}

Also, Jon did this weekly at no charge for Chad because insurance would not cover the costs. And that is why I would like to make the insurance companies understand and see that they should cover these kinds of treatments, because they work. My prayer is that through my book and through sharing our story about our son's accident and the recovery process, that the insurance companies will see so many things that they could consider and many more patients would have a greater rate of recovery.

We had definitely come to a time where you put your trust in God. I had surely done this up to this point and everything was going so much better.

I have to admit, I worried a lot the night before Chad was to go to see Jon, I thought he had already had all those needles for such a long time while in the hospital, with all the IVs and the shots for pain and pokes for getting his blood sugar tested every single day. So I did wonder if we should put him through more needles? That's what worried me. But...again...faith pulled us through to Chad improving even more.

In fact, Chad and I had talked about this going to his appointment that day. Agreeably, we both decided he would try this treatment one time and if it hurt at all, we would ask Jon to stop and we would discontinue treatment.

To our surprise, after Jon inserted the very first needle, the needles themselves were so tiny and thin it was a piece of cake! Chad did admit the only ones that hurt were the needles that Jon inserted in Chad's head. And they only hurt when Jon pushed the needles down further and when the needled needed to be twisted. But by doing that, Jon was trying to stimulate the nerves and we believe it worked and that's why Chad was progressing! And in all honesty, Chad inserted a couple of needles in himself, as Jon instructed Chad to do. I believe God allowed this type of treatment to happen and everything worked out because God was still watching out for us.

{Vibe Machine}

VIBE Treatments

This machine in itself was awesome! The purpose of it was to shake or vibrate the old scaly cells off Chad's nerves and make them alive again. We would do this treatment three times a week for six minutes each time. The first time we used this machine, I was scared, and it was like a huge wave of electrocution. I sat there and thought I had lost my mind. In fact, I remember Chad and I sitting there after we were a couple of weeks into using the VIBE machine, laughing uncontrollably because it was just so weird! Here he was looking to me for direction and I was making choices like this?

I kept second guessing myself and wondering if what I was hearing from God to do this was in fact really God. But it was. Also I would like to say, the machine was very loud! It's like you see in the Frankenstein movies all the electricity you hear and the noise and the lights! I first thought what kind of Mother would even put her child in this machine; let alone, join him and laugh about it! Chad was always teasing me by saying he was going to touch the machine and touch me. As I said, please read up on this; you'll find it very interesting therapy. And this was installed at the U of M where Chad was three weeks after he left and came home. So see, God knew what He was doing, Chad got a three-week jump on using this machine!

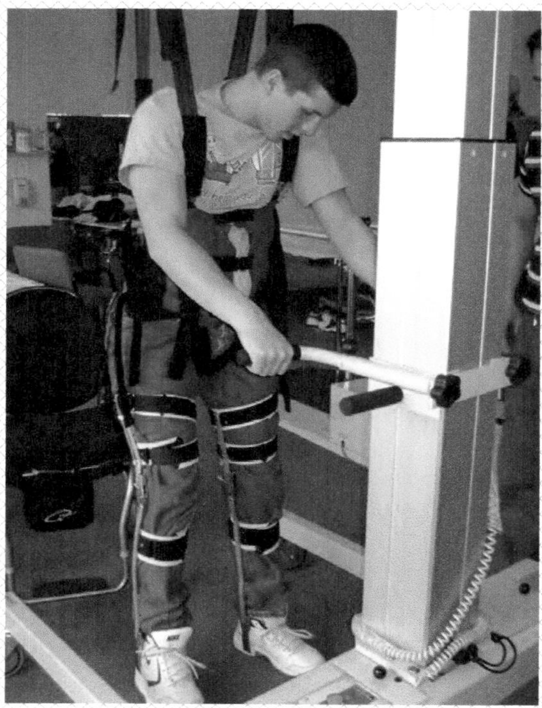

{Chad using machine to help him take steps with leg braces}

Chapter Fourteen – The Accident

{Chad and his brother, Noah – the bike before the accident}

{Chad's bike after the accident}

The day of the accident was a Sunday. During the summer months the boys would get wood for the following fall and winter months ahead, as we heat our big old farm house with a wood burning unit. Therefore, wood was gathered and then, Chad told Scott he was going to go get cleaned up and get a haircut. And off he went on the motorcycle. After leaving the haircut place, which was *Bo Rics* on Bay Road, he drove down Fashion Square Boulevard to Trautner Drive, here in Saginaw, Michigan.

The actual accident began when a black Lincoln Navigator accidentally cut Chad off. As Chad swerved around, an older couple in another car had to quickly react in order to get out of another driver's way. This driver hadn't seen Chad there on his motorcycle; so, he lost control going around a curve. Seconds later, he was hit by the Lincoln Navigator, who bumped Chad from the passenger's side. Chad hit the curb, flew over the handle bars and flew about 75 feet in the air and hit a tree. That's where his story began.

The Story from Chad's Point of View:

Chad later explained to us that he knew he was going to crash. He remembers the black Lincoln Navigator bumping him and then the next thing he remembers is waking up looking up into the sky with the taste of blood in his mouth.

With our son's first waking moments after the accident, he said to himself, *just get up*. Then, of course, he realized if he could just get up, he would be fine. Right away, he tried to move and said it hurt so bad he couldn't stand it. He kept telling himself, *just don't cry*; he'd tell himself over and over again, *just don't cry*. Chad admitted that he tried to move but couldn't and passed out. But before passing out, he saw all the blood on the visor of his helmet. When he told me this all I could do was think how scared and alone he must have felt. Yes, I also thought about the fact that we had not been there. I know now that it was a blessing for me not to be there because if I had been there and had seen all of the accident, I probably would have had to be committed. Seriously, if I had of seen him fly through the air, I would of freaked. I would have been no good and could not have fought the long battle we had ahead of us.

He tried many times after he came out of the coma in the ICU unit to tell us what happened. Of course he couldn't talk because of the tube in his throat, but he managed to draw us a picture of what had happened. Chad was frustrated because he couldn't talk and explain to us what was on his mind. We too were frustrated. Scott and I wanted to know what happened.

To see what we finally learned and had to come to grips with - please see picture below.

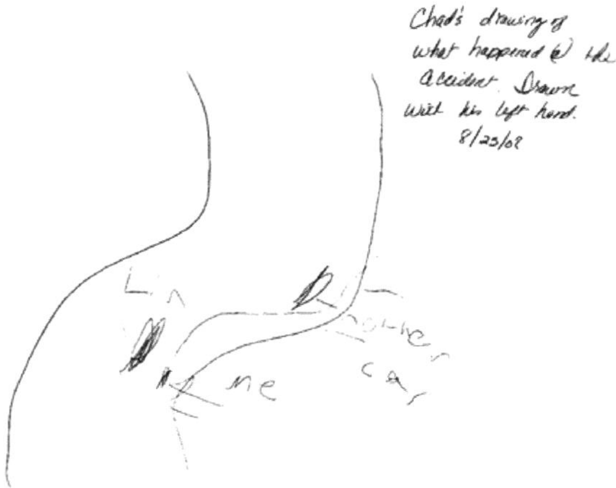

{Chad's drawing with left hand trying to explain the accident to us}

Chad had asked me several times if anyone else had been hurt. When Scott told him *no*, Chad was so relieved, he cried. That didn't stop him from asking us several times again and again for days on end about the condition of his bike and if he really did not cause anyone else to be hurt. It broke my heart to lie to my son, I didn't have a choice, he was so critical, and anything sad like that could have possibly done him in. I knew we needed to give him something to fight for, so I told him time and time again that the bike was alright. Scott kept telling Chad that the bike wasn't important, he was and we would talk about the bike at another time.

Still, Chad knew by the look in my eyes that the bike needed to be fixed. He did have a very good friend from his childhood by the name of Tadd; I know, kind of a funny thing, huh about their names? Chad and Tadd? They were *two peas in a pod*, as they say!

Tadd came over for several days and nights and put Chad's motorcycle together again. Chad was really surprised the day we brought him home! That was the first thing he wanted to look at before going in our home, well, that and he couldn't wait to see his dog.

Chad was so frustrated because he was in so much pain and wanted to talk. We did our very best to understand him but failed a lot of the time. He would just get frustrated then and cry and try to pull out all the tubes, from time to time. On such occasions, this left the staff no choice but to restrain him. And with a shattered wrist you can only imagine how painful that was. There was a time when he was so drugged up on three different pain killers that he became violent. He would plead with us to take his restraints off. And, yes, we talked the doctor into it, but only if we were standing right by the bed. Scott had to make sure he was there if we did this because Chad would just go crazy. It was so hard for Scott, especially to yell at Chad. He was in so much pain, and we didn't know how long in days or hours we had with Chad. What parent wants to yell at their child upon their deathbed? The truth is we also wanted to be honest with him; but then we had to be careful on the same hand.

Chad finally succeeded three hours before he was supposed to go into surgery to get his trach out after all this time. It had been eight weeks since the accident while Grandpa Clark, who was staying the nights with Chad now so Scott and I could get some sleep, Chad decided he was going to pull his trach out. And that's just what he did. Afterward, he had to have it put back in for another two weeks; his lungs were just too weak to function on their own. One can only imagine how that must have hurt. His throat and voice box were so sore at least for the first five weeks we had him home.

Chapter Fifteen –My Journal

During the middle of August of 2007, we were still at the U of M Hospital with Chad and he was still in ICU. He had been in ICU for four weeks and we had no idea when he would be discharged. Still, I had no choice but to trudge on with all the hope we could find. I had a strong commitment to keep a daily journal of what medications he needed to take on a daily/hourly basis. Also, I had to keep track of what the doctors said to us each time they came in to see Chad. There was so much information that Scott and I had to monitor, and with hardly any sleep, and with all the worry, it simply was hard to think, much less do all we needed to do to help our son. Keeping the faith was the only way. They were way understaffed at U of M hospital but still it was important for Chad to receive his meds at the right time so we monitored that as well. On top of everything else, his sugar had to be checked every hour and he had these boots that we had to keep on his feet for four hours at a time to keep the circulation in his legs.

Another thing was that WE learned how to suction out his trach, because he had caught pneumonia. So constant watch had to be done on that end or Chad might choke and his oxygen level would drop. There were times when the machines would go off and his heart would stop. Our situation was very scary, and we were trying to do this with no sleep.

We had to make sure the chest tubes draining the fluid on his lungs were doing their job. If they were not working properly, the pneumonia would get worse. At times, I would go out in the courtyard and scream at the top of my lungs for God to just take Chad. I felt I just couldn't do this and watch my boy be in so much agony and come so close to death so often. The whole ordeal was so taxing on my frayed nerves…constantly, watching him at death's door and still refusing to believe he was indeed at that stage – so I fought, I fought even harder and we'd both refused to give up…and then when Scott left to go back home to work, I was so overwhelmed.

Day and night I spent in Chad's room. I only went out of that room to get something to eat if the nurses would tell me I was no good to Chad if I wasn't well myself. And I found that was true. And not to mention the guilt I felt when we discovered there was no insurance on Chad's motorcycle. This too I would write down in my journal because I couldn't believe I had done something so stupid.

Another thing was that we were constantly facing the fact that we couldn't pay for what Chad needed. Deep, deep down inside my soul I kept feeling if we had more money to care for him he would have a better chance of getting well. And, believe you me, we could use extra money. Anyone and any family in our situation could sure use the money. If I was in a place to purchase needed items for Chad I would see something I needed or another member of our family wanted and if it wasn't something necessary, I would think only for a second about purchasing it and then I'd pass on getting the item. Every extra penny that we could gather together that wasn't put toward keeping our home and vehicles together simply had to go toward caring for our son.

~

The Internet

You see, I was new back then at this 'going on line' thing. Little did I know that even if you give a credit card payment to the insurance company and it is after hours in their office it doesn't go in effect until the next business day! Oh yeah, I blew it big time. I didn't read the fine lines. I thought because I could print out a receipt I was covered and it went into affect right then and there. Wrong!

So – long story short – there was no coverage on the motorcycle up until that Friday night when I bought coverage! He bought the motorcycle on Thursday. Chad needed to get the endorsement of the motorcycle so he could take a road test on Saturday. Hence, I had to express my anger in words and that is what I also put inside my journal.

~

I began not only journaling the things about Chad and his needs, and instead wrote in my journal about how I felt and what my needs were. I am really glad I did this...as now looking back and reading those journals, I have learned a lot! Wow, I was a totally different person before Chad's accident! In fact, had I not looked at the handwriting, I would have never believed some of those entrees came from me or my words! That is how bad it was! I was shell shocked to see how much healing I have had and what peace I have learned. Also, I'm shocked to see how far I have come. Yes, I still remain to this day a different person. I don't think I will ever be the same Charee I was before this accident; I mean, really how could I be?

For me...I did not write in any fancy looking diary...you know the kind...the ones with an actual key. My notes were written on just plain hospital paper. Some were written on gum wrappers – instructions for Chad and some were notes written on my hands, which I later wrote down in a notebook. It was not a pretty sight. In fact one of my journals talked about how the staff just came in his room and started barking orders at me. They were saying how I needed to learn these things and gave me nothing to write their instructions on; I thought: *how rude is this*?

ஃ-ஃ

I really learned a great deal about myself; one thing of which was that I really did feel so alone. In some of my notes it showed how desperate I felt at times. I don't think I have ever in my life been sooooo desperate! And I was so hurt, even today as I review my manuscript, I recall all the pain it brings tears to my eyes. In fact, talking about this right here reminds me of when I was writing this book and that my notes and these chapters prove out loud to my hubby, he absolutely hated it and kept telling me he couldn't read the book with me because it brought back so much pain. And when I would beg to read to him anyway, he would have tears streaming down his face, which is why I am nervous putting this book out to help people. I don't want to hurt anyone.

Back to my journal: I did think about this and in fact did write in my journal that 'some day I should write a book to warn people how to talk to doctors and what to look for if their loved ones should ever be in Chad's shoes'. I also wrote within these pages how I am sure I helped people. And this...my friends...is how God works and how all this started!

Below are some sad, but heartfelt, notes that came about because of my trying to be *real* and really honest. I wrote the information on a Kleenex box in the ICU room: August 10, 2007 @ 4:55 a.m.

"Today is supposed to be a wonderful day of celebration God! How could you do this to me? How? What did I ever do to deserve something this bad? Do you hate me that much? AM I REALLY that bad of a person? You never give me any help. You brought Scott and me together on this day. WE were married in your house and in your name. I prayed to you that if you would allow Scott and I to get married when we were dating in high school that I would do my best. I did my best God. I gave it all to my marriage and my kids. I stayed home with them and took them to church. They knew of you and knew you well. Why can't you help me? Bring Chad out of this! PLEASE! This is hell watching him like this. I suppose you will choose to take him home with you on this day also, so that for the rest of my life I can remember Chad died on our anniversary. Lord, we got down on our hands and knees what more do I have to do. Don't take Chad. Please don't take Chad at least not today. Please

bring Scott some joy today. He has been such a super Dad and wonderful husband. That's my gift that I want to give to him today. Because I am stuck here and can't get out to get him anything. Are you listening God? Do you hear me? Do you even care?"

Another note was written on September 3, 2007 @ 3:12 p.m.

Today is my Grandpa McCrossen's birthday and yesterday I had to spend my baby girl's 21st birthday with her here in this place instead of at home or someplace where she could feel her birthday was special. I am so mad! I would have never thought that Kayla would be here and it would be like this when we celebrated! Poor Kayla; I just look at her and she is so stressed. God please don't take Chad on Grandpa's birthday. And don't take him tomorrow on my Dad's birthday.

I am so sick of people coming in here telling me do this or do that. God, please help me to be kind to these people. They are just doing their jobs. But really, this is going on for so long. Will it ever end? I am so sorry for anything I have done wrong, please forgive me! Will Chad ever wake up? He has been sleeping all these weeks. How much more blood can come out of those stupid tubes in his sides?"

Chapter Sixteen – Nurses We Call Family

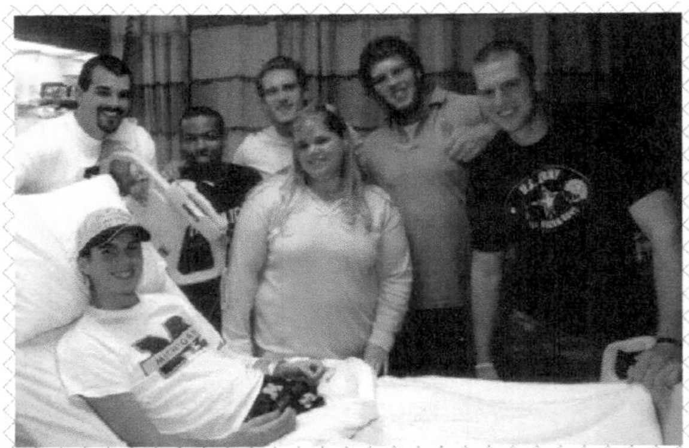

{The U of M football team inviting Chad & Kayla to their V.I.P. game}

When you see the same nurses around the clock, they become family. Chad's nurses would cry with us, and cover me up with a blanket in the chair when I would fall asleep from exhaustion. They would sneak me in soda pop or food and give us words of hope; they really went all out for us. That's really why Scott and I kept track of different things; plus they showed us how because they knew it would benefit Chad.

There was this one nurse who would request Chad to be her patient every night that she worked. Her name was Jenny Chang. She had two small boys herself; and she did all the little extra things for me. Nurse Chang would tell me to go take a walk and call me on my cell phone if Chad woke up. The nurse would bring me something back if she went to lunch. We were most grateful of all because she prayed over Chad and treated him like her own son. Her being there was a blessing from God. There were numerous nights Nurse Chang stayed after her shift with no extra pay if Chad had had a rough night.

You know I am convinced that God does place special people in your lives just at the right time, and I don't know why I am so amazed at His great and mighty works, but he places people in our lives that we don't even know with the special purpose to help us! God gives us these dear people just at the perfect time! I would think He would always use family members, but He doesn't most of the time; well with me this is true, but that's why I am so honored to call this staff family. There wasn't one day that went by that I didn't thank God.

He has showed you, O man, what is good. And what does the Lord require of you? To act justly and to love mercy and to walk humbly with you God.

Micah 6:8

Another nurse I was thankful to have was named Karen. Her last name escapes me, but at the time she was like the mother I needed at that time.

I remember when Chad was coming around and getting ready to move to the rehab floor, he had given me the finger because he was so agitated at the time. Afterward, Karen was first to scold him and say, "I don't care how much pain you are in; you don't flip your Mother off! She has been right by your side since you got here." And Karen made him apologize to me. I really believe that the devil had entered Chad's body because his eyes looked scary; Karen assured me that the meds were really strong and Chad was on a lot of them; and that often, the meds make people crazy. After all, Chad was on Oxycodone, Oxycontin, Morphine and Valium all at the same time. Not only did this make him crazy, we also had to make certain our son would not become addicted to the drugs which were actually considered in some circles to be street drugs!

Chad's favorite nurse was Clara. She was young and pretty; her eyes just lit up when she talked to you. She was the one that gave Chad the nickname, 'Stud Muffin'. It was so thrilling for me as a Mom to be able to sit back and watch my young handsome son interact with these young beautiful nurses. I did think to myself as I sat by and watched quietly that this was something most moms didn't get to see, and if it hadn't been for his accident, Chad would never have brought a girl home for me to experience this of him, as he was always too shy for anyone to meet us! It was right then that we started to see things for what they really were.

I remember when I came home and Kayla was caring for Chad; she did this so I could spend some time with the little ones. My goodness, I was missing out on a lot of things with them! I missed out on so many of Noah's firsts! His first days in 4th and 5th grades; you know all that stuff they do in the later years of elementary right before the kids graduate to middle school. Anyway, I got this call on my cell and it was Chad! Clara had made him call me. It was the first time I had heard my son's real voice since the accident! I expected it to be Kayla calling me with her usual hourly check in and report on Chad. But to my surprise it was Chad!

He said, "Hi, Mom. I love you, and I have some good news!"

I couldn't talk; all I did was cry. His call was another huge blessing from God, because if you haven't heard your son's voice on the phone in about two months, you forget what it sounds like. Plus, on top of that, I didn't really expect that I would be talking to him ever again, especially on the phone. I got the words out that I loved him too and I was so happy he called me. He said "Clara wanted me to call you and tell you that today when she tested the feeling in my legs, I could actually feel it a little bit!"

By now, of course Clara was in tears and asked to talk to me. She said when she tested Chad's feet on the bottom, even without looking, he could tell her what foot she was touching! I finally got the nerve to tell her that this happened to me while tending to Chad and when I reported it to the doctors of course they told me it was normal for a spinal cord injury patient's body to do this. To my surprise, she just told me, "What do they know?"

Clara had seen it many times before and some of the people she saw this feeling awareness with are walking today, even after they were told by those same doctors that they would never walk again either!

She and I agreed we all serve a greater God than that and only He would know and heal Chad and make him walk again some day!

The Promise

Well, that was my sign from God. That's all it took to convince me that it was all in His control and this was going to be alright somehow. The feeling did not stay in Chad's feet, but it had been there. It was there! I knew it was going to be a long, long road ahead, but now we were certain the miracle would one of these days happen. I just had to learn how to trust solely on God, and be patient. I am still learning how to do that to this day. Don't get me wrong, there were days that I thought this would never get better. I still did nothing but cry a lot of the days. It was hard for me to get through the days, even when the days and nights ran together. And then there were some really, really, long nights and days. And even today, as I write this book, I feel the same way. That's when I let the friends I have pray me through. There were a lot of times, and still are today, that I had to rely on those friends and family to pray for me. I have made peace with that. I had to, and once I had made peace with God, I was okay. If He decided to take Chad home with Him, and Scott and I still think that way today.

Although I don't understand it and probably never will, I see what kind of a life my son would have had back then. We still think that now as we struggle so much with different things like, blood clots, a hip that keeps coming out of the socket, pressure sores, urinary tract infections, so on and so fourth. In fact, I still wonder what kind of a life Chad will have and even when, 'yes', I said, 'when he walks, just how different his life will be. Our son can never get back those five and one-half years now that he has suffered through this accident. And I always tease Chad and tell him that's the first question I am asking God when I see Him face to face – is why He allowed this to happen to my son and why in the world it took Him so long to give Chad his ability to walk again. I have come to the understanding that we may never know why God allows what He does for people to go through, and 'probably' – I tell my family, 'when I get to heaven I won't even care to ask because I will stand in awe of God!'

The Lord will guide you always; he will satisfy your needs in a sun- scorched land and will strengthen your frame. You will be a well- watered garden, like a spring whose waters never fail.

Isaiah 58:11

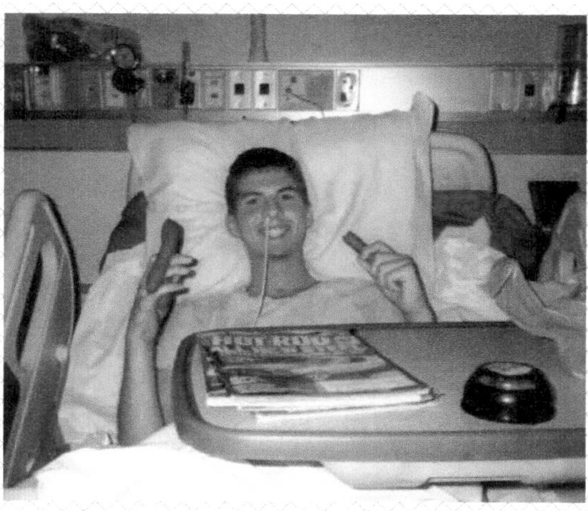

{Chad enjoying his favorite beer slicks from our local meat market, Ted's Meat Market; they kept him well supplied}

Chapter Seventeen – God is Still Faithful

One day, I was down and depressed because our family who does everything together, had been torn apart. I missed all of us being together. I fell to my knees and asked the Lord to make our life better. I pleaded and begged Him to do something; give me some kind of hope; tell me it was going to be alright if Chad didn't walk for a while. I was so desperate. It was the night I got the phone call from Chad. He was on the phone informing me that this precious nurse who's name was Clara, had told him to call me. They wanted us to know that when testing Chad's foot, by touching the bottom of his foot, it had moved!

I was in tears because although Chad didn't feel it, that to me said the nerves were working! I thanked God and then not only seconds later was told by the doctor there that this development probably didn't mean anything. When people have spinal cord injuries the legs and feet have spasms. I was crushed, but I prayed and got this calm feeling that the doctor was wrong. I pleaded with God again to show me how to go about knowing that Chad would walk again. That's when I learned a couple days later when we went back for the weekend to visit Chad that there were several nurses there, especially the ones that prayed over Chad who advised me that they had seen several people just like him who had done the same things and they walked! News like this was always a good sign; if the legs and feet move that is wonderful progress. The nerves are not dead!

And once again, that's what Satan loves to do. I played this game with him several times throughout the time Chad was in the hospital. You see, not just Satan, but other people (for whatever reason) love to steal and take away the hope that one needs to keep fighting the fight. So I thought from that moment on, no one was ever going to steal the hope away from me again. I got sick of having the wind knocked out of my sails. I knew that I had to find hope and keep it, and no matter what, I had to dig down deep and find that hope and hide it, because after all, I had to fight for my son; there was no other way. My mind was made up that no matter what the doctors told me and after all, they were humans. And, so, I would have faith. God gave them a brain and hands to work on my son, but I knew they themselves were not God; though it is nothing for God to move mountains. He created this huge big beautiful world. So I knew it was going to be God and Him alone who would give Chad the ability to ever walk again some day.

Come to me, all you who are weary and burdened, and I will give you rest. Take my yoke upon you and learn from me, for I am gentle and humble in heart, and you will find rest for your souls. For my yoke is easy and my burden is light.

Matthew 11:28-30

Later that same day I learned that it was God looking out for all of us again. We were told that Chad had never severed his spinal cord. He had just stretched it, which meant that it would in time, and probably a LONG time, grow back together again! If the spinal cord had been cut in half, it could never be repaired and there would be no hope of it growing back together ever! X-rays showed the stretch but not anything severed! In fact, when the X-rays were first done, they showed Chad was not only injured at T4 and T5, but in C6 and C7. Months later when Chad was starting to feel his abs was about the same time the swelling was gone in the C6 and C7 injury! So to this day, he is classified as having a T4 and T5 spinal cord injury. That...my friends...was all of God's doing!

~

Well, the day came when Chad came home! The home inspection that the hospital had passed and was done. Because our home was an old farm house that meant it had extra wide doorways so Chad's wheelchair could easily go through, we had a bathroom attached to the bedroom we were going to put Chad in on the first floor with a shower stall just for him! Our countertops in the kitchen were already low. The only thing I had to do was to bring the microwave oven down off the shelf and place it out on the countertop. Was that a blessing or what? God knew what He was doing I believe when we purchased our home. I can't help but think of the amount of money it would have cost us to make improvements to our home. Thank you so much God!

~

This is the part of the story I really like. Scott and I were asked by our Pastor if we would stand up before our church, because it was about Thanksgiving time again, and they couldn't think of anyone who had gone through as difficult a year as the Pilgrims had, except our family. We agreed to share our story; after all, our whole church family had supported us and prayed so faithfully for us. It was the least we could do. Plus, it was also the first time we had seen many of them in awhile and this was going to be the very first time for us to go public with details of Chad's accident, hospital time, further surgery, recovery, and 'yes' even the lack of recovery in some areas.

Boy, our sharing our story was hard to do, but we did it. I had a mission and needed to tell my church family that God is faithful. I wanted them to know first hand that He never leaves you ever...like He promises. And although this was a horrific thing to happen to our family, we had no choice but to still be thankful to God.

With tears flowing down our faces, we shared our story: Chad's story.

We told about how God was right there at the scene of the accident. Our point was made when we shared that it was our belief that Chad hadn't been alone.

Scott and I told about us praying for a quarter of a lung capacity and within three hours, Chad had reached the desired level. We shared about how we prayed for Christian staff members to work on our boy, and we got them.

My husband and I were thankful for a place to stay at Mark LeChard's house. We shared how there was a time that we needed a second car there and we didn't know we would...but my darling daughter, Kaitlyn had just turned 16, and like most teens, really wanted a car!

Buying a car was the last thing we wanted to do, but she got on the Internet and found one about thirty miles from where we were. So we drove there and Kaitlyn fell in love with the car and we bought it!

They were all leaving to go home after we had purchased the car because school was starting for the fall, Kaitlyn handed me the keys to her car and said, "Here, Mom, take my car, you might need it because Dad is coming home with us!"

She never even got to drive her new car until I came home three weeks later. See, God knew Scott and I needed another car at U of M! We didn't know it at the time we got the car! God is faithful.

There is so much more. We had people bringing in food for our kids, and school shopping was even done for them!

Then the time came when I needed to come home because the rest of the kids were in school and I needed to sign paperwork, go to conferences, things like that – the type of things that every parent does to keep up with their child's progress at school. Scott really needed to return to work and Chad was now out of the woods. He had started rehab at the hospital.

Most of the time it was hard for us as parents to choose what we were going to do next. Again, God came through again. Our eldest daughter Kayla had just graduated from college, three weeks before Chad graduated from high school. She was in between jobs and was able to stay the remaining three weeks at the hospital with Chad while Scott and I came home. That was still hard but Kayla and Chad checked in with both of us throughout the day every day while they were there. Oh, little did we know that the day of Chad's accident was the day our now new son-in-law, Anthony had asked our daughter Kayla out on a date after work. They were supposed to go out that evening but then Chad's accident happened. It was still all part of God's plan, because through all of this Kayla needed someone, and God sent Anthony.

Anthony knew exactly what Kayla was going through as his older brother a couple years before Chad's accident had gotten into a car accident, crushed his knees and was told that he too would never walk again. So Anthony talked with Kayla every night encouraging her that Chad would or could walk someday like his brother is doing now. Oh, how great our God is to put different people in our pathways and love on our daughter and take our place when we couldn't be there for her!

People took care of my beloved pets, as well as my house in my absence.

My huge garden I had put in that spring was a worry for me. After all, fall was coming and everything needed to be canned and picked.

I remember praying in the hospital chapel several times for funds to come from somewhere because for the 7 ½ weeks Chad was in the ICU unit it costs us $400,000! The life flight from Saginaw to Ann Arbor was $7,000. Where were we going to get the money to pay these bills? Our youth group at church all put together a bake sale and raised just enough to pay the life flight bill right to the penny!

Oh there is just so much God has done for us! He is really faithful. Somehow my bills were getting paid.

The amazing part is the family business was going under and our house was about to be repossessed, but when we got back home, everything had miraculously gotten taken care of; our business was still striving and to my surprise, the mortgage company had called to say they found a $6,000 mistake. We were $6,000 ahead on our mortgage! God is really good!

> *And my God will meet all your needs according to his glorious riches in Christ Jesus.*
>
> Philippians 4:19

It was so hard for Scott and me to share our story especially with our children sitting in the pews looking at us. I had a hard time even listening to Scott tell his side of the story without crying, and I found I couldn't even look at the congregation because there wasn't a dry eye in the whole church.

As I started to share my side, Scott put his arm around me and I took a deep breath to take his turn sharing. For the first time ever, right then and there I couldn't bare to look at the hurt on my kid's faces. I found myself not looking at anyone and just staring up at the balcony at the back of our church praying in my head for God to get me through this. And then I found something! I felt all the love these dear people felt for us! I am not kidding, no words can explain it. The accident was a terrible thing to happen to our son, but through it came so much love. I have heard people my whole life tell me they love me, but when you feel it for the first time, I swear it was like feeling God's love for me through these dear people at my church.

That day at the church it was gut wrenching sharing our story, but there was so much to tell about God's amazing love! His word is true, I know I was there and I lived it! And I KNOW that this is what changed me into the strong Christian I am today. Even as I was sharing my story on Chad's accident, I felt like I was going to throw up! And for a minute there as I was explaining how he looked in that emergency room when we got the call I could smell the smells in that room. Smelling those smells and trying to share what had happened was way over the top for me!

The day I stood up and told our story was the first day it hit me in the middle of my sharing that God was there and He held Chad and I knew He had my son's life in His hands! As I was talking, it really hit me right then and there; God spared Chad's life for a reason. And then flashes of God holding Chad and possibly breathing life back into my son filled my head. Oh, there were some glorious pictures I was having during my talk.

❧

And as if God didn't give us enough miracles of love, at the end of the service is where we met Josh Holt and his Mother Susan from the Care Pages for the first time. They drove three hours just to be there and meet us! So after church we came to our home and had pizza and exchanged stories of our boy's accidents. We talked about therapy and things to help one another but mostly we came to realize that we had God in common!

Chapter Eighteen – Sammi

Chad's dog's name is Samantha Rose, "Sammi" for short. This is a dog that was given to Chad when he was at U of M. A family by the name of Kennedy, raised and bred pure yellow labs.

{Little Samantha Rose – Sammi}

Joni Kennedy had asked me from reading the Care Pages and keeping up with Chad's story, if she could bring Chad a puppy. She said her family had prayed about this and that God was telling them to bring Chad this puppy. Well, I didn't know what to do. So I prayed, and that became one of my sayings. "It pays to pray!" Anyway, Joni assured me if the situation didn't work out and it was too much trouble, that she would take the puppy back and hold no hard feelings. She asked me to think about it and told me to take my time.

Now I love labs. They are the nicest dogs, but we already had a black lab of our own, named Bear. However, during this time, he was getting old and it was nice to just have one dog in the house. Plus, I was thinking about how hard it was going to be adjusting to this new life and then house breaking a puppy? Scott and I struggled with this decision. We would do anything to put a smile on our son's face. Anything, no matter how hard it was going to be.

The day came when even though Chad still had the tube down his throat, he communicated with us from a spelling board. Scott and I prayed about the puppy and if we should get it or not before we asked our son, "Do you want the puppy?"

Of course he wanted her. I explained everything to him and told him who Joni was. We tried to make sure he still wanted the puppy.

"Yes," Chad stated.

So, on September 25, 2008, Sammi became part of our family.

That day came. Joni asked, "How about if I bring the puppy to Chad at the hospital?"

She so wanted to meet Chad. I didn't think this was possible, so I asked the hospital staff and to my surprise, they said they highly recommended it! In fact, the hospital said that Sammi could stay in Chad's room and actually live there with him! I couldn't believe it! In fact, they said it would help him and most likely the dog would be great therapy. Plus, we also learned that we could take the dog to a special school where she could be trained by Chad to help him with needs he might have. Everyone learned that Sammi and Chad would grow to be very good for one another!

Sammi's Arrival

I waited and waited in the hospital lobby for a woman I had never seen or met before in my life to be carrying a puppy for my son. Chad was sleeping so I went out to get some fresh air. Then I waited. I prayed while I waited. We had said 'yes' to the idea of getting the puppy for Chad, but we didn't think about a crate, food, etc...none of us had immediately thought about all the puppy things you need. Also, I hadn't gone out to get the needed supplies, and here the puppy was coming to us...and there was no way I was leaving Chad alone to go shopping for them.

Being at a turning point, I told God, "Well, this is all in your hands. If you want Chad to have this puppy, you will need show us how I am going to be able to come up with the supplies." At the time, I was just incapable of worrying about one more thing or my head was going to explode!

Well, lo and behold, this woman came in with the most adorable puppy! And of course everyone stopped her to see such a cute puppy!

We hugged and shared tears and I knew this was a true gift from God. Joni shared a story with me of how she had been in the hospital and had been very ill. She explained that she stayed a long while in the hospital; so, her husband had gotten her a puppy. The puppy had made her feel better and really helped her to recuperate.

And to my surprise, Joni had thought of every single thing for a puppy and then some! She brought a brand new crate filled with puppy food, toys, collar, a leash, bowls, puppy wee wee pads...you name it, and it was all in there! Now was that God at work or what?

Chad and Sammi Meet

During the time that Joni arrived, Chad was asleep. Therefore, Joni and I talked for a while just the two of us. Chad and I had put in another rough night and he needed rest. I needed to hear what Joni had to share with me and so, we played with Sammi. This was the first real joy I had had since Chad's accident. It felt so good to smile and see this new gift of life. Besides, I am an animal lover and missed my big dog, Bear at home as well as my cats. So this felt really good!

I asked her to please meet Chad and share her story with him, as she had shared with me. I thought this would help him. We both dried our tears and put on smiles and walked down the hall to Chad's room. We put the puppy on his bed, and the puppy immediately lay across Chad's legs and went to sleep, only one time did she look up to us as if to say, "What? I know what I am supposed to do!"

From this time forward - actually from the time Chad woke up and saw her lying on his bed, he was instantly taken with Sammi. She also was from that time forward the best puppy ever. She never barked or whined and was always calm. It really saddened me that Chad could not get down on the floor and play with her as he is a big dog lover himself.

The doctors and nurses there always carried Sammi around the hospital and played with her. This was fun to watch but I know it made Chad a little sad because he was confined in bed and couldn't show off his dog.

The day came when I had to make a hard decision, and that was to take Sammi home with Scott and I because Chad was really busy working with his therapy now every day and I couldn't bear the thought of keeping that adorable puppy in her kennel while Chad was away doing his therapy. Scott and I also thought it was time for us to get Sammi used to her new home, which she probably thought by now was Chad's hospital room. So I suggested to Chad that I take Sammi home with us and bring her back on the weekends when we came back, that way he and Kayla wouldn't have to worry about her. He sadly agreed and I know by the look on his face he was sad and depressed. I felt horrible but knew it was the best thing.

ঌ-ঌ

I will never forget when we left late one Sunday evening to come home for the week. I picked up Sammi from Chad's bed and felt I was doing something really wrong. My fear was that I was hurting my son so deeply; so I cried walking out to the car with her.

{Sammi learned to wink ----- Graduation Day for Sammi}

Scott listened as I told him I thought we were doing the right thing. *Yeah right*, I thought, as if Chad wasn't hurt enough I go and hurt him again!

Depression

As you would have figured, depression had set in because Chad was not so doped up and had started rehab. He hated therapy because he flopped around like a fish, and everything always hurt on him, plus the fact he couldn't walk. Our son knew he had lost at least three weeks of his life being put in a coma and he couldn't ever get those weeks back. Not to mention, he wanted to come home and knew he had weeks of therapy ahead of him. This broke my heart, I felt hopeless and I wasn't even the one in Chad's shoes, I was outside looking at everything revolve around him and his life threatening situation.

After deciding to bring Sammi home with me, I managed to housebreak her and get the pup used to the house before Chad came home. This made Chad upset, but he was in far too much pain to play with her anyway. I kept my promise with him and on weekend, she came with us, which ended up being a great idea until every Sunday evening arrived - and we had to leave.

But time healed Chad and he finally got to come home and now he and Sammi are the best of friends!

{Chad and Sammi snuggling}

Chapter Nineteen – Fundraisers

Fundraisers were becoming very important to Chad and they were also providing his needs. We found out that the insurance company would only cover so much of our costs to find the healing for our son that we felt he needed and deserved. What we learned instead was that unless a person had the top of the line insurance, which we didn't have, there would surely be areas that they would not help as much as needed and in some areas, not at all.

The very first fundraiser was at Ames Church. It was here that the youth put on the bake sale, as I mentioned earlier.

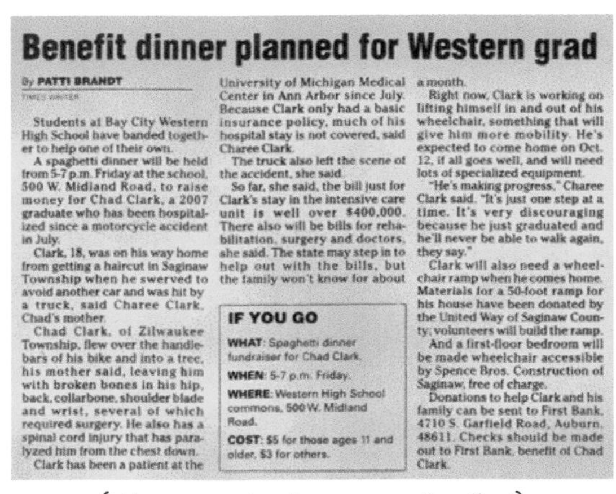

Benefit dinner planned for Western grad

By **PATTI BRANDT**
TIMES WRITER

Students at Bay City Western High School have banded together to help one of their own.

A spaghetti dinner will be held from 5-7 p.m. Friday at the school, 500 W. Midland Road, to raise money for Chad Clark, a 2007 graduate who has been hospitalized since a motorcycle accident in July.

Clark, 18, was on his way home from getting a haircut in Saginaw Township when he swerved to avoid another car and was hit by a truck, said Charee Clark, Chad's mother.

Chad Clark, of Zilwaukee Township, flew over the handlebars of his bike and into a tree, his mother said, leaving him with broken bones in his hip, back, collarbone, shoulder blade and wrist, several of which required surgery. He also has a spinal cord injury that has paralyzed him from the chest down.

Clark has been a patient at the University of Michigan Medical Center in Ann Arbor since July. Because Clark only had a basic insurance policy, much of his hospital stay is not covered, said Charee Clark.

The truck also left the scene of the accident, she said.

So far, she said, the bill just for Clark's stay in the intensive care unit is well over $400,000. There also will be bills for rehabilitation, surgery and doctors, she said. The state may step in to help out with the bills, but the family won't know for about a month.

Right now, Clark is working on lifting himself in and out of his wheelchair, something that will give him more mobility. He's expected to come home on Oct. 12, if all goes well, and will need lots of specialized equipment.

"He's making progress," Charee Clark said. "It's just one step at a time. It's very discouraging because he just graduated and he'll never be able to walk again, they say."

Clark will also need a wheelchair ramp when he comes home. Materials for a 50-foot ramp for his house have been donated by the United Way of Saginaw County; volunteers will build the ramp.

And a first-floor bedroom will be made wheelchair accessible by Spence Bros. Construction of Saginaw, free of charge.

Donations to help Clark and his family can be sent to First Bank, 4710 S. Garfield Road, Auburn, 48611. Checks should be made out to First Bank, benefit of Chad Clark.

IF YOU GO

WHAT: Spaghetti dinner fundraiser for Chad Clark.

WHEN: 5-7 p.m. Friday.

WHERE: Western High School commons, 500 W. Midland Road.

COST: $5 for those ages 11 and older, $3 for others.

{Write-up in local newspaper for Chad}

The next fundraiser was put on by the Carrollton/Zilwaukee Eagle's Club. This was so great! People came from all over to help our son! How wonderful was that? On this heartfelt night, even the people who worked at the Eagle's Club gave not only their time, but their tips! A lot of local businesses donated items to raffle off in an auction.

Eagle's Fundraiser

We found out when we came home that Chad's insurance would only cover one wheelchair and Chad had to keep the wheelchair he picked out for five years. No exceptions! He had heard of this standup wheelchair that would allow him to stand up and of course the insurance would not cover it. The doctor reported Chad needed this chair to allow the blood to flow which would allow the nerves to keep working. This particular chair was a must! So the Eagle's Club heard of this and approached Scott saying they wanted to raise the money for Chad. Thank you God! They had raised a lot of money but this certain standup wheelchair was going to cost us $14,000! Yep, can you believe this? In spite of all the hard work that the Eagle's club did, we were still thousands of dollars short! What were we going to do? My whole family and of course loved ones and friends again started to pray. We just had to have this chair for Chad!

Little did we know that God had brought our local TV5 news media to the fundraiser for a reason.

I received a call one afternoon from the Standing Wheelchair Company, which was the company of course that fitted Chad for his chair. They had called to tell us that someone saw the news clip on the TV about Chad's fundraiser for the chair. The story inspired them to pay the whole entire bill on Chad's behalf! That was definitely one of God's angels!

With this standup chair, Chad is able to go work out in the pole barn like he used to and today he changes the oil in our cars. He has even put new brakes on my van! Chad still struggles and of course things are harder for him, but this chair has made life a lot easier for him. However, he has mastered playing the Wii in his standing wheelchair and has even learned how to dance in it!

&-&

Another fundraiser was put on by Mike and Stacey Wilcox at *The King Fish* in Bay City.

Chad Clark

Auction & Comedy Benefit Dinner

Sunday, October 12 2008 @ 5:00 p.m.

1019 N. Water St. Bay City

Only $20/person: See Contact to Purchase Tickets

DINNER * AUCTION * COMEDIAN

All proceeds go directly to the Clark family to help offset medical expenses

Chad Clark, 19 a 2007 graduate of Western High School was in a very serious hit and run motorcycle accident and has incurred many medical bills, and costly treatments. Chad is paralyzed from the waist down, but with your generosity he hopes to walk again one day.

{Flyer for another Fundraiser for Chad}

We needed more money due to the fact that the insurance company said that Chad had exceeded his time in therapy. We were told he couldn't have anymore unless we paid for it for the next six months! Keep in mind now we had no choice because feeling was coming back within Chad.

{Tickets printed up for Fundraiser}

"He needed it NOW," Dr. Sears said. And the insurance company said 'integrated medicine' was not medicine! So that's how and why the money from this fundraiser was used.

Mike and Stacey were friends Scott and I had met from elementary school. Our Kaitlyn and Kaycee are friends with their girls, Tiffany and Ashly. What a nice family they were to do this fundraiser for us!

The Western Fundraiser

In early fall, Western High School put on a fundraiser for Chad, which consisted of a contractor coming to our home to put in French doors that extended out to a deck in Chad's room. There was also a new heating system so Chad's room would be warmer. Other additions like new carpet, a new mattress and box springs for Chad's bed, a new recliner and a TV were made available.

Cash was collected and used to start a trust fund for Chad for later expenses! (which we found out later again that God was looking out for us because when Chad burned his feet we used that money for gauze and supplies that the insurance company would not cover!) Oh and did I mention God knew Chad was going to want something to do while being confined to a chair for a little while so He allowed someone from this fundraiser to give Chad a brand new Xbox! Actually it was the Halo3 system that he had been asking for even before his accident occurred. This was a double blessing to have this because the Xbox gave Chad something to do in the hospital while recovering from three different surgeries!

The best thing about all of this was that the school had a home football game and Chad had been a football player in high school while there at Western. So before the game they had a spaghetti dinner and while at halftime on the football field, the school released balloons in honor of our son. Everyone also wore stickers with Chad's picture on them to remember to pray for him to recover! How awesome was that! Scott, Chad and I had to miss it, but we have wonderful pictures to enjoy! Boy, the love was so overwhelming! There were all true Warriors!

Many more fundraisers will have to be planned I am sure in the future. One thing we really need to do is to put together a tax-free trust fund for Chad.

Chapter Twenty – Accidents/Humor

{Chad trying to dance with Mom (Charee) in stand-up chair}

{Kaitlyn trying to make Chad smile at a doctor's appointment}

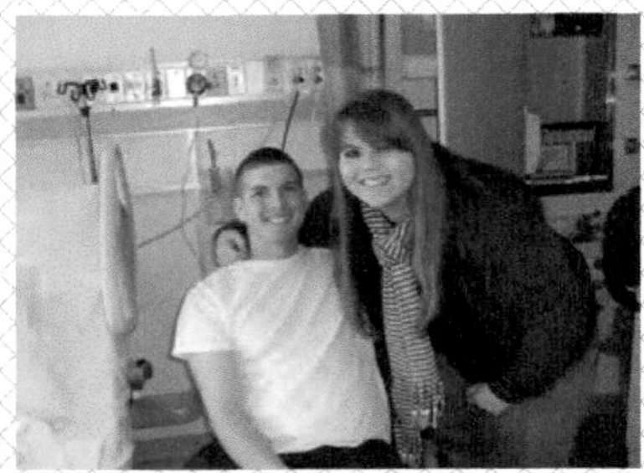

{Kaycee spending the night with Chad before hip surgery}

{Our first vacation after Chad's accident – The Creation Museum}

{Charee and her Kiddos – The Creation Museum}

Accidents

Yes, we have had plenty of accidents with Chad at home, other than him burning his feet I mean. They weren't ever planned. I guess accidents aren't supposed to be, or else they wouldn't be called accidents, now would they?

The one accident that comes to mind because I just got finished telling you about Sammi, is that, we had signed Chad and Sammi up at *PETSMART* to take puppy classes. Chad went to the very first class and that was all, because after that was when he had the shower incident and his feet got burnt.

I recall we pulled into the parking lot at *PETSMART*, and it was raining. This was one of the first times out alone with Chad, and I recall that as I got the wheelchair out, I let Sammi out and hooked her leash on the back handle of Chad's chair. While I was trying to get my son out of the car, Sammi tugged on the chair and away the wheelchair went and then down on the parking lot Chad went! All wet - he was, and while I was trying to get Chad back in the car or the chair, Sammi took it upon herself to run all over the parking lot. To make matters worse, we were already running late and now I had this wet kid, with a wet puppy and a wet leash.

I looked around for someone to help me lift Chad up or to help me get the puppy, and that early in the morning there was simply no one around.

We went into the class, tears in my eyes, and Chad looked up to me and said, it's okay Mom, I can't feel if I am wet anyway!" We both cracked up laughing and by the time we got into the store, I had tears in my eyes from laughing so hard and like I said, Chad and the dog were all wet! If you are in a living situation such as we all found ourselves, it was soon clear to us - you have to find the laughter in these things or you will go nuts!

❧-❧

Another accident we had that comes to mind was, when Scott and I took Chad out for the first time together, Chad was still admitted in the hospital, but we were allowed to take him out. We had gone to *Dairy Queen* because Chad was having cravings for Butter Finger Blizzards. This treat probably felt soothing on his throat; plus, it was one of the very few things he could eat at first.

We came out of the store and Chad asked us to please let him try to go down the curb so he could get a feel for what he had to do. We agreed and he fell right forward and if we hadn't been there to catch him, he would have fallen right front-wards, chair and all. Needless to say, Dairy Queen was packed that day and we had tons of spectators! Chad and I laughed, Scott was in tears.

Yes, Chad and I have learned laughter is the best medicine.

❧-❧

There were also a lot of times when we first got home with Chad that we had to dress him and it was hard. Often, we would bang heads, or his feet would flop off our knees trying to put on his shoes.

Chad would also flop forward and we would bang heads if we weren't watching. One time he got a little cut and made a huge deal out of it! No stitches required!

Hellion Days

There were often days that Chad would be a little hellion and I would get mad at him and smack him lightly on the legs or on his behind. He would laugh and say, "I don't know why you do that; it doesn't hurt, and I can't feel it. You know that don't you?"

No one knows when you are used to disciplining your child that now he won't be able to feel when you hit him, you don't think of that. Still to this day, I do that and he says the same thing! And I have never been one to use time out. That to me is for sissy Moms. I would talk to my kids and explain the situation. Then if the behavior persisted, they would get a smack on the butt or hand. Some things are just too dangerous to let happen too many times.

Oh there have been many, many more accidents that have happened and still do. You just learn to go with the flow and handle each accident as they come along. I mean no one prepares you for these things and we have no instruction manual.

Warning

I have tried and tried to tell people all throughout Chad's accident that motorcycles are dangerous! It's not that I dislike motorcycles; other drivers just don't see the cycles as easily as they do the cars. This means that motorcycle riders are in danger all the time. This is what happened to Chad.

I have had MANY people tell me, "It won't happen to me;" or they have said, "I'm in complete control," or my favorite, "I can handle it!"

"Wow!" I say. If they only knew what I do now! The truth is that they are so foolish if they think it will never happen to them or to someone they love.

My whole point was that people, who own motorcycles or drive them, have to think about their loved ones. Why take chances and possibly lose your life, only to leave your loved ones with hardship if it's not necessary? If someone was single and never wanted to be married or have kids, I would say fine, ride a motorcycle all you want. However, young people like Chad who certainly had a great many loved ones he'd possibly leave behind...and in this case, he did take that chance. He wanted the motorcycle, purchased and drove it...yes, it was his choice to own and drive a motorcycle that fateful day. Chad took that chance that he'd leave loved ones in a world of hurt.

Still, people don't want to even think of that. People in today's world are selfish and greedy. Our whole lives have changed now because of the choice Chad made one day and I say that's not fair. No, I do not resent my son; it's just if I could teach one person and change one person's life, then this horrific thing we went through would be worth it.

In my personal opinion, who in their right minds would bring such hurt and torment to their loved ones? You see, this really bothers me because if people wouldn't be so selfish and think about other's needs before their own, this world would be a much better place.

Life has been hard with Scott and me seeing the hurt our other children have had to go through because their brother is in this condition. All of it really makes me sick.

I know the accident was not Chad's fault. I know God had a purpose for allowing this, but every single day we suffer with the affects this has caused. And our once good life we had is changed and gone forever. People just need to think; Chad thought he was bullet proof. A lot of people think they are, so that is my point with this whole section. Your lives could change in a blink of an eye; mine did and I used to be one of those people who thought this could never be me, but it did, and it was in the blink of an eye!

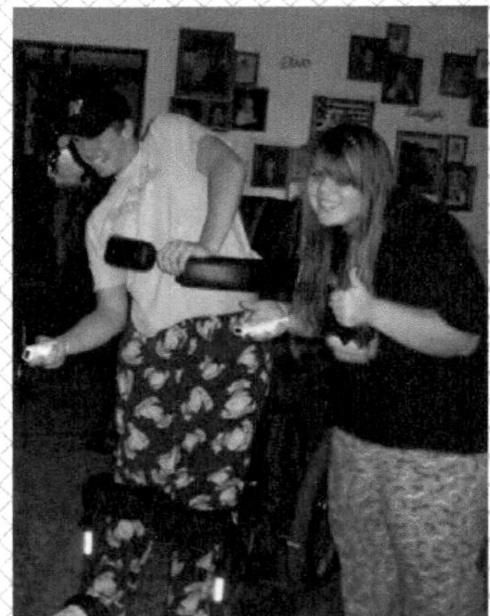

{Chad and Kaycee getting Chad to exercise by using the stand-up chair and his new Wii System}

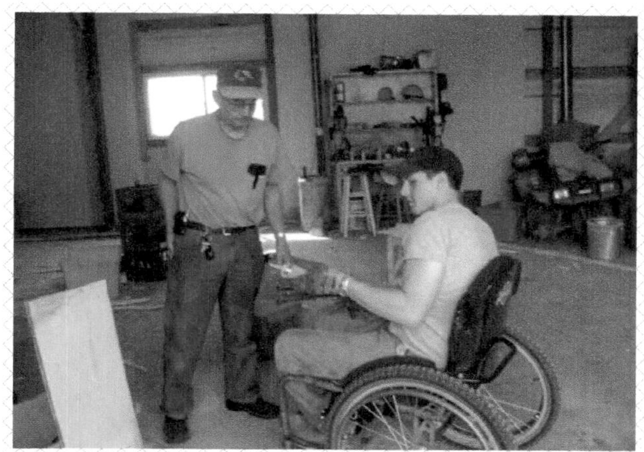

{Grandpa DeShone (Tom) and Chad building a log splitter}

Chapter Twenty-One – Our Family and Beyond

{Chad's Baptism}

Our Family

Now, to communicate the whole story to my readers – I now need to move on to a serious side. I must tell you about the effects all of the events from the moment that Chad was in the accident to now – as anyone can imagine, this brought so many new emotions to our family. The rest of our kids found it really difficult; not just because Chad took time away from them. Nevertheless, it was hard to go out in public, not because it was embarrassing, but it was all so new and different.

Noah, my youngest, found it frustrating because Chad was no longer the big brother he had been so close with and had always done a lot of things with. He saw the strong Chad he once knew who was now becoming very frail and weak because he had so much with which to deal. Noah missed playing football, riding four wheelers and just talking one-on-one with Chad.

Chad was always in a lot of pain in the beginning because of the broken bones and he inadvertently took a lot of that out on Noah. Not only was this a trauma for Noah, as well as for Chad, but we had told Noah at the hospital in Saginaw that we would be home after a little while. We had no idea that Chad would get flown to Ann Arbor. Nonetheless, we didn't come home for three months and that was very hard for Noah to regain trust in us again. Not only that, he still has issues with knowing where I am and being apart from me. If I told him I would be home at a certain time and was late he would fall apart, so Scott finally convinced me not to give him an exact time as to when I would be home when I went away with Chad.

Kayla, our oldest, she pretty much was able to keep her emotions and thoughts under control, although she had a lot to deal with, as she was being left in charge with the other kids here at home. They cried a lot because they were scared, they missed me and all of us being together. See, I made sure no matter what, we always ate dinner together every night, that was one thing Scott and I really agreed on when raising the children. Thank God she didn't see the immense amount of time and tasks Scott and I did with Chad. It was hard enough for her to see Chad when she stayed with him in our place after he got to rehab. Kayla also found it frustrating with Chad and his situation, my goodness; she spent her 21st birthday in the ICU unit celebrating with us all. She had also been given the task of telling and preparing her siblings that Chad may not make it.

{Chad and Kayla}

{Charee with Kayla and Chad}

Kaitlyn, my second oldest daughter, was having a hard time dealing with this all too. She helped Kayla keep things in order at home, as best she could. She was turning 16, and the world was hers; at least she thought it was.

Kaitlyn has aspirations to become a physical therapist. She'd like to specialize in spinal cord injuries. She now is a senior co-oping at Bay Medical in Bay City, in the physical therapy department. Go Kaitlyn!

{Kaitlyn, Chad and Kayla}

Kaycee, my third oldest daughter, was 'partners in crime' with Chad. Kaycee and Chad had been buddies from the time Kaycee was a baby. They are very close. I will never forget the look on Kaycee's face when she first saw Chad after the accident. It broke her heart, but I am so very thankful to God that Kaycee kept her faith through it all. In fact, Kaycee went away to *Bay Shore Camp* – a Christian camp and made sure she called and found out how Chad was every day. Kaycee kept asking everyone she would come in contact with to please pray for her brother.

I tell you all this, to help you. This affects everyone, and it doesn't go away until you deal with it. My once close kids were now all fighting and saying hurtful things. The stress was so thick all the time around everyone, and when they would see me up at the hospital, I would cry as soon as I saw them because I missed them so much. I couldn't help them because I was so consumed with Chad.

This one other time I had to go out in the garden at the hospital and scream to God, "This just wasn't fair. These kids didn't deserve this. They went to church every Sunday, they all did well in school, got good grades, made the Honor roll, didn't do drugs, etc..."

I couldn't figure out why God would allow this to happen to our family. This was another time I had to cling to my faith as I found it very hard to forgive that person who hit Chad. That person was living a normal life, their family was not torn apart, and they were going on with their lives and got to be with their family. What was the deal? They didn't have to watch their son suffer and go through the days not knowing if he would live or die.

Chapter Twenty-Two – Viewpoints of the Family

Kaitlyn: Her Outlook on the Accident

My daughter Kaitlyn shared with me her feelings and outtakes on Chad and his accident. This is what she said to me and her feelings of how things are today.

The first time Kaitlyn saw Chad the day of the accident she viewed him from the doorway of the hospital room. Before she even entered to be with him, she said all she could see were the tubes he was hooked up to and that his face was so swollen she got scared. Knowing it was serious, her heart just kept beating faster and faster as she got closer to his side. Realizing the seriousness of the situation, as she walked closer to Chad her fear to touch him was overpowering. All she could hear were people talking about how he wasn't going to make it.

Kaitlyn thought her first visit was like walking through a dream but knowing that it is real. She also has told me that even though everyone was saying Chad was going to die, she felt like it wasn't going to happen.

However, my daughter did say that when she saw Grandpa Aveary and her daddy go behind the nurse's desk and personally talk to the hospital in Ann Arbor about flying to come and get Chad that she felt relieved. But she did however worry when she heard talk about Chad not surviving in the air flight to the hospital; but she felt peace that it had to be done.

As time went by, Kaitlyn didn't believe it when anyone told us Chad would never walk again. It was in the back of her mind all the talk and the things that were said, but deep down in her heart, she knew that if her older brother could fight and live...then walking was certainly in his near future. Another problem she had besides believing that Chad would never walk again was the way people stared at him and our family all the time. She thought the first time she saw Chad in his wheelchair, he was retarded. Now keep in mind, he had a tube in his nose, a trach in his throat, from not eating he had lost so much weight that it didn't even look like her older brother. And all this was hard for her to endure and yet have people stare. It really bothered her when people would stare. It was like she felt their stares meant we weren't good enough or that people viewed Chad as being retarded also just because he was so young and in a wheelchair. To better describe her feeling was that she thought people assumed we were abnormal. Kaitlyn feels like when people stare at us that they pity us. She said she felt like a second class citizen and that she had a hard time dealing with it and still does to this day.

Another huge mountain for Kaitlyn to climb was trying to answer the phone calls while we were away from the thousands of people asking questions about Chad's condition. She didn't know what to say and didn't know any of the answers to the questions people were asking. And when on the rare occasion she did know the answers, Kaitlyn was afraid if she should say it or not, afraid of the person's reaction when she told them the answer. Like for example, people would ask her if Chad would be able to walk again.

Kaitlyn did tell me though that another memory she had was the day we brought Chad home for the first time after his accident. Although the house was a little different with a new ramp and extra things to help Chad get along now, that Scott and I did a good job trying to keep everything normal. She indicated that even though there were new things, that warm safe feeling was still there and it was clear we all had the love for one another that we shared.

And on the way home that first day we brought Chad home we had all stopped at McDonald's to grab some lunch because we felt things were going to be pretty hectic when we finally got him home.

She remembers her father and me being afraid to take Chad into McDonalds because we weren't sure about getting him in and out yet and we had Sammi the puppy with us, so Mom had made the decision to eat outside. But this she felt was normal and good, maybe it was because they were playing with the puppy, but anyway, it was fun to her and she thought that all this new stuff wouldn't be so bad!

Another memory Kaitlyn has is also on the first day Chad came home and he hadn't seen her new car yet. She was sure he would have noticed this new car in the driveway when he came in but that's not what happened. They had talked about her getting a car together as soon as she turned 16 and how excited Chad would be, so while he was in the hospital, we bought this car for Kaitlyn. She talked with Chad a lot and months passed before he was going to be able to see the car. She thought for sure that would be the very first thing Chad looked for when finally months later, he got to come home. But he didn't ask about the car right away. Therefore, she told him to go look out the window and he responded to her that he couldn't see. The windows were up too high. That broke her heart, not only that he couldn't see her new car, but that he couldn't even see out the windows.

Today, Kaitlyn puts Chad's needs first like this wedding she is planning with her fiancé, Kirk. He will be in her wedding and she doesn't care if the other people in the wedding party say things about why the wedding party will not be on the altar with Kaitlyn and Kirk while saying their wedding vows because there is no way for Chad to join them up there. It now has just become second nature to her to do this for Chad. She also tried really hard not to pity him when helping him and has a hard time being tough when she knows what will be good for him to do on his own.

It's a daily struggle to see a loved one have to live in this way but Kaitlyn also knows that Chad is healed and is just waiting for God to give us that one huge miracle she prays for day after day and allows Chad to walk! She struggles with seeing him in the wheelchair, as this of course was something that never crossed her mind while growing up with him. He was so active and never sat still.

Like me, she finds it hard to understand how someone could do this to her brother – and then abandon the scene - and just leave her brother there to die.

Kaitlyn feels the loss for Chad she tells me every now and then. And it's so sad but this is reality. She often tells me it would be different if Chad were a lazy person who did nothing all day, but he helps people. In the past, he did everything all the time; never was he one to just be still for any length of time. This reality is hard for our daughter to accept.

What Kaitlyn would like people to know most is that her love for her brother has grown through the experiences the two of them have gone through because of his accident. Love endures where there is hope for things unseen. Her belief was strong and continues to be so.

Kaycee: Her Thoughts on Chad's Accident

My third oldest daughter shared her thoughts with me about our life these past few years as a result of her oldest brother's motorcycle accident. I have to tell you that her take on Chad's accident did surprise me in ways I never imagined. Interviewing her really made me think and caused me to realize things that I didn't even think about before. In fact, I find this chapter shocking and yet a little sad. But the positive thing is that in everything else I found in her words, feelings and thoughts, I also found good things and you will see as you read this chapter.

Today is July 17, 2012. My Kaycee is now 18 years old and she graduated just a month ago from high school. She now works in our family business with my oldest daughter, Kayla. Kaycee has plans to go to college in the fall and become an optometrist along with going into the field of becoming a missionary. Her goal is to fix people's eyes so that they may read the Bible and study God's word. And this is her take on all this.

As with all my kids when I asked what their first thoughts were of the first time they saw Chad in the hospital room, Kaycee thought she had been in a dream. Actually, she believed she had been having a nightmare. Everything was really chaotic, but she didn't think he was going to die. Kaycee said as she looked around, she felt really scared. Chad's clothes that had been dripping with blood was something she remembers seeing and they were cut all in pieces all around him. As she looked around, she saw Scott and me crying and looking really scared for ourselves. This I'm sure was frightening to her to see her parents scared. Right away, Kaycee felt like throwing up when she faced this scene.

Kaycee also remembers Kayla telling her not to cry because it would be more upsetting to everyone...and so she tried not to cry. Instead, Kaycee told me she went into the bathroom to cry. When she told me this, I cried. It is so sad to think my child went alone into the public bathroom, to cry because she was scared and her heart was breaking. And my daughter's thoughts were not to make Scott and I anymore upset than we already were. We are so blessed to have girls like these!

She also admitted that she felt all alone and like God had just left her. Kaycee said she felt like God just didn't care and that he wasn't around anywhere. She kept praying though and tried just to be calm. Kaycee said she didn't know what to say or do and everyone looked so sad. All of it caused her to realize she had never felt such sadness before. Nevertheless, she remembers that she kept praying very hard, as often as possible, and more times than any other time before!

When the medical team put Chad into the helicopter, Kaycee thought then that this was going to be the last time she would ever see her brother, Chad. And she said she tried to prepare herself emotionally and secretly for this. Also at this time, she felt things would never be the same. She said as she looked around because it was late at night and noticed all was still and quiet except for the noise the helicopter was making and that also scared her. There was a strange split second that she thought I was gone too. And that our family would forever remain apart.

I asked Kaycee to give me her thoughts and feelings as to the first time she saw Chad in Ann Arbor, Michigan. Again, she explained to me that she felt God had for sure given up on us. Rather than let Chad see her cry, Kaycee held back her tears. She tried to be strong; I do remember the look on her face in that hospital room that day, it just killed me! I held so much pain for her. She was so strong, and I too thought God was done with us.

At the time that Kaycee heard Chad was not going to ever walk again, she said she never once believed it! She knows one day he will walk.

You know, by now it is beginning to feel really great that my children were never struck with a belief that Chad wouldn't walk. They all believe in miracles. Which brings me to the next part — the walking part. Kaycee said that when medical staff told her Chad would never walk again, they also asked her if she was okay with it. My daughter said she was devastated. She remembers telling them that she was just happy he was alive and that we could visit him!

Being home with Chad when he finally, after all those months in the hospital came home - Kaycee admits those were intense times; but that after we got a system down, she shared with me she felt the same warmth and love in our home that had always been there even before the accident. All the 'new stuff' such as the ramp and chairs she said were just a part of Chad. Kaycee said she thought of those items as just something he needed for *right now time*; and that those necessary medical-type items would soon go away.

When I asked Kaycee to share more, she said her memories of all the different people that came into work with Chad; she felt was awkward even though they were nice. She did get sick of coming home from school and seeing different people in the house but she said that became easier to live with because it was good for Chad and as time continued, it became easier for her. She knew it was the best thing for his health. Plus, she had begun to realize that the things we were getting for Chad helped me care for him, so she put up with it.

One sad memory for her happened one day when she came home with exciting news about being nominated to be on the Queen's Court at school. However, after Kaycee rushed home to share the news, everyone was so busy with Chad and making sure he had the best of care that she sadly had to wait to tell me. There were other times that sharing about her senior year would have come natural but it was too hard to interrupt me because I was busy learning something about how to better care for Chad or I was busy taking his vitals or whatever. Yep, and learning of the times Kaycee needed me definitely cuts right to my heart too!

ᘛ-ᘚ

There were so many things going on at once...and it was all these little things that I was going through that just broke me; I was a broken woman. Our children had a broken mom and every new day brought something new to break my heart, which I thought was already shattered at the time. It's one thing if it were a sibling of mine or a parent or a spouse that was in this type of urgent care need — not that it wouldn't hurt so much, but, honestly, when it's your own children who are depending on you for every little thing; well it is different.

ᘛ-ᘚ

Kaycee mentioned that when Chad came home from the first hospital stay that seeing everything he had to go through had actually served to make their relationship grow stronger. They had always been close and even called each other 'best buds'. When Kaycee was born, for some reason Chad had taken a 'liking' to this sister the best. Maybe because at the time he thought with three girls, three sisters, that he was never going to get a brother so, Kaycee would have to do. I'm not really sure but am so thankful for their relationship.

It is my belief that God knew what he was doing way back then because Kaycee has been the one all along to talk to Chad about his feelings and beliefs about God. In fact, Kaycee is the one who got Chad going to Bay Shore Camp, which is a Christian camp in Sebewaing, Michigan. For the last five years he has been a counselor there for the kids. He's been sharing his story...a story that he would not have been able to share if he had not been in this accident. Chad has brought so many youth to Christ and he has touched their hearts as well. I am lucky if I have brought one!

In seeing day after day what he had to do, Kaycee said she tried at first to help Chad and do it all for him, but soon learned that she didn't want to take pity on him either. So, she would tell him he could do it himself and she would stay and help if he needed her. However, most of the time she tried to encourage Chad to do things for himself. Yet, our daughter was also able to sympathize with him about how hard it was to go through what he was.

There were those tender times when she told him how proud she was that he was brave and was doing it himself! And she too, like me, would have to go away and cry as it broke her heart to tell him no! Now think about this, Kaycee was only 12 at the time of this accident.

When we were still living in Ann Arbor with Chad not knowing what the outcome for the rest of our lives was going to be, Kaycee went to Bay Shore Camp. She went with our church youth director and his wife who had four little ones whom Kaycee had babysat for many times. They asked if they could take Kaycee with them that week at camp, not only to help with their little ones but to get Kaycee's mind off of everything. You know, I don't even remember saying 'yes' she could go, but somehow, she ended up going. It was there Kaycee said she *found* God.

Every single person at that camp, the youth, the visitors, the staff, the parents of kids who attended, prayed every day faithfully. Everyone prayed at dinner times, at worship times, at events, etc... Kaycee said she was overwhelmed, and to tell you the truth, we felt all those prayers at the hospital! Chad started getting better each day during that entire week Kaycee was at camp! Our dear son wasn't healed, but he had escaped death! We knew for sure he was going to live!

Kaycee confided to me that her being only 12 years old at the time made her feel as though she might not ever really get to experience her own normal childhood. She went from being 12 to 18 and she says she doesn't know where time went. To her it felt like from the time we came home from the hospital with Chad after his accident, that she had to become an adult.

This is the part of Kaycee's side that shocks me, but I find it true myself; I guess though I never had the guts to admit it or voice it until now. The part about family — she said when some members of our immediate family first saw Chad they took pity on him and us as a family. Some people she would hear blame Chad for doing this to himself and that they would talk about how Scott and I weren't good parents. Kaycee heard people say they believed Chad deserved to suffer consequences for making the choices he had made to purchase the motorcycle in the first place. Also she heard that her brother was being punished for things he had done in his past.

She didn't like family get-togethers because there was always someone who was saying mean things about us and that hurt her feelings. Kaycee knew a lot of what she heard was false and that what people were saying were lies and gossip and harmful to her and her entire family, especially to Chad. In fact, after talking about this one part of our experience, all of my kids have confessed that they too heard the talk all the time and didn't want to say anything in fear they would hurt my feelings. They knew this would only add to mine and Scott's pain and that we had already been through enough. "It was hard," Kaycee said. She couldn't understand at the time because the people would be so different when they were around us but when alone and with other family members, they would say the things they did, which some of them were cruel and untrue!

When Chad burnt his feet; that to Kaycee wasn't a big deal. This also shocked me. She said she remembers seeing me clean the wounds and thought to herself it looked and smelled gross and again made her want to throw up; but also she remembers when she would see me tending to those burns that she just figured that's what Mom' s do. It was like changing a diaper and cleaning up puke! So this didn't seem that different to her. As far as caring for Chad's feet, the only real negative thing she knew and thought to herself was that every time I was taking off the old bandages that it was going to smell.

Another thing that upset Kaycee was when family would make hurtful remarks about that and 'yes', some said that Scott and I, but me especially because I was the 'stay at home Mom' should have known better. Kaycee actually overheard others say that we should not have allowed Chad's accident to happen! Now I have to be honest; I am human, and those remarks especially from family members really hurt me as well. But I know it has all made me a stronger person today!

I am so thankful to God that He was there when these ugly words were being said about me and my family. I am also thankful because I know beyond a shadow of any doubt that my kids know that God is a God of love, and He definitely does not punish us like this and He uses the very bad to make us better people so He can use us for His own good. I tell my kids all the time just as I will share with you, that I believe God has put me and my family through a test and I believe with my whole heart we have passed this...and many other tests. And it is true, God must really love me and think I am a strong woman of faith and He wants to use ME to do his work, because He never gives us more than He knows we can handle! There I said those same words, the words that I hated when people would say them to me! This is how much I have grown and I see it for myself. Today, in fact, this knowledge gets me excited! And there for a while I was on my high horse thinking wow, God didn't allow this sort of thing to happen to many people; so that must mean He is not going to use them as He has us. Not true! Don't worry, God made me come down and see He just has a different kind of work for me. Because believe me, I do not think I am one of God's favorite people by far. It is my hope to get to heaven someday and ask Him, just what did He think He was doing by allowing this terrible thing to happen to Chad and Chad's family and why for such a long time?

Who knows, maybe it will take another 28 years before Chad walks, and I pray I will see it in my lifetime. But I do know God is right there with me every step of the way and it has changed me into the person whom I love today!

Kaycee is convinced that this had a really big impact on Chad and his life. People take him differently now. He is more in tune to God. She said that she feels had it not been for this accident Chad would not be as close to God as he is now. I believe it also. It has made him an awesome man of God and I just know he will be a pastor one day. I know that is his calling; just like I knew Kaycee would be a missionary one day.

And yes, when asked the question 'how she felt when we went out in public for the first time', Kaycee said she held her head up high! She was never embarrassed of Chad and our situation. My daughter said she knows God is using this for a greater purpose and that the day Chad walks will be the day God gets the glory and we feel His love to the full extent! She didn't care if people stared; they were always staring at her anyway for her weight or something she was wearing so Kaycee used this to help people. She was real with them and people were attracted to her. Kaycee reached the kids at school who had a handicap or weight problem. She started a ministry right there at her school on campus to reach people and share God's love with them. She said Chad's accident helped her draw people to herself. It just takes my breath away to see this and learn that this type of 'good' came out of our situation! Like when she was chosen not once...but two...years in a row for Queen's Court in high school; this is a good thing; as usually it is only the popular girls who get chosen.

People love Kaycee and she loves people, all kind, and colors, wealthy, poor and needy. They are all the same in Kaycee's eyes! That is another blessing God gave me. It's one thing just to say you're proud but my goodness, I feel it! To feel this proud of our daughter; it is power! In fact at Kaycee's graduation ceremony one classmate announced and thanked Kaycee for her big heart! Now my daughter could be the most 'beautifulest' girl in the world; (and to this mother, she is. Yes, of course, I think all my girls are!). Nonetheless, it's far more important to me to know they do have a good heart and they show it to others! All of this never would have happened, I don't believe if it had not been for Chad's near death accident.

When I asked Kaycee how this had changed any of us for the good or bad what were her thoughts; she said this: on baby brother

Noah, it's sad to see all the things he never got to do that the older ones were able to do, such as vacations, camping, and fishing. Also she mentioned that Noah got robbed of his childhood, in that he feels pressure now to do all his chores and sometimes Chad's too; and to be the man around the house to take some pressure off Scott. Her Daddy changed because he now worries more, and looks sad most of the time. It's hard for her to see him feeling stress and he hardly laughs like he used to. And me: she said I am way over-protective, that I hardly ever smile, and that I seem pretty much frustrated most of the time. Another thing she admitted that the thought was that I take things way too seriously and that it doesn't seem like I enjoy life like I used to before the accident.

Overall, Kaycee and our other children have said how this accident has made the marriage between their parents stronger and the love of God is more alive in our home. She's glad she learned that God comes first and miracles happen in front of their own eyes. And that no matter what happens they know the love Scott and I hold for our children and they feel it! So even as I write this and heard her say those words, that Scott and I are different, and as hard as it is for me to accept those words, I am so proud that she sees the strength in our marriage. And that they know that no matter what happens, we are all here for each other and they KNOW the love of their heavenly Father!

I am going to close this chapter on Kaycee with her final thoughts: She thinks that Chad will walk one day. But before that happens, something has to happen; that there is something missing. There's going to be a piece to the puzzle. Like the accident happened and then someday Chad walks but that there is going to be something in between. That he is not going to ever walk with any medical things or people, that God will make him walk so that God gets all the glory. Her example of this to me was, like one morning no one will expect it and Chad will just get out of bed and start walking. And when he walks it will strengthen people's faith. Especially the ones who have held out so long; watching us as a family and reading our lives as I put it on Chad's Care Page. And I agree with her. I have said it so many times, that 'yes', God does give us wonderful intelligent doctors to help us out, but only God can do miracles!

We all pray too, that there will be at least one - if not thousands - of people who read the story of Chad's accident and that it will lead them to us and they will be able to fill in that puzzle piece that interlocks all of what God sees already together.

Noah: What He Thinks About the Accident

When I asked my youngest or my 'baby', as I call him, just what he remembered about Chad's accident, I must admit, his answer made me chuckle. Noah's response to me was something like this; "Mom, you know I don't remember because I was too little, I was only 9!"

So, I asked him to sit down with me and share some things that bothered him or things he did remember about the accident. Today, Noah is 14 and is willing to allow us all a glimpse at what he remembers. This is what his feelings are as of today with all this.

Our youngest son, Noah stated that he never thought Chad was ever going to die. In fact, he doesn't remember how Chad looked at all the day of his accident. However, he does remember watching Chad go into the helicopter and he thought it was so cool that Chad got to go in it! The sight of all that at his age caused him to think Chad was just going to fly away! Maybe this was because he got into an accident and people felt sorry for Chad...so, Chad was going to the moon!

He didn't recall the hospital room at all, or have any recollection of the people that were there with the family.

After that, Noah says he remembers coming home and all the kids sleeping in the living room on the floor and he couldn't figure out why the girls were crying. He got sick of hearing them cry, he remembers.

My 'baby' remembers missing me. He was unable at the time to figure out where I was. Noah tells me he also remembers Kayla and Kaitlyn yelling at him but Kaycee was really nice to him. Then he says he saw Kaycee cry and he was sad so he cried but didn't know why he was crying too!

Noah shared with me that he knows he kept telling everyone that he didn't know where I was and he didn't like me to be gone. And there for a while, he didn't think I was ever coming back. To my surprise, Noah thought he had done something wrong and I had left him because of it! You have to know that one sentence just breaks my heart.

Later on, because he was so young, he couldn't understand why Chad was unable to walk. Noah also said that he was blown away because even though Chad wasn't walking, Noah thought that just like someone who has a broken arm, they would just go and get a cast and then in a little while the cast would come off and then they would be healed. This is what he thought it would be like for Chad when we told him Chad couldn't walk for now.

To Noah, who is now, as I said 14, still struggles with hurt feelings of him and Chad not being able to do what they always talked about doing together. They would say as soon as Noah got old enough, they would do some special things as brothers.

Noah told me he does, however, remember me changing Chad's bandages when Chad burnt his feet and how awful the smell was to all of us. Also, he recalls seeing Scott with a huge tub of ice for Chad's feet but doesn't remember anything about how Chad's feet looked except the feet were really red! And that we left to take Chad to the hospital again and Noah couldn't figure out why we were going to the hospital for Chad's feet when at times if he got burnt when he was little I would just run the burn Noah had under cold water or give him ice to put on the burn. And he did confess to me that he was mad at me because Chad took up all my time and frustrated me so.

Something I found interesting is that for as little as Noah was, he admitted he did feel embarrassed when we took Chad out in public because people would stare and Chad was so slow.

He did think that our home was all situated and thought we were all done with Chad but couldn't understand why we were still rushing and running around all the time. To my 'baby' that seemed weird.

One thing that Noah found to be weird through this whole ordeal was the healings services we took Chad to. Noah had trouble accepting the fact that I could no longer work at his school, and that everyone treated him extra nice. Admittedly, he felt awkward that the teachers treated him so nice. Actually, it scared him and then he started to think that Chad might die.

Another tough time for Noah was when he would come home from school. People who were helping Chad such as the visiting nurse, therapists, etc...would come in or be there and he would have to be quiet and it felt awkward again if he tried to watch cartoons and they walked passed him and said hello! And he couldn't grasp why Kaycee was always sitting by Chad in church and why Chad wasn't bringing his standup wheelchair to church so he could stand up with us and sing! Leave it to a little one to not understand just how heavy this chair was to lift in the vehicle!

When I asked Noah if there was anything he could think of that was good that came from this accident, to my surprise, he said, "yes"! His reply to that question was that he thought the puppy,

Sammi was cute and he liked to play with her and thought it was cool to run around the hospital halls with the puppy.

Noah liked going to the hospital to visit Chad because he got to see me. Our youngest son thought the hospital was huge and cool! He also said that without Sammi, he wouldn't have a dog named Hank! Hank is Sammi and Bear's puppy that we kept. Little Hank ate antifreeze and we just couldn't give him away knowing he may have problems in the future because of this. To this day, Hank is fine and we loved our big, ole Bear dog so much, we wanted to have an offspring of Bear's because Bear is so old now.

In another conversation I had with Noah, I asked him what he thought about this whole thing since we are going on five years now since the accident the 29th of this month because it is now middle of July 2012 as I am writing this to you. He said things are more different now than before because Chad can do more by himself, Praise the Lord!

Chad still isn't walking as of yet and is still in the wheelchair but things seem happier. Noah admits he still blames the guy who hit Chad and doesn't hold any hard feelings against Chad for buying the motorcycle and getting into the accident.

As far as helping his brother – Noah believes it's a big pain because he is the one that always has to now put Chad into his chair if he falls out. At the age of 14, he weighs over 200 lbs and is 6 feet tall, so it falls on him to do a lot of the physical things that it takes to care for Chad. Noah takes after his Dad in size and so he is the one that picks Chad up for us and moves him around. But Noah said he would still keep doing that for us and Chad.

Noah views our family as different because since this accident, Scott and I get frustrated dealing with Chad and all his needs, especially when Chad is depressed and wants to give up and not try anymore like at therapy. Noah admits it is hard to work with Scott in the family business because Scott seems to get crabby easily while working and he can tell Scott is stressed and worried about me taking care of Chad and getting burned out. All of this is a lot for a young teen boy to think about and in many ways, these experiences will help carve Noah into a stronger man because of the things he's been subjected to and that have come his way. Still, I have to admit it is often a sad situation.

Many times Noah has also explained that when he and Chad are doing a project together that Chad just doesn't have the patience explaining to Noah how to do things anymore. So, he tells Noah to get him out of his chair so Chad can get down on the floor and do whatever they are working on himself and then Noah has to pick him up and put him in his chair again.

I will leave you all-in this chapter, with something that Noah told me that I just thought was hilarious and I hope you will too; it's like I often tell people and I know I have said it to you throughout this book, 'you have to find the laughter in things'. When Chad had been home for several weeks, he, Kaycee and Kayla helped Chad get on the four-wheeler. I know I have shared this story with you all somewhere in this book, but when they did that and duct taped his feet to the pegs, Noah was really scared and worried he was going to get in trouble by us. Therefore, he told Chad to hurry up and ride away! Chad assured him that I wasn't going to be mad at him. He thought I would be mad at Chad for asking the others to help him, and Noah replied to Chad "No, Mom won't. She will be mad at me for putting you on here because you can't walk, Chad!" And Chad said to Noah, "Well buddy, at least you can run away from her. I can't!"

Story from Chad's Point of View

Now I know that I was not in Chad's body to experience what he did at the time of his accident, but I can share this chapter with you as he and I had nothing but all this time to talk about details. So I wrote this chapter from Chad's point of view.

I remember seeing this awesome motorcycle on the side of the road coming home one day from work. *Man*, I thought, *I just got to have this baby! It was so sweet!* So I stopped and asked how much and got all the info about the bike I could get. Afterward, I got back in my truck and headed home to have dinner with my family. While I was driving, I was thinking to myself, *There is no way Mom and Dad are going to let me spend money on this bike, especially after we already had two in our garage! I know they want me to save my money but this bike was really cool! Way cool, and I can do so much to it!*

I knew Dad would think the bike was cool, but he really wanted to see me save my money and Mom well, she was a Mom, scared her baby boy would get hurt; you know how Mom's are. So at dinner that night, I told my parents about the bike. Just as I suspected, the usual was said. But then to my surprise, my dad said, "Well, Chaddick, (that's what they call me, it's not my real name but Chad was just too short when I was little to call me when I was in trouble for some reason. I don't know...it's a parent thing, probably). "I guess, son. You have been working really hard and you have been tithing so I will go look at this motorcycle with you."

Mom just gave dad her usual look; the look when things are scary to her and she thinks my dad is off his rocker, so to speak. Before I knew it, my dad and I had plans to go look at this bike.

On a hot, Thursday night, July 26, 2007, when I handed the owner of the bike my wad of cash, I felt on top of the world! I bought something I had been saving money for so long and did hard work and long hours to obtain it!

The next memory I have is of the following Saturday morning...getting up bright and early to go get the endorsement on my driver's license to be able to drive this great bike I had just purchased. I was still flying high with excitement! Couldn't wait to take off on that thing all by myself! And yes, there is something to dad being right. All my childhood years growing up I had thousands of arguments with him about being safe and doing the right things when it came to driving my mini-bikes or snowmobiles. He and I had the same conversations about my dirt bikes and motorcycles. So, this was not news to me that I had to go and do this with Dad. We needed to make sure I was street legal. Plus, he wanted to be able to watch me himself and know that I know what I am doing. And I kept thinking to myself I have to go all through the next day which was Friday before I could go get certified!

Kayla's 'look-back' at the Accident:

Kayla replied when I sat down and talked to her about her thoughts like this:

When Kayla first saw Chad in the hospital room she started picking up all his torn bloody clothes all over the floor. She was mad to see they had just cut and torn all of his clothes like that. She remembers looking at Chad and thinking, 'there was a ton of people looking at him'. She couldn't see him anyway because they had all these ice bags and backboard and collars on him; and all the tubes and wires were attached to her brother...not to mention he was on a respirator and we could hardly see him.

Our daughter explains that she does remember attacking Uncle Dave – thinking he was one of the little kids – as he came in the room because she didn't want the little ones (her siblings) to see Chad in the condition he was in at the time. She feared they might be scared. The hospital officials cleaned Chad up some before the rest of the siblings got to actually come inside and see him for the first time.

Her memory of leaving Chad's room to go find the rest of the kids: She went back to the waiting room and there were so many more people there than what there was when she left to go to see Chad. She says she remembers feeling quite angry because some of the people would see the rest of her siblings and just go up and start crying to them and hug them. This scared her younger siblings. So Kayla remembers gathering the other three up and taking them into the hall. She began explaining what was going on, and she sat Noah in a wheelchair to keep him occupied and stayed out in the hallway to stay away from other visitors. Until Pastor Mark called her to bring the kids into the room again.

After they took everyone back into the room where Pastor Mark prayed with everyone, Kayla remembers Dad and Grandpa talking to the staff at U of M to come and get Chad in the copter. She remembers Dad meaning this was serious business and when he talked, everyone started to move. When we got ready to put Chad on the copter, she remembers watching them resuscitate him again and thinking it was odd how his body jumped up. Then she remembers them finally getting him in there and quickly taking off. Noah, our youngest son, just kept crying.

As everyone left the hospital, she remembers stopping at my in-law's house to let their dog out. She came home and the kids hadn't eaten anything yet so she fed them at 4:00 a.m. when they arrived. It was hell; she was beyond tired and the kids just continued crying. Kayla didn't know what to say to them because they kept asking her if Chad was going to die. The kids cried for over two hours. She finally got them all to sleep and was able to pass out at 7:15 a.m. At 7:55 a.m. that morning, only minutes into her sleep, I called at 7:55 a.m. and woke them all up with an update!

She remembers seeing Chad at U of M in the ICU and she remembers being afraid to touch him. The staff kept telling her it was okay. There were machines making noises, especially the one that kept breathing for Chad, that she remembers. As I write this, she is making the noise as it sounded when the machine breathed for him. Also Kayla remembers that the staff didn't seem very nice to her but now knows they were working hard and taking their jobs seriously to keep her brother alive.

Chad's sister, Kayla says every time she looked at Scott and I, we looked spaced out and extremely tired. She said she was scared because it looked like we weren't ourselves. That in itself was very frightening, she said. Kayla admits that whenever she saw us, she said she was scared for the rest of the kids to see us and she remembers we looked very thin and I looked frail. She had never seen me like this before.

By the time the kids came and were able to see Chad two weeks had passed and she had been keeping them verbally up to date on what was happening to their brother and at the same time she was trying to prepare them. She said the phone rang off the hook here at home and she really didn't know what to tell the callers. Some callers were in shock and couldn't believe the horrible news and were unable to believe how bad Chad's injuries were.

Kayla confesses that when she was out in public with Chad, she wanted to smack people because of the way they stared and treated us. It seemed to her that they judged us and they don't know what the situation was. It's everywhere you go people look at you, especially when we were new at getting Chad in and out of the car, in the wheelchair, and when we attended family functions with other relatives.

She says still to this day, people don't know how to act, including family. They judge everything we do and think either that we should do things better, or that they could handle the circumstances better. Sometimes people said how we should do something with Chad even though they've never experienced our situation yet.

People still treat us today like we are not normal; like we are all frail. It's not just Chad; it's all of us that get judged. Kayla said, 'you overhear people talking about you, and their words can sting'. When this happens, she doesn't have a clue as to what to say in return to them.

Kayla also doesn't know how she felt when she came home with Chad from the hospital. It was a completely different house. She had been away taking care of Chad in my place when Chad was out of the woods and in rehab and she said it was like walking into a different house with all the new things for Chad, which really weren't a lot because by that time, we didn't have to do a lot of repairs. However, she said it was still different.

When Kayla was at rehab with Chad it was really hard for her to watch because she would have to sit back and watch him struggle with himself. It was hard not to help him. At times, it was very difficult to hold back her real feelings when he was around...she said she always just wanted to cry, but didn't most of the time. She wanted Scott and me to be there and she was angry at the person who caused the accident. A lot of times when they got Chad in his chair to go to therapy, Chad ran her over and it really hurt; so that was a struggle and she hated getting him ready to go to therapy.

Although – then and now – Kayla cannot imagine what it was like for Chad.

When the medical world told Chad that he couldn't walk, Kayla thought they were crazy; that they did not know Chad. All she could think of was that no one could keep him down. She said that she was angry all the time with how they treated him and they always wanted to just give Chad a pill to make him happy. Kayla admits she was depressed because it seemed as if the staff just didn't want to take the time to help her brother. It was just easier for them to say he would never walk again. In her opinion, the staff was not helpful. And sometimes they were rude. She remembers taking classes with Chad and it seemed as though they really didn't care about how anyone felt. When they got up to the rehab floor, there were some staff members that were helpful, but for the most part, they just wanted to show Chad how to get in and out of his chair and how to live life in the chair. The medical staff members just seemed to treat her and her brother like they were in a chair.

Kayla said she is different today because of Chad's accident. She is completely independent and confident in herself, as she learned to be. She doesn't care what people say about us as a family or her personally. Our daughter doesn't have any trouble going out in public. She no longer cares about how people stare at us. She is confident in herself and Chad, knowing God doesn't make any junk.

She views me, her mom, as a person who is very confident now...almost like I would have never been confident to write like for example this book, or join our church choir. She says that Scott on the other hand now shows emotion and she finally thinks he is human! Scott and I are stressed more, and we are really hard to separate. We always have to do things together. Her thoughts are that her dad and I are a lot closer and truly do things together more. Kayla confides in me that her dad is a lot clingier to me. Over all, she thinks Scott and I are better now.

In closing, Kayla still believes that Chad will walk someday, and it will be in God's timing. Her brother's fate is not in man's or modern medicine's hands, and when Chad walks, he is going to be a better person and that he will get married and settle down someday. She says that she has gotten closer with God, and takes her walk with God seriously, and likes who she has become.

Kayla has had to live with her husband, Anthony's aneurism. She believes Anthony will go back to work and his outlook will change on things. In her opinion, Kayla believes that Chad's accident happened for a reason and that if this accident hadn't happened something worse might have taken place.

Scott's Point of View of our Life's Trials:

This interview was hard, not only for Scott but for myself. For me, it was hard because it's like I told you all in the beginning of this book, when I would ask my husband to let me read the chapters to him and/or ask him to proofread them with me, he wouldn't because he had terrible memories and this brought back such sorrows. He did though give it his all and try, but during the interview I gave up and said we were done. It was the end of the chapter because I couldn't bring so much pain back to him.

I remember not too long ago, Scott was talking to Chad and telling him that he had to trust in God. Scott still doesn't understand it and he has pleaded and begged God but he has got to just trust in God and know God is good and loves us all so much. This happened for a reason, and every day it breaks his heart to see Chad in a chair, but he knows Chad is soooo much more than that chair. He told Chad that that chair doesn't define the person Chad is, and that as hard as it is for him to be in that chair, it's hard for us as parents to see Chad in that chair. Scott told Chad that the chair doesn't make Chad the person he is today, that Chad makes Chad who he is.

Scott admits it is hard, but feels our marriage is about as strong as he thinks a marriage could be. He views things differently now with everything. His relationships with his kids are different and so much more important. My husband knows now what it means when it says in scripture that when a man marries, he must leave his original family for his new family.

Reflecting back, Scott divulges that he is a better listener and says he hangs onto conversations and rethinks things people have said a lot more now. He knows that there are times of sorrow but the good times God blesses him with, will outweigh the bad times. Our having to live through the accident and all the trials has made him a more compassionate person. He takes things more seriously now.

It kills Scott to see me struggle with all of Chad's needs but Scott knows I can do it. He sees me as a much stronger more confident person today. There have been times he admits that he wishes we had funds to just hire Chad's needs to be met, but Scott knows the good Lord will be merciful and supply all our needs for our son.

My dear love also shared with me that he values friendships and things here on earth differently because now Scott realizes you can't take those things with you when you die. He also knows that money and all the things money can buy and all the things people have that he and I don't have aren't important to him. It's the quality you give to people and he knows that we made the right choice for me to stay home and not work when our kids were little. Because of this decision we didn't always take vacations and/or get to take our children fancy places to see the world. However, we have stuck together and I was always home when my kids came home from school; this Scott knows they themselves value and will pass onto their children one day, that things and doing everything for everybody else and trying to create a name for yourself and to show people what you can do to impress them isn't it. It's family, your spouse, your kids whom a man should impress.

Chad's father also agrees with me that God has something really special for he and I and perhaps our children to do for Him in allowing this situation to happen. He shared that God may have allowed this in order to make us strong. I recall him telling our children the other night as we said *grace* before our meal that he was going to be like Job in the Bible; he was going to continue to give thanks to God even if all his things were taken away as Job's were.

My dear husband also admitted that he never really gave it a thought before and cherished what some people said to us...like at church when people made comments about us 'all having to do things together as a family', or that 'whenever one of us went we all went', or when people would say, 'your kids are so nice and kind and polite and we just love being around your family', those are all gifts we have received, Scott feels. I agree!

It's so special as a parent to see the love your children have for you and each other, and really we are all so much closer and if Chad's accident hadn't happened I don't think my eyes would have ever been able to see that.

I closed this heartfelt interview up with my wonderful husband; and, I did so by asking him what his thoughts were.

Scott would like to close with what he said to me and I have to admit, I cried! In a happy way, a prideful way, but in a way most of the talk almost caused me to weep just to hear him say these words. I can still see it on Scott's face when he told me, "I am one blessed man. I have a wonderful wife I have known for over 30 years now; been married to her for 28 of those wonderful awesome years. I have five beautiful children whom steal my heart away every single day when I look at them. Also we have two wonderful son-in-laws soon to be, a house full of love, and this most wonderful, great big, overpowering, bigger than any storm God in my life!"

He is just waiting now for God to reveal a miraculous miracle and allow Chad to walk again!

Chapter Twenty-Three - Thank God for Chad!

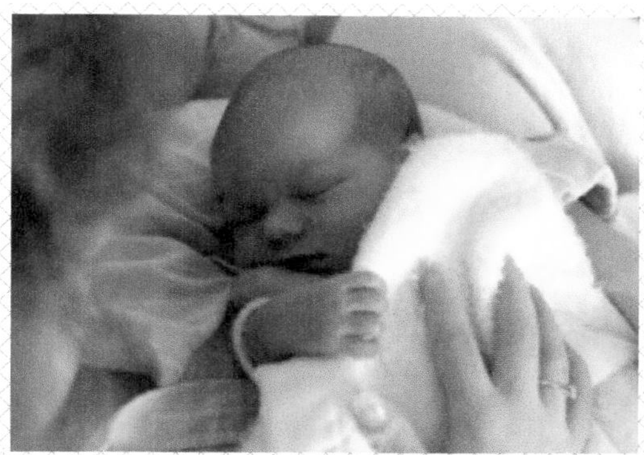

{Chad at Birth}

You see, I believe that Chad Clark has a calling from God, and like it or not, he's going to work for God! Maybe he isn't going to be an ordained priest, but you don't have to be ordained to be a priest. It was evident that Chad, through his article in *The Township Times*, and later in *The Saginaw News*, and his being on the television, was going to bring people to Dr. Sears. I strongly believe that Chad's testimony will provide people all over the world – hope.

{Chad playing football in his younger years}

{Chad Clark before accident}

{Chad's Dad (Scott), Chad and his brother, Noah}

Chad Clark and his mother, Charee, feared Chad would never walk again after his motorcycle accident last July. (Courtesy Photo)

Doctor's faith helps teenager defy all odds

By JENNIFER HOEWE
The Township Times

Countless doctors agreed: Chad Clark would never walk again.

After a horrific motorcycle accident in July 2007, the 19-year-old suffered injuries leaving him paralyzed from the waist down. Seven weeks in an intensive care unit followed by rigorous physical therapy led specialists to believe Chad would remain permanently wheelchair-bound.

"Medical science had given up on Chad," his mother, Charee Clark, said. "We were dedicated to finding someone who would quit saying no."

That someone was Dr. Andrew Sears. As medical director of The Living Well, 3190 Christy Way, Sears welcomed the distraught patient.

"The people I want to help are the ones the doctors have told, 'There's nothing we can do,'" Sears said.

But Chad's discouragement was twofold: a bleak prognosis coupled with extreme financial strain. His family's funds were running low since he lacked medical insurance at the time of the accident, and the initial hospital stay had accumulated an extensive bill. With little hope, Chad scheduled his first appointment with the optimistic doctor.

Sears willingly offered his services.

"Am I going to turn away a 19-year-old just because he can't pay?" Sears said, holding back tears. "I would rather be dead."

The Living Well provides uniquely therapeutic healing processes to its clients. Massage

See "FAITH" on Page 3

Dr. Andrew Sears helped Chad Clark regain feeling in his legs after being paralyzed from the waist down. Sears predicts Chad will walk again by August 15, though other doctors said it would never happen. (Photo by Jennifer Hoewe)

FAITH

Continued from Front Page

therapy with essential oils, bio-feedback sessions and acupuncture comprise a partial list of available treatments. Sears makes the initial diagnosis, while he and his colleagues perform the treatments based on their individual specializations.

As a formerly abandoned patient, Chad said he found new hope with Sears' methodology.

"I had a lot of faith initially, and Dr. Sears helped restore it," Chad said. "I learned how important it is to have a positive attitude."

The constant stream of negative feedback Chad received from other doctors belittled his chances of full recovery, Sears said. Thirty-four years of practicing medicine has led the doctor to believe any miracle is possible with enough faith.

"Jesus is the only physician," Sears said. "We are just his helping hands. I trust that God will make Chad walk again no matter what other doctors say."

An innovative approach will have Chad back on his feet by August 15, Sears said. Adding three additional senses to the scientifically-acclaimed five equates to an increased chance of success in healing, he explained. A sense of purpose, common sense and a sense of humor turn the science of medicine into "the art of healing," Sears said.

"Whether people heal depends on whether or not we can inspire them to heal themselves," Sears said. "We all have the power to heal ourselves. All we need is the willpower."

Chad and his mother found that willpower through ongoing consultations with Sears. The Delta College student has regained feeling in his legs and was recently fitted for leg braces, Charee said. Without Sears' help, Chad would never have made it this far in recovery, she added.

"This has given me hope and the drive to keep fighting," Charee said. "We should never just accept what medical science tells us."

Her son agreed. Chad said he is "100 percent confident" he will walk again.

{Article that appeared in The Township Times}

My son was making a difference and we didn't even know it! There were two young men that came from Port Huron, and some other place that escapes me now. One young man was Chad's age and he had been in a car accident on July 3rd, just days before Chad's accident occurred. This young man was also paralyzed. He heard about Chad and all that was taking place with Chad's treatments at Dr. Sears' office. So this young man came to meet Dr. Sears. We didn't know it but we showed up for one of the same type of treatments.

On this miraculous day...here was this fine looking young man waiting at Dr. Sears' to see Chad! They went in a room alone to talk together and I believe that if Chad hadn't been in that chair, in the same position, stooping down to that young man's level, our son would have never brought that young man to God. Here was a great blessing, Chad, at the age of 19 at that time, now being instrumental with other people by helping them see God. In fact, he has brought more people to God than I have in all my 43 years living on this earth! There are other people who come to see Chad now and the treatments he is receiving. It's so nice to meet new faces and these people I have learned are my dear true friends, hand-picked especially for me from my Master Himself! So everything started to make sense! God will heal Chad I know it, but in GOD'S time not ours!

Testimonies

Yep, here was my son talking powerful words of powerful things that later had become testimonies! He stood up in our youth group at church and told his story; and, that night two young souls came forward to dedicate their lives to Christ. He went to Bay Shore Camp, which is a Christian camp that our church and so many others support and told his story there; and, they had four young kids give their lives to Christ for the very first time! Wow, imagine how proud I felt and how really blessed we were by God.

This was far better than Chad walking, I thought. Don't get me wrong, with my whole heart, I still longed for him to be able to walk. But what he was doing now was so good and pure. Chad was beginning to see he had a purpose. The following is my second favorite scripture.

> *I waited patiently for the Lord: he turned to me and heard my cry. He lifted me out of the slimy pit, out of the mud and mire; he set my feet on a rock and gave me a firm place to stand.*
>
> Psalm 40:1-2

Chad Changes Lives

The thing I forgot to tell you all in the beginning is that I had no idea that my own son, whom we took to church every Sunday from the time he was born, had gone through confirmation, was in Sunday school, and sang in the church choir, went on youth events – you name it – Chad had already been through so many church functions. However, all of this experience did not necessarily mean he believed then that he was going to go to heaven.

{Chad having fun with a Popsicle}

He was not wholly convicted that Jesus died for him...or as I said above, that he was going to Heaven! Yes, you heard me; I thought when we had him baptized and brought him up in the church that he knew all this. But the truth was he didn't know. I thought God was punishing me now for sure. It was almost as if we, as a family, continued going to church but had never really ever sat down and had a 'heart-to-heart' talk with him about the true 'meat' of spirituality.

On the day Chad gave his own powerful testimony on a CD that our church was giving to the local kids that needed help, I learned the true him. As I listened to what was being recorded in Chad's own words, I felt a sick feeling in my stomach! And it was right then and there I got on my hands and knees at that church and cried out the words, "I have failed and I am so eternally sorry, oh God!" And it was also at the same time I shouted out, "Thank you dear Heavenly Father for this gift!" The gift I could hear through the recording was that Chad was now very close to God. He has come to the place where he knows his place will be in heaven some day. But you see – knowing that my son was now able to identify that he was going to heaven, in some ways made me regret not helping him realize this earlier in his life. The most important thing is that he knows 'his truth' today and it is no longer necessary for me to harangue myself for not getting him there sooner...the important thing was I could tell by listening to the CD that Chad was convicted God loved him.

I found out that Chad had totally given his life and all that he was to God! That was the biggest miracle of all. Had it not been for this accident, my son may not have known the Lord – he may not have gone to Heaven when he dies! And I found out that no matter how much we give of ourselves as parents, or how much we teach our children, you just don't know what they actually have learned. You have to trust in God and believe He is watching over them.

Day After Day

I would like to tell you all that those things that I just told you about healed each of us and made us all better. But the truth is we still struggle and the hurt is still there every single second of every single day.

We long for our old life, but I have to honestly say, it's all good, just to know that Chad has changed some people's lives is really a gift.

Our family still has a lot of bad days and our family has changed. I struggle to balance the time between my other children and helping Chad. My husband and I have only gone on one date night alone since our son's accident. I have missed a lot of *lasts*, like Noah's last year of elementary things and events. I missed my girls going to 'homecomings' and proms. Our daughter, Kaycee made the Honor Society and I am sure I would have been there more for her in her school events if our life had not changed so drastically.

It's hard because of Chad the length of time we spend at church services was cut short due to us having to be home for medication times. Noah struggles with reading and math and school work in general. My pride and joy – my house, yard and garden have suffered from lack of attention. And yes, it's so depressing, but I do know that this is where I am supposed to be. And if it never changes, which I certainly hope it does, I am fine being where I am now and doing what I am doing. Because I know it's of God.

People always ask me, "Does it hurt that you lost friends because of your faith during this whole ordeal?" Or, "Isn't it hard to give things up?"

Of course it does...but when you obey God...and you listen and give Him your all, you have a peace inside you that cannot be destroyed by anyone or anything. And I have to tell you, for all the friends I had who laughed at me; God has replaced them with better Christian friends. Really, I am blessed. And when we get our miracle and Chad walks one day, what will all those people then say – the ones who laughed at me? Won't they see how faith in God truly works?

Turning Points

There are a lot of times I can't help but think all about the 'what ifs'. I always wonder what if I had stopped and simply accepted the fact that Chad would not walk when the doctors first told us the worst of the diagnosis. And what if the driver that hit Chad would have stopped and stayed and possibly rendered aid or called 911 at least? Or what if someone nearby had rushed to his side and given him the proper treatment right away? What if they would have iced his spinal cord right away like they did that football player who got injured and is now walking? What if maybe I would have been at the scene to make sure everything was done right away to help Chad?

Surely the results would be different if our insurance had been the top of the line insurance; but, would it have helped Chad walk by now? And suppose we would have caught the driver who hit Chad and sued him like everybody tells us we should have done...though would our son's health be better? If only we would have hired a lawyer to reopen the case and find the person who hit Chad. As you can tell – the list could go on and on!

You learn to get past these doubts and turn the corner. If you don't, you never get better. You will never be able to accomplish anything. You will stay stuck in a place where you don't want to stay. It's true, you have to find it within yourself to go on and forgive. And nobody can do the forgiving for you.

We found that as we learned to forgive, it was easier to go on and things turned around quicker. It's really true! But it's also really hard to forgive someone who has basically destroyed your life and left your son to die, and to see him in the state he is now than from what he used to be.

It really drove us nuts when thinking of all the 'what ifs'. What really makes me sick on this subject is the things people say to you without thinking. As if this whole thing we are going through wasn't bad enough, this is no lie, I ran into someone from our old church one day. At first they asked how Chad was doing. Next, they actually said to me, "Maybe there is a lesson in this for ALL of you."

Well, like I told you, I have learned to be bold and open my mouth. So I asked this particular person just what she meant by this. And of course, she answered, "Maybe you and Scott should have been better parents and not let Chad have a motorcycle!" Or, "Maybe you shouldn't have let him go get his haircut by himself."

My goodness, Chad was 18 years of age! Really was she the type of parent to tell her eighteen-year-old child what to do every minute of their life? I don't think so...cruelty is such a burden.

One of my favorites was the day I was at the gas station, and this person came right up to me and asked if I was Chad Clark's mother. I said, 'yes,' of course. He said he had seen Chad's article in the newspaper. This man asked me what kind of Mother I really was to give my son false hope. Didn't I think I should be a real Mother and help Chad cope with this and not build his hopes just to have them shattered. Because after all, I wasn't a doctor.

And to all the people who tell me I am crazy, and that they can handle their motorcycles, and that mothers do not stop their children from getting right back on the bike and ride again. Shame on me for doing all these things.

That's what I call turning points, because I no longer have the desire to even respond to the people who say these things to me. I do thank God though because I have the confidence to just keep my mouth shut and say nothing. I am a good mother and I know it now.

God has a way of dealing with these types of people and He does it in His own way and time. It's not up to me to prove anything to anyone and especially to those who attack me or my family. In the past, I have already done that, because had I not kept pushing, Chad would not be where he is today! I already told you, you reach a point where you feel all the guilt you can feel and you cry all the tears you cry until there aren't anymore!

Ideas

I feel I must share with you that there are some things that haven't changed in Chad. Like Chad's desire no matter what to come home from the hospital and drive things like his four-wheeler. Later, he actually had Kaycee, Kayla and Noah help him onto the four wheeler and duct tape his feet to the pegs so they wouldn't fall off.

Another idea Chad had was to try to play NASCAR going down the ramp. One day he talked of doing wheelies around the corners and wanted to do it on one wheel. Chad also thought it would great to learn how to ride the escalators with his wheelchair! Yes, he actually had the therapy people work with him on climbing steps and riding the escalator. This he has not mastered yet!

Chapter Twenty-Four – Compassionate Encouragers

Below are notes, letters and/or email snippets from friends and associates who made certain 'we hung in there':

Charee–

When it rains it pours. It seems like you just can't get a break these days. I hope all of your worries and troubles don't swallow you up. You sounded strong in your email - like your old self. But I know all of what you wrote must weigh very heavily on you. You are a strong person, everyone knows that, but you're dealing with a lot right now. You're *always* dealing with a lot, but all of what you wrote to me sounded like it's more than usual.

I wish there was something I could do or say to help Chad. I don't think anyone can actually imagine how it is for him. As far as I am concerned, I try to imagine, but I know his pain and frustration and anger are way beyond anything I can grasp. I wish there was an easy answer. He's got a hard road, that's for sure. It's just so incredibly unfair.

He's got so many good qualities though. So many things he's good at. His potential isn't diminished just because he can't walk (for the moment). He still has tons of ability. His mind and his hands and his heart are all strong. He's full of personality and charm, not to mention his natural mechanical ability (which is truly impressive). And I'm sure that his having gone through all he has, has actually given him other qualities and sensitivities which very few other people have. This is a dark period but it will pass. It might just be something which he has to go through basically on his own though. I don't know. But it will get better. He will see the light at some point, and then he'll be alright.

I guess meanwhile you've got to continue to have the patience of a saint. Love, you've got plenty of. You've got enough love inside you for a hundred people. However, I can imagine patience is a harder thing to come by. But again, with all of your strength, wisdom, courage, common sense and pure grit, you will get everybody through this. That's how it's been and I'm sure that's how it'll always be. It's a lot of responsibility and I know it can't be easy, but you're up to it. Even when you've been completely exhausted mentally, physically and spiritually, you've always come back. I don't know how but you have that ability. You might get down but you are never out. Never. You've proven that time and time again.

So, try to take heart and keep the faith. As always, I wish you good luck. Stay strong. I'll be in touch again soon. I'll write to Scott too.

Take care -
Mike

∞-∞

Dear Mrs. Clark-

We would be honored if you would cordially accept our invitation to speak at our next public meeting and talk about your ideas for new motor cycle safety. We have been keeping up on your son Chad's progress and feel with your reputation, and your ideas you could make a huge difference in many lives and we value your comments.

It is just amazing to see how far you have come with your son, and to see all Chad's progress and your story is just so inspiring to many. We know your time in pretty much taken up with the care of your son, but you have so much to offer to us all and many would love to hear you share your story if you are willing, this I believe would benefit more than you know. Your compassion for people and your words of hope and encouragement are so important especially in today's world with many of our parents and youth.

We are holding you and your son Chad, and the rest of your family in our prayers. God be with you and please keep doing what you are doing, spreading the light into this dark world.

Sincerely,
James Corderly

∞-∞

Charee-

You need to hear these words I believe the Lord has placed on my heart. I can't begin to tell you that we are all so encouraged by you and what you stand for. It seems so unbearable what you are going through with your son, but you make it look so easy, how do you do it? We would love for you to come and share your story at our next women's group, would you be willing?

I am so glad you have such a heart to help people, I value your friendship and would like to keep encouraging you as you keep all who are watching you going. I am so happy to call you friend and have you in my life. I have heard people say that they want what you have, that being a relationship with the Lord, if you could speak at our next meeting that would be a blessing to many. Please get back to me and see what you think.

Yours in Christ,
State Street United Methodist Women's Group

Dear Charee-

I have to tell you that I have been watching you know and keeping up with Chad and his updates, I see you every Sunday and you come in to church with this huge smile on your face like as if nothing every happened. I say these things to you because I believe that you need to know how you have an effect on people like myself. I am not facing what you are in your situation, and my problems seem so small, but I would give anything just to have one quarter of what you have for my little problems.

I see you up there singing your heart out to the Lord, praising him, and I think "how can she do that'? I look over at Chad who is just watching his mother sing her heart out and my heart just leaps! You are such an inspiration to us all. I cherish your friendship. You make me just feel so happy when I see you. You are so upbeat with your words and actions. You give us all so much hope and life! Please keep being the person who you are, we all need more people like you. God sure does love you and when I see you sing, you can just see the love you have for God!

Your friend,
Amy

Chapter Twenty-Five – Care Pages

The Care Pages are something that was started when Chad first went into the ICU unit. These were people that were told about Chad's progress every day. These updates and posts were started up by Kayla would post to everyone what needed prayers we might have for Chad. Also, she would post if he made it through the night or if he had an upcoming surgery, etc… because, of course, we didn't have time to keep everyone informed by phone or in person on a daily or per minute basis.

In the beginning it would have been impossible to share each day's events when Chad was really sick in ICU or in critical care situations. So, what we would do was…I would report to Kayla and she would pass it along via the Care Pages. Most of the time, we were with Chad and couldn't have our cell phones on because of the different machines in the room, which were busy keeping Chad alive. And we weren't about to talk on the phones keeping everyone informed as bad as that might sound.

So, after some time I am now the one trying to keep up with Chad's posts. Actually it ended up being another blessing from God as this really helped me to have a support system. I will explain why next.

Prayers Around the World

Through Chad's Care Pages there were people leaving us messages of hope. People with kind words and thoughts, which actually kept me going, posted and then Kayla would either show me the post or tell me about it. The notes came one message after another, and when Chad was able to stay awake later on in the hospital, I would read these to him, which I believed gave him the fight to stay alive.

However, and most of all, there were prayers going all around the world from this thing we call the Internet! I am not kidding. There were prayers from people in other states and even other countries that I have never met. What a blessing this was for us all. I know without a doubt that as these wonderful people kept praying for Chad; we believe that God heard and answered a lot of these prayers…perhaps it was because God got sick of being bugged about healing Chad and pulling him through!

I didn't know it at the time, but Care Pages were really for our support as a family, for us to hook up with others who maybe have been in the same situation we were, and some people did in fact email and tell us that they knew what we were going through. In fact, through the Care Pages is how we found our new wonderful friends the Holt's.

Josh Holt ~

Joshua Holt is someone we met through the Care Pages as I said. It started when his mother wrote and sent us a video of Josh in his therapy. Josh was hit by a car on Mother's Day 2004. He was hit and thrown in a ditch by the driver of the car. Josh had been on his rollerblading and while in the ditch, he didn't get blood flow in his legs and his spinal cord was also damaged. He too is still paralyzed. Josh is Chad's age also, but like I said, he has remained paralyzed for the last four years. Josh is working hard and making progress also.

Anyway, his mom, Susan Holt, kept in touch with me by emailing me through Chad's Care Page. We discovered that they lived in Grand Rapids, Michigan. His Mom and I have become very good friends and she offers a lot of support to me. Still to this day!

See the letter we have placed here (written by Susan – word for word) that she sent to Chris about Chad. This is the type of wonderful support we seen from people.

Sunday, November 16, 2008 8:37 a.m.

Chris,

Charee Clark sent this to me. I will definitely be praying. Just like Charee's son, my son is paralyzed as well. My son was hit by a car while rollerblading in May of 2004. My son, Josh, is going to physical therapy and trying lots of different new things that are out there to get him walking again. We will never give up hope. Josh is now 20 years old, has a job and a girlfriend. It took a long time to get there. He is out deer hunting right now and just called us yesterday that he got an 11-point buck.

If God doesn't heal your nephew right away, there is life after paralysis. It took my son 3 1/2 years to get there, but it took much less time for Charee's son, Chad. As soon as I read about Chad on the Carepages.com, Josh and I reached out to Charee and Chad and encouraged them. I hope many reach out to your nephew's family to help him. ***That makes all the difference in the world****. My son was 15 when the accident happened and spent his 16th b-day in the hospital. These young men (or any age) can go through some prettey "dark" times trying to* *deal with this, but with a lot of encouragement, they can make it through it. I will be praying for your nephew and also that he would grow closer to God and grow as a person through all of this. I think God allows these things to happen so that we all slow our lives down enough to really get to know Him better and do His will. Life does come to a stand-still when life-changing things like this happen. I think Charee would say the same: Both our families have grown so much because of our son's accidents.*

Be assured that there are many people praying. I had never met Charee before these things happened to our sons, and probably would have never met her, but I am so thankful that I have met her and her family. We needed each other. We need this network of people who will encourage, pray, and share experiences and treatments with each other. Your nephew and his family will need others to help them through all of this. I will keep praying. If there is any other way we can help, please let me know.

If you would like to pass Josh's website on to your nephew, please do. It shows Josh's journey and progress. I know it encouraged Chad and Charee. Also, you will probably want to meet, or least see, Chad's Care Page, for encouragement as well. Here is Josh's website: joshwholt@blogspot.com -- Chad's Care Page: Go to Carepages.com, then type ChadClark2007 in the search box. I know Charee won't mind that I gave that out because she would love for you to grow and get encouragement from their experiences.

All my love and prayers,
Sue Holt
Grand Rapids, MI

P.S. I also have a son in the Navy. God has kept him safe for the last 4 years. He has been on 3 deployments over in the Persian Gulf and surrounding areas. God has watched over Caleb, for which I am extremely thankful.

On the morning we stood up in church to tell our story about Chad was the very first day we met the Holts. Sue and Josh had driven to our church to surprise us and meet us. I will never forget after church, as we were being hugged by a lot of our church family, someone came and said there is a surprise for me outside in the hall. That someone had wanted to meet me. I was thinking it was someone from my church family that I hadn't met yet, you see, our church is so big with two different services that I never have yet met them all.

So, I went out in the hall and I saw Josh and Sue. I had recognized them from seeing video on Josh's Care Page. It was great! I thought to myself, *why in the world would this family come all this way just to meet us*? When they did come, it was the day I was there up in front of the whole church trying to tell my story without breaking down, and not only did they come for the first service, they stayed and heard our story again for the second service! "Somebody up there likes me!"

So, after I made my way through the people in the church, I found Susan and Josh. What a handsome young man Josh was. You could just see how much love and all the life this fine young man held inside through his eyes! So much was going through my mind. I wanted Josh to meet Chad. Chad hadn't come with us on this particular day. It was very important for his feet not to get bumped because of the skin graphs. Plus, I really didn't want Chad to hear us tell our story on him; it was bad enough he kept seeing us cry at home when people would come over and see us and hug us or say how sorry they were. Our dear son already felt guilty and at the time, I didn't want him any more depressed than what he already was.

We had made the decision to bring them back to our house for lunch to meet Chad who was probably still in bed. I told Sue that my house was probably a mess but surly she would understand, and if Chad were crabby she went through all that with Josh. Sue said they'd like to try and if it ended up not being the right time to meet him, she and Josh would head for home. So that's what we did.

The boys hit it off over pizza and pop! And we parents hit it off as well. What a kind loving person Sue was, and yes, she had really walked in my shoes! This really helped, both of us I believe.

As we listened to Chad and Josh talk about hunting and guy talk, Sue gave us tips about wheelchairs, and medical things and where we could go for help with questions. We still communicate at least a couple times a week. Because of this horrific accident and the Care Pages we met the nicest family!

Chapter Twenty-Six – Afraid

I try to tell people of my experiences so maybe it could help them. If they could learn from us, it may make their lives easier. I will never forget when Chad was out of the ICU unit but still had his trach in. At the time, he was able to swallow, but only liquids. We asked him to leave his room and go to the cafeteria with us. He kept putting us off until I got mad and demanded he tell us why he didn't want to go out of his room. It just wasn't right. You don't stay cooped up in your room for months without seeing the outside and then just be okay with staying there after you were told you could go out. The problem was that he didn't want people to stare at him in his wheelchair and see his scars. Plus he had a rubber feeding tube sticking out of his nose.

Finally, one day we talked Chad into going to the cafeteria with us. I found out what he was thinking and feeling as I felt it too. People did stare at us. They do treat you differently, and you do feel like you don't fit in or belong anymore. Thank God that has changed! But the truth is you don't think of all these things until it happens to you. But for a long, long time this is how we all felt when going out in public with Chad. The last thing in the world Chad wanted or we wanted for him was for people to have pity on him or for people to treat him different. But then again, some people really don't know what to say to you or how to act. And that's when you learn to laugh!

Anger

The hardest emotion I feel that is also extremely hard to deal with, at least for me anyway, is ANGER! Wow, I am finally sharing this out loud! This accident has made me so angry. I am angry that the person who forever changed my son's life and made my son paralyzed, who forever changed my life, my relationship with my kids, their relationships together, this one person ruined our home life. He just got away scott free; the person didn't even care enough to see if Chad was going to have any help of any kind before he fled the scene of the accident. I wonder how he can actually live with himself and I wonder if he ever thinks back on the day of the accident. True, the information of this reality may never be provided us...but still, I wonder.

Day after day, I prayed that God would heal Chad and then I thought it would be easy for me to just forgive this person and to just go on with my life. I always thought in the back of my mind, this was a horrible thing to go through, and it has been for sure, my worst nightmare, but if Chad were to just have all his broken bones heal, and he recovered from his surgeries, and most of all if he had not had that bad of a spinal cord injury, it would have been easier. Nonetheless, as the days went by, and I could see Chad was recovering from his broken bones, we then we watched him recover from all the surgeries. We all still had to realize that he was still left not being able to walk, I got even angrier.

Anger really took over me every time Chad would cry, or when he would flop around like a fish out of water when he tried to move while doing therapy. I was mad – thinking *he is so young*. Our 'still very young' son had has his whole life ahead of him. What do you do when you are hit with such a horrific thing?

And then there were other things that set me off, like my husband Scott, who was hurting so badly. It was so unfair for a person to be so hurt. You could tell Scott's heart was broken and for the first time in my whole life, I knew what it was like to have a broken heart. And to this day, I tell everyone my heart will never be whole again...even when Chad walks one day.

Anger set in again during the many times the rest of my kids would cry for me to come home. I missed them so much, and because of this poor soul who hit my son, I had to be away from my kids, my home and all my pets! While this person got to keep going on with his life, my life had fallen apart!

> *Here my cry, O God, listen to my prayer. From the ends of the earth I call as my heart grows faint; lead me to the rock that is higher than I.*
>
> Psalm 61:1-2

I remember reading in the Bible passages that kept saying to me, "be forgiving!" And no matter what day or time it was, or where I chose to start reading in the Bible, there was always something there that said something about God commands us to be forgiving.

Well, it was about that time when I read again the be forgiving part, that I started really getting mad at God, as I sat by my son's bed day after day, night after night, I would yell at God. How dare He tell me to be forgiving? How dare He tell me that I had no choice; that's what God commands me to do. Then I started thinking about Jesus' words from the cross, "Father, forgive them for they know not what they do."

Well, this person who hit my son sure knew what he was doing! And I also remember that one of the weeks that I was left there alone with Chad while Scott came back home to work, and Chad was going through that spurt where he would code every night, I yelled at God and told Him, even he chose to take His son to heaven after he endured so much pain, Jesus didn't walk around here on earth disfigured from all the beatings He got while being crucified, he didn't have to go through the rest of His life in a wheelchair. Why wouldn't God just take Chad up to heaven also and end Chad's suffering? At least up in heaven, Chad would not just be walking, but running, he would be happy. In heaven our son wouldn't be watching life pass him by in a wheelchair. I was so mad at God, and yes, I must tell you I am so ashamed of this anger...I am putting it down in black and white to tell you all, that it is perfectly normal to get mad at God. I later discovered that at least I was talking to God instead of shutting God out of my life. I learned that God never left me as He promised as I stated earlier in this book.

> *Create in me a pure heart, O God, and renew a steadfast spirit within me.*
>
> Psalm 51:10

I am learning still that there was a reason God didn't take Chad. Our precious son has a purpose. God is using him, and I am so very thankful for that. I learned also that if God would have taken Chad as I requested...that Chad could have possibly gone to hell, because although I had taken him to church, almost every Sunday, from the time he was born, and he was involved in choir, Sunday school, youth group, etc...as I said earlier in the book. Also, Chad still had no idea if he was going to heaven or not. There was no real assuredness. So you see; God saved my son's soul by this accident. In the end – all in all - it's pretty hard to be mad at God for that!

Another anger issue I had was while in the hospital, I prayed for God to give me people that were all Christians to work on Chad. God did send a lot of those special people, but not all of them were Christians. I got really mad when every morning in the ICU it was routine for all the doctors and the interns to go to every patient's rooms and discuss their conditions. I had to stand outside Chad's door in the hallway and wait every morning at 5:00 a.m. and make sure none of them went in and told Chad he could not walk. And every time I asked them not to say that in front of Chad, they treated me as if I was a crazy mother in shock or not facing reality, or as though I was a mom giving her son false hope.

> *A hot-tempered man stirs up dissension, but a patient man calms a quarrel.*
>
> Proverbs 15:18

Finally, I got sick of trying to explain that it says in the Bible that God heals everyone. I mean scripture after scripture it says God healed the lame. If you believe it so shall it be, etc...I couldn't figure out why God wasn't healing Chad. I believed it was going to happen. I spoke it to everyone there every day in that hospital for several weeks, for several months and by now, have believed it for years. So, why wasn't God healing Chad?

Then one night, as I was praying, God spoke to me. He said, "I will heal, but in MY time not yours!" Then I knew, and as hard as it was to accept that, I did. Probably if I wouldn't have been relying on my emotions and feelings and if I had stayed focused on God like He says to do then I would have seen that God was healing Chad all this time since the very beginning of the accident! What I needed to see and what my family and Chad all needed to see and learn was that the main healing was He chose to keep Chad alive!

This is something I hope people do read in my book and do learn from – so I'm glad to be sharing it now.

*

The one other thing that I found hard to deal with when I was angry was rude people. I shouldn't say that because looking back, I don't think the people were trying to be rude. Some people are just not good with words.

I remember when we were first home with Chad, I would take him out to the store and it was probably the first of November. Where we live it's just about this time when it starts snowing, and I was trying really fast to get the bags in the car and Chad was waiting to get into the car. There was some lady who pulled up and yelled at me and told me I was a bad mother and that I should have put my son in the car first! I held back the tears and thought I really was terrible, but it was all new to me, breaking down the wheelchair, and just being out in public with a son now with special needs! I tried to hold back the tears but Chad just looked at me and said, "It's okay Mom. We will get this down." It's just so hard when you are hit with this all at once without any warning. It does get better, as the days pass. You do the same things like break down the chair, get Chad into the car things that you must do on a daily basis. It's just that no one really knows until they walk in your shoes and when people open their big mouths without ever knowing anything to me is just disrespectful!

Chapter Twenty-Seven - Angry Right Down To My Soul...

This is the part of the book I wish weren't my favorite but in all honesty it is. This chapter has allowed me to release some feelings that were withheld and hidden. With all that has happened up until this point so much has been so difficult that it was not easy to share how I 'really' feel with others. Now being able to write this and allow others to see some true honesty about the type of anger that came to me...honestly, it feels good just to come right out and say it. To get my true thoughts and feelings off my chest, so to speak.

The reason this is my favorite chapter is because this part of the story is where I say I finally found healing. Well, at least to the extent anyone could who has gone through something this horrific! It is not my intention to ever hurt anyone's feelings by anything I say, but people need to know the truth if they really want to make things better for those who are in a situation like mine in the future.

By this point in my life, reality had really sunk in and I was living our 'new normal' life, like it or not. Each day brought me a new set of anger issues. Each and every day it was: dress Chad sometimes five or six times a day, change his bed daily and sometimes up to three times a day, keep track of meds all day long. Also I made him meals for him and helped him through the different types of therapy. Other chores were to wash and bathe him (twice daily), change bandages and dress new wounds, lift him everywhere he went, empty his commode several times throughout the day, keep track of his blood pressure, be his appointment keeper and prescription re-filler, as well as schedule visitation times for friends and family. Did I mention do his laundry several times a day? In addition to all of Chad's new needs, I had his burnt feet to deal with and all the work that comes with that as I mentioned earlier in the book. So if you add all this with my list of daily household chores I did for the rest of my family being a stay at home mom and wife, you end up with quite a busy position for me. Did I fail to mention spending time caring for our pets?

I'm sharing with you all of this plus the fact that I never got a good night's rest, I hardly slept. Of course, Chad would definitely call me as he fell out of bed or had to get up or needed something during the night. In fact I can tell you there was about a week's span where I honestly can admit I would go to bed at night and it felt as though I hadn't even closed my eyes to sleep! I am a person who has to have sleep. I am still a night owl, and have learned to take what I call 20-minute naps here and there to get through my days.

If all the tasks described here weren't enough for any one person to endure, I had my regular things I was committed to, such as church committees, 'room Mom' events for my other kids in school. A room Mom is someone who organizes holiday parties, sets up field trips, or someone who comes in and helps out with activities within the room. I had business dinners and meetings to attend with my husband with our family business. With all of this, where in the world was time for ME? What about the things I longed for? I mean after all, my kids were no longer infants, and they were at that age where I was starting to feel my first taste of freedom.

My heart's desire was to pick up my singing career or go back to school because I gave those dreams up to be a 'stay at home mom'. I don't regret it. That was one of the best things I have ever done.

Oh and let's not forget my daughter, Kayla announced she was getting married, so I then had a wedding to plan! And I was not about to miss that! I promised her from the very beginning that I would help her plan this wedding. However, it was important to both she and I to do this; we both waited for this all our lives since the day that baby girl was placed in my arms!

Now let's talk about the part where I never really had time to grieve on the loss of the son that he used to be...I needed to grieve the part of him that now couldn't walk; therefore my dreams and goals for Chad were all changed because of this person who hit him and left him to die on the side of the road! And, oh yes, let's not forget that with every single day of my life now being a living hell, I had to learn to forgive this person and hear from a thousand people about "God never gives you anymore than you can handle". And my Favorite daily saying from people, "God must be punishing you for something you've done!"

The thing I'd share would be that all of this was mixed in with the cries of my other kids scared and adjusting to our new lives and having family members whom I really thought would help me out never show up! I had no one! I mean no one! And that's where I found God! I had him and I learned that He was all I needed after all! And let me tell you when you are as tired as I was day after day, you start to hear things and you start to imagine things. Well, that's until God pulled me up out of the muck and mire I was in and thank goodness I began to recognize his voice! Seriously, I am telling you the truth, lots of people said I needed therapy, which no lie I most likely did, but where was I going to fit in yet another emotionally exhausting thing? And besides, our insurance wouldn't cover therapy for the parents and I needed every ounce of money I had or could possibly get to put towards Chad's needs! And that's when God said, "Trust in me, I will be right by your side every step of the way, Charee".

So with all that which I just explained to you in order to help you to see what my days were like, being forgiving did not come easy for me. Learning how to forgive was a battle every minute of every single day for me. From people telling me 'no' and slamming doors in my face about helping us with Chad and telling me he was never going to walk, to people telling me my two favorite phrases as I mentioned above to family members always making excuses not to help me when I would ask or hint around.

Just one little thing I forgot to mention: this was going to be the year of my 25th wedding anniversary with my wonderful husband! I had dreams of us renewing our wedding vows and my boys bringing me down the aisle to greet Scott and my girls standing in for me! And now, one of my boys was in a wheelchair! Not to mention, the man that I married 25 years ago who was smart and funny and loved life was now wearing his broken heart on his sleeve for the world to see. And his young blonde hair was now old and gray from seeing our boy at death's door and seeing his wife struggle to take care of our child and all the special needs that went with that.

{Scott and Charee Clark's wedding day. . .before Chad's accident.}

{Scott and Charee Clark – after the accident}

I mean my heart just broke when I had to see not only Chad's face but the look on my other kid's faces every day with depression and disgusted looks. And most of all, all the fear! I had to put on a straight face because I found out I am the glue that holds this family together. If I fall apart, my fear was they would fall apart, which I never knew this until this accident. And to you who may be thinking that is good for me; let me assure you it's not! Believe me I did not view it as a compliment. It's tough to be in that position, especially when all these cute little faces are looking at you and you would never do anything to ever do them wrong and you would cut off your right arm to save them from harm.

Let me be really clear before I get myself in trouble. I hold no hard feelings against anyone for them not helping me, and I have learned through God's grace that some people, sometimes even relatives cannot handle seeing a loved one in a wheelchair or with a disability. I have learned that people get angry and stay away because it makes them feel uncomfortable to see a loved one in this position.

I learned all this on an Emmaus Walk that I went to from our church in early October 2011. An Emmaus Walk is a small lock-in at a church from Thursday to Sunday evening. You get a whole weekend to experience God, there are no phones, clocks, and you have no sense of what time it is or what day it is. All you concentrate on is hearing from God! You don't get any word from home so you can't worry about things at home with your kids or husband. On this walk, they even go as far as to put paper up on all the doors and windows so you can't see outside at all! I agreed to go. While there I prayed and God kept tugging at my heart. I have to tell you, I hated it. I even went as far as to sneak my cell phone in just in case something was to happen to Chad. You see even cell phones were forbidden during the weekend. It took me until that Saturday evening to realize what truth was staring me right in my face! I must tell you that my husband went on the same walk the weekend before me, so he knew what I most likely would be going through. This trading of weekends is encouraged so marriages will get stronger, but when the guys come back they are not supposed to tell their wives anything, which my darling husband was good at, at this particular time. But I knew when he came home that he had changed! I could just see it on him. Scott looked so happy and peaceful, and to be honest, I got angry; so much so that I started a fight because he wouldn't tell me anything. My husband not telling me what had changed him ate at me and all Scott kept telling me was it was *good*, and I would like it!

So back to the cell phone that Saturday night I went. Soon, I called Scott and told him I hated it and started to cry. To my surprise, my husband told me to get off the phone and to go do what I was supposed to do. I couldn't believe my ears! My face was blue with such anger! It was that very night, I found God in a brand new way!

Never in my life had I been more embarrassed for being so angry with God! I was falling on my face in front of that church after the testimonies I had heard from people who came to help people like me! I don't think I cried so much in all my life! Not even seeing my son at death's door! It was that very night that I slept in the very same sanctuary where I had experienced such a revelation just hours earlier. However, only after I found out about the grace that my dear Lord had for me...the grace and love He held for me and then coming to know that He was there when I wasn't at Chad's accident...that He held Chad as Chad lay fighting for his life. God was with Chad during the ambulance ride over to the hospital, and He held Chad as they hooked him up with all those wires and tubes, when I couldn't be there. Most of all I was grateful to God for Him giving Chad a second chance at life by this point!

It was also at this time that I found out how much hatred I had and really how angry I was. I had so much anger for family who made excuses to be with everyone else instead of with me in the hospital every day, as my heart broke and I was so scared my son was going to die. Truth be told, I know this is going to hurt which, is why I said earlier I didn't want to hurt anyone's feelings, but I was even mad at my Mom for doing things with my nephews who were healthy and fine, and not being by Chad's side as he fought for his life every single second, of every single day. I mean after all, I know the relationship I have with my girls...neither they, nor I, could function without one another!

I was also angry at my Dad. You see, he was retired like Mom and I thought had nothing better to do...but still he didn't come to be with me and with Chad! I was and always will be a *Daddy's girl*, but still he didn't come.

Although my sister did come once to see Chad, I was still mad at her. My thinking at that time was – 'here her boys are so healthy and this is her nephew, the one who favored her when he was little'.

I was angry with my friends and often wondered *where are they? Didn't they know my world had crashed also with Chad?*

Well, on that Emmaus walk I took, I learned that God was there. He took care of me and that was all I needed. God was drawing me near to Him to use me later on for his purpose! There were no other ways to reach me and grab a hold of me than to test me with the life of my son! Later I learned that I couldn't ask my sister who had a daycare in her home to miss work and come be with me, and my Dad, I couldn't expect him to drive a two-hour trip every day to see Chad and I, when he wasn't in good health himself! And I learned after that Dad had been taking care of my garden and my children. My kids were striking up a special relationship with their grandfather. They had time to bond while I was away, probably because I would try to control the relationship my way.

The relationship between my father and I had been strained at best since my parent's divorce and that strain had trickled down to my children. Heck, I even found out Dad bought them pizza for dinner one night and they all ate together. Up until this point, he would never come in my house, let alone eat dinner with us! In addition, I found out later through much prayer time with God that Dad couldn't bear to see Chad in such a way because they were a lot alike. I have always said Chad looks and acts like my dad from the time he was little.

Everything just kept piling up more and more on my nerves and it was too hard for a person to take. And Mom, well, she did come a lot to see us, and she did pray; I know that. Also I know that she was hurt to see Chad in his condition. She was really close with Kayla and Chad before my parents divorced and she had other grandchildren such as my sister's two boys. My sister really needed Mom's help, she's a single mother.

My friends, well, they had families also to tend to and jobs to go to five days a week or more and they didn't know what to say. Later I learned that I was blessed to have them because even though they weren't there with me, they were praying to God faithfully for the life of my son!

Nevertheless, I did learn and really came to appreciate the fact that God did give us Scott's parents. They were there to help us after about the fifth week in ICU. Aveary, my father-in-law, stayed there all through the nights with Chad. He slept in one of those awful recliners so that Scott and I could go get a decent night's sleep and we could try not to worry about Chad. My mother-in-law, Becky was there to keep me company and pray with me. I learned and thank God for my being able to realize that this wasn't a situation just like everybody else's. They had their faults, but my father-in-law is a very devoted Christian and he was very faithful to God. God knew that I needed someone like him at that time, and also for Scott who was the head of our household. Scott needed a strong father figure for what was ahead. And nobody was going to show him that but his own father. God knew what he was doing!

I also came to understand that God gives us all choices in life. He allows things like accidents and illnesses to happen to test us to see how we will react. Because how could he really use us and have us on a close walk with him if he doesn't see what choices we will make with what He gives us, to see how we will handle it? Are we going to run away because we cannot stand seeing something? Or are we going to tackle trusting in Him no matter how hard the situation is that He's allowed us to be in for His reasons? And when I truly think of how God could do this to me...allow me to suffer watching my son for all those weeks fight for his life, to see day after day that my son was not walking; I humble myself, because look what we did to his son Jesus? Because of our sins, God had to watch his son suffer on that cross. Not only did His son suffer, but God planned His son's torture and death just because He loved me so much so that I may be with Him for eternity. It was there on my Emmaus Walk that I learned this. I can't imagine ever, and it shoots shivers down my spine, thinking about me planning the death and torture of my son just so everyone had a chance to be with me in Heaven for eternity.

So after I learned all this, the anger didn't go away but the things that I did learn on my walk sure helped a whole heck of a lot! It was scary to me. I was so angry and nothing and no one would be able to take the anger away. I hate to say it or admit it, but it was like I was in a whole different body, not mine at all. My anger just controlled me; although I tried really hard not to let it show. In fact, I tried so hard that people would tell me how strong I was and that they admired how well I handled everything. They would say that I made it look easy.

The reason I tell you these things is because I know that other people go through this at times during hardships. But with God's help, you can do it! I'm not kidding.

I want to be totally honest in my own words; just as I promised in the beginning of my book. I probably am going to be looked down upon by members of my church when this book comes out; but, it's all about the truth! There is a saying that 'truth sets you free' and it really does! I was so angry there for a while. I was the one looked at by some members of my church as *having it all together*. But I actually was mad to the very core of me and was so hurt to see the families of my church come in with the same kids that were in Chad's youth group! It's like I told you before during the Emmaus Walk. 'Here I was in God's house being mad at His people once again.' They would all stand up and sing and praise God and here I was peering down at Chad who was in his wheelchair! Their kids got talked and praised about for their accomplishments with college, jobs, or something they did at church to get recognized. Yet, here was my son in a chair, with scars all over his body...not even able to walk. If that was not bad enough, the rest of my kids had sad looks on their faces because they too felt what I felt, and was hurt to see their parents so sad.

Still it didn't end there. We would see family members for holidays. My nieces and nephews were all laughing and running around having great times with their parents. They were going to family reunions and this was really hard for me to see when we couldn't attend. The reunions would always be outside and it was hard for us with the wheelchair and all of Chad's needs. And when we would say, "maybe we shouldn't come," they would all question us as to why? Others didn't understand how hard the events in our lives were for us now.

When you have a spinal cord injury your body doesn't regulate your body temperature,. Hence, if it were really hot outside, Chad would get sick, or if it were too cold he would get sick with a cold. Being around everyone hugging on him, we risked infection all the time. So interacting with a lot of people just wasn't fun for us at all! This coupled with people who would say to us, "it's not your fault; Chad did it to himself. He made the choice to get on that motorcycle not you!" That made me angry too! I thought, *really. If it were really your son, could you be like that with your own child?* How do people have the nerve to say those types of things to grieving people? I am telling you, if it weren't for God I would be one miserable, hateful person!

Another thing that was really hard for me was when I told you in the beginning of this book about my nephew Kyle who had broken his neck. I don't know why and will probably never understand this because it's just one of those things, but everyone kept telling me that Kyle ended up walking the next day after his accident. What a miracle!

{Chad and Kyle after Kyle's broken neck injury}

And, yes, he did break his neck, but my goodness, at that time we sure never thought that we were going to be going through similar circumstances...but, of course, that went on much longer. His complications were a great deal more difficult because of the infections and hip replacements, and more.

Kyle never had all the other complications that Chad did, such as the crushed lungs, and all the broken bones Chad had. Chad's accident was much more severe than Kyle's was! And to tell you all the truth, I was really mad at God for not healing Chad after we prayed as a family for Kyle the night of Kyle's accident. Here we were all as a family for the first time praying together and God answered our prayers! Can you imagine what proud parents Scott and I were showing our children what good things come out of prayers? Especially when we all pray together as a family? I felt I looked like a total failure in the eyes of my children! And that made me so angry. I thought, *God how could you do this to me?* If he healed Kyle that easily why wouldn't he just do that for our son Chad?

Which brings me to this part: I know now since my nephew, Kyle who spent some time staying with us this summer feels guilty to some extent. Not that we are honestly sore at all or mad because God chose to heal him and not Chad right now. Praise God! I love this kid with all my heart! He and I have always been close since his accident. I know that's because Kyle knows how hard I prayed for him. I thank God everyday for him! But I think my sister and brother-in-law feel guilty or scared knowing that every time they look at their son Kyle that it could have been him in Chad's place. So that's why I say I couldn't fault them either for not coming and helping or visiting more often. That's a hard thing to see.

I will never forget the looks on their faces when they came home for a holiday and Chad had just burned his feet. I was changing bandages and although they didn't say anything, you could tell by the look on someone's face when they first see things like that! And really Kyle is so cute. He doesn't say anything, but he tries to be at Chad's level still after all the years those two have been together. Kyle gets in one of Chad's wheelchairs and goes around the house with him or he goes outside to do things with Chad. I think he kind of wants to experience what Chad is going through to help him more. And that is a blessing itself. No one asked or told Kyle to do that, he came up with the idea all on his own, that is a huge blessing, which I consider to have come from God!

People still are like this today at certain times. Yes, even my own family members, not all but some. But I keep in mind that God deals with those people now not me! Thank God! Like I said, 'He gives us choices' and I always think to myself, if God allowed this to happen to me in the blink of an eye – then it could happen to anybody! So I pray for people a lot and that really helps me feel better.

Chapter Twenty-Eight – Chad's First Step!

On February 24, 2009, Chad took his first itty bitty step at Bay Medical Center Rehab in Bay City, Michigan, and was later able to actually walk 185 feet! Oh that was such a day of joy for all of us! It was like watching him start walking all over again, which he was but as I thought through this all, I could see God had given me yet another glimpse to see my son take his first step again! How sweet is that? Honestly, I knew not every mother would want to have to be in a situation where she had to see her son have to learn to walk again.

There wasn't a dry eye in that rehab center! I remember the look on Chad's face! This was the big moment! Scott didn't believe me when I called to tell him! This was just four days after Chad's 19th birthday. So it was 19 years after his first step as a toddler that I got to see his legs move all over again!

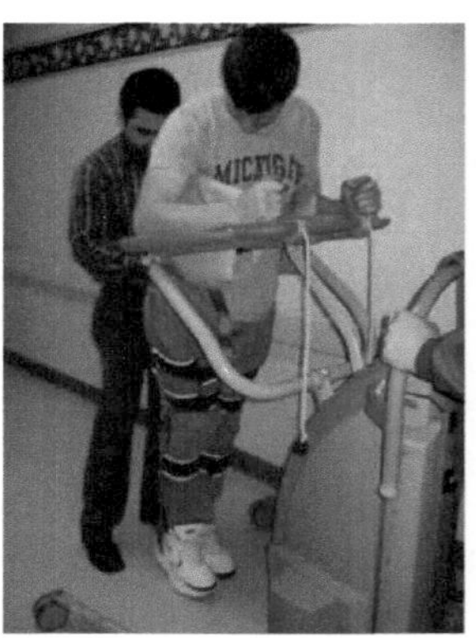

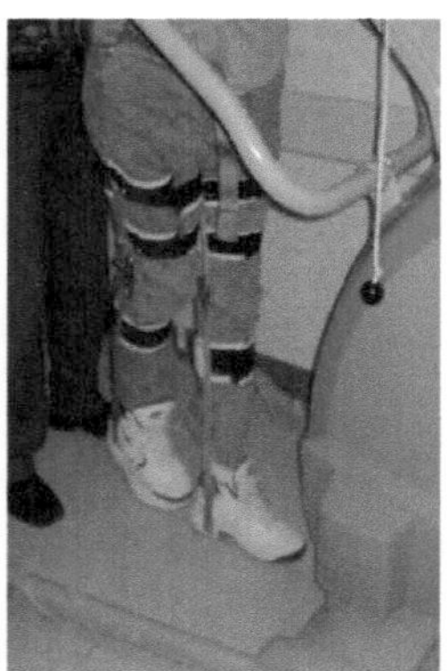

My daughter Kaitlyn had a co-op job at the center and she had been the one to suggest that we take Chad there for therapy. I thought why not? Kaitlyn actually had the idea that if I dropped Chad off for his appointments, she would be able to bring him home after her work-day was finished. We thought it was a great idea because it would give me a break and free my time up for me to spend more time with the rest of the family on that particular day.

Kaitlyn had come up with this idea because she said while working at *Bay Med*, there was a mother who had brought her son in every day for therapy from an accident of which he had been involved. My daughter stated the patient reminded her a great deal of Chad. As I observed this young man, I saw he could be a handful at times just like Chad. That's when Kaitlyn thought it would be great for me to have a break.

It was by the grace of God that I was present to see Chad take his first step. I had happened to stay that day to see what his therapist John was going to do with him as far as new treatment. Every rehab facility thus far was only interested in working with Chad to gain more upper-body strength. This was frustrating to me because I had been saying for a long time, "Chad needs to get up and at least stand!" No one would listen. Lifting weights was something Chad had been doing at home; but we needed someone or something that would assist him with standing and eventually walking.

John was really good for Chad. He said that seeing Chad walk was his goal from the first day he worked with our son. John used this device called the *Lite Gate*. It stabilized Chad's trunk so no one had to hold him up. With Chad's leg braces on, John was able to pull the *Lite Gate* machine by its wheels and Chad could try to swing his hips to walk. This worked! It's a true miracle of God! Even though the medical staff maintained that this would never be possible...on this day, it had been miraculously accomplished!

~

I was so happy that day. Chad was in disbelief. I decided not to report it on Chad's Care Pages due to all the grief we suffered when Chad never did walk as predicted on August 15, 2008, as predicted by Dr. Sears in *The Township Times* article earlier in the book. Some might say it was such a small step it might not even count as a step. To us, this was huge step forward for Chad! It was hope, after all. I thought to myself, *a step is a step no matter how big or little it is*!

So finally after praying about it for a while, I decided to tell everyone I could about Chad's miracle...I did this, of course, in hopes that someone else out there needed their hope to be refreshed and alive again. I figured no matter what I reported, people were going to render their own opinions and there was nothing I could do to change their minds; so, I might as well say it and speak about the things that were on my heart. And with telling our truths, I presented the first photo titled, "Chad's First Step!"

The First Step!

This was so awesome – words just can't explain it! Me seeing his step and the progress actually happening was too fantastic. Here was a second chance to see my son take his first steps again. And to be honest, it was even better than seeing him take his first steps as a toddler! I was so proud! As I said earlier, he was still in disbelief and if you ask him today, Chad will tell you he just got lucky. He would say that he is not walking fully yet so it doesn't count. Sure I have it on video and took pictures but it just doesn't do any justice until you see the miracle in person.

Sadly, there was a downside though to all of this. I don't know why people have to be so cruel, but Chad was so full of pride he...without any of us knowing...posted the video I had taken of him walking his 185 feet on U-tube. Tons of compliments appeared but there's always that one person who can open their mouth and spoil it for everyone. There was this one comment on the site that said, "This is just a kid swinging his hips this is not walking!"

The comment was so cruel, I thought! If this person who obviously opened their mouth before they thought, actually knew how hard our whole family had worked to see this one step happen...and how much effort and work had taken place on Chad's part to make this happen, then they may not have been so cruel. Chad tried to hide that this comment hadn't been hurtful, but we all knew it had been. And then that's when the new rule at the Clark household came alive. "If you can't say anything nice then say nothing at all!" And yes, it applied for all of us. My children would politely remind me of this when I would get mad at someone treating Chad badly with their comments saying they find it hard to believe he would walk!

I can do anything through him who gives me strength.

Philippians 4:13

Emails and Testimonies

The Care Pages was an Internet service that The University of Michigan offered to all their patients in order for them to be able to interact with one another about their injuries such as spinal cord or cancer, things like that. I had never heard of such a thing. It was also a way to let family and friends all at once keep up on what was happening with Chad.

These pages of posts were about people we had met and they assisted people in saving time, as well as the cost of long distance phone bills. Throughout all the time I had been posting updates on Chad's Care Pages, I had no idea that so many people around the world had been reading these posts! To be honest, I was updating Chad's pages to keep mostly family and friends updated so I wouldn't have to be on the phone all the time. I am not a phone talker, but still I knew people wanted to keep up on Chad's condition and progress which I felt much honored about.

I must confess that keeping up with the postings was good therapy for me also. It felt good to get some of those things out that were brewing inside at times. My goal became just to make people aware that things can be prevented in life and when that is not enough, and life deals you a bad hand you just deal with it and go on. No, that's not always easy to do, especially when you are watching someone you love suffer and your whole life has changed, but you find it must be done. I can't tell you how many people shared their stories with me. I was pleased and surprised to see the new friends I had not even met but had become family to me. I must confess, by reading how these different people got hurt and what they endured, what they had been able to do that day and what they struggled with on a daily basis, made me quit crying and feeling sorry for myself. The different posts made me fully realize and take to heart that there was always someone out there who was a lot worse off than us! And I believe that this also gave me the strength to fight. And I thank God for putting those people in my life!

Let us not become weary in doing good, for at the proper time we will reap a harvest if we do not give up!

Galatians 6:9

I never gave it a second thought that my postings were being read all over the world! This made my family not so happy with me because my life and our family life had become an open book. The way I looked at this was that God had given me a second chance, and changes needed to be made, and it was going to start with me. I felt in order to help someone...I needed to be honest. I needed to be real and I needed them to see the real side of the pain. Also, I needed them to see that with one accident, in the blink of an eye your world could be ripped away. But more so than all of that, I needed people to know that I had walked in their shoes, which meant that I had felt their pain. I had been where no one else had been unless Chad had not been in this accident, and I had to practice what I preached to my children!

Always, I have told them in order to tell the world about God and His love for us, you have to attract people to yourselves. We should go about attracting people in the world who are going to want to come and talk to you. If they think your life is perfect – if they think everything is wonderful for you all the time, they are going to stay away from you. People want to talk to others who have been where you have and felt what you felt. And so the Care Pages came alive!

And here is where I share with you once again people and Satan attacks, of course because they can't stand it when you are helping others! The green-eyed monster comes alive! My wonderful husband couldn't stand it if I misspelled a word, or said something that he felt wasn't appropriate! My kids were mad because not only was all their time taken up with being their brother Chad's caregiver, now they had to share me and with other people; and yes, I became a prayer fanatic for these poor other people and their families. So, that meant our family prayers were longer at mealtimes or bedtimes, but I knew in my heart I was doing what God wanted me to do. It meant that there were a lot of people judging me for things I'd said or even felt. Also, it meant being put in the spotlight and having to explain even when it was no one else's business but mine. It didn't matter to my family though, and *yes* that was very hurtful. Many nights I cried myself to sleep.

One day the joy overflowed when I got an email from someone saying how I had inspired them to push through, and because of me, this or that had changed in their life or situation. I began to be like Chad now; I felt I was to bring people to Christ! What an awesome feeling!

My other family members, cousins, etc… would try to call up my in-laws or Scott and start a fight because of something I wrote on our Care Page. I never wrote about any one of them and had never used their names at all; only my kids and my husband's. I had permission to use the name of doctors or whoever helped Chad or did something with Chad to post their names on the Care Pages. Later on, the Lord pressed upon my heart that these people who were trying to stir up trouble were feeling guilty about something and thought I was referring to them. Who knows! I learned a lesson, well, actually a couple of lessons: 1- that unless you are there in person to let people hear your tone of voice in what you say, then for someone to read what you wrote might not be a great idea. And 2- that some of these people that were complaining to my dear husband and in-laws to try and get me in trouble so to speak, must have had guilty consciences and maybe God was dealing with them individually! Besides those who really knew me and the person I really stood for would know that this is not where my heart was or is!

I prayed for thick skin if I was going to have to be dealing with these kinds of people. I remember saying to God one night,

"Well, God, if you really want me to do this and write on these Care Pages you better do something then to help me out! In no way do I want to waste time by putting out these fires when they would flare up. I had a much bigger vision than to have to be frustrated all the time. It's hard enough on my marriage and now having a child who is now in a wheelchair, to have to fight all the time with relatives who just don't get it!"

And God answered! Oh, the complaints didn't stop, and my husband did get a little perturbed from time to time, but I got the thick skin I asked for! Which to this day helps me out so much more than I ever dreamed it would. After all this time, I have had to fight for every single thing from insurance needs for Chad to the care he receives from professionals. I am not cutting anyone down at all. It's just that like I always say, *if they aren't walking in your shoes they have no idea what you need*. Even people who specialize in spinal cord injuries have no clue because – all they know is what to tell you to do – but doing what they tell you to – the way they tell you to – doesn't always work for everyone! Therefore, my prayer is for them to open their eyes to that! All I know is I had a mission in that I was not going to accept this from people believing that Chad would never walk again, and all this getting me in trouble stuff was going to have to go or I needed thicker skin because I had no time for nonsense! And most of all, I wasn't out to impress anyone but God. He knew my heart and that was all I cared about! Let Him be my judge!

Oh and one more thing, my praying time started to get longer and I found that God was indeed listening to me and helping me. I started to feel I was protected and thought that it was alright to always speak the truth and call on His name in time of need and if I did, God took care of everything! And I still run into this today. It happens in my own home, and church, with my own family members.

Chad's accident has really changed me and I believe for the better although I know a lot of people would disagree. I feel better for the person I have become. Now I can go to bed at night and when my head hits that pillow, I have a peaceful sleep. How you treat people is what comes back to you.

Funny thing is I used to be the person who would go out of my way to avoid someone especially if I knew they didn't care for me and even didn't want to talk to me. Now I am the person who says to myself, *we are all brothers and sisters in Christ;* so I am the one who goes up and starts a conversation or I am the one who says hello first. And I think when I see them and I know for sure they are going to avoid me I am not going to let them get away with that. To my surprise, I have had it happen that some people thought I was the one who didn't like them and that's why they didn't talk to me. Silly stuff guys! Get rid of it in your lives, let's talk to one another. And yes, it was a rude awakening for me, what I was doing myself to make anyone think I didn't like them. I'm just sharing these things with you all to simply tell you that I would have never learned these things if Chad hadn't had this accident. And this accident is the whole reason for this book. I have a much closer walk with God and I am a better person today because of my closer walk. So, in a nutshell, I am showing all of you who are reading my book how to save your own selves...so that a horrible thing like your child being in an accident doesn't have to happen to you to make you wake up and see life like it has been for me.

> *Be gracious to me, O God, for people trample on me; all day long foes oppress me: my enemies trample on me all day long, for many fights against me.*
>
> Psalm 56:1-2

So, this is the happy part of Chad's story! I had emails saying that because I shared my heart people were going to church for the first times in their lives! I had emails asking for me to pray for people who were also paralyzed by an accident. I had one Mom say I needed to share with her how I got my faith and how she could be more like me with her fifteen-year-old paralyzed son. And yes, I actually had a Mom who begged me to pray for her three year old daughter who was hit by a drunk driver and left paralyzed one day before her fourth birthday. My heart ached for these people. Then I had the desperate parents who told me they had lost their children. They just wanted me to pray for their pain. I felt so honored to have been asked to do that. And I must confess that as I posted about how badly I felt from time to time, I felt like such a fool because through emails, I found people who were worse off than me! How dare I cry about Chad and his situation when some parents don't even have their child with them.

Fortunately, I met lots of new people that I would have never met before. I found out many new ideas of treatments for Chad. There were many people who had stronger faith than mine. To me, I felt as if I was able to reduce some of their pain just by saying I understood them as we shared our stories. But to tell you the truth, my life was so much richer for meeting these people.

God did replace the people who found fault with me by allowing these wonderful people to come into my life. I have people now who are closer to me than my own relatives and you know that's okay too. I learned that some of Jesus' own family members hated Him and mistreated Him and turned away from Him. Makes me feel good actually; hey, I am more like Jesus than I thought! I must be honest, I have friends in high school that will say to me on occasion they never knew I was so religious. I say shame on me! My own pastor thinks I ought to become a pastor, who knows where the Lord will lead me. But I am open to anything! As long as it is good and the Lord has put his seal of approval on it!

I don't know if I should say this but: there's no stopping me now with all I have shared with you all so far, but, I know I have a very hard time sometimes keeping this religious stuff to myself. There are times I tend to overkill...to preach at people, and sometimes, I know that people are not ready to receive the things I say least of all how I say them. I have a huge problem especially with my kids and husband with trying to make them do things. I am always saying to them and this is wrong, I know; but, I tell them maybe things are still wrong and that's why Chad still isn't walking. I say things like – I don't know about them, but I have really learned with this accident and maybe they haven't learned anything by the way they are acting. Yep, I say it! And that's when once again my favorite verse comes to mind, "Be STILL and know that I am God!" He is simply saying to me, you don't have to shoot your big mouth off and force them to change, and you, Charee, don't have to judge them. Be still and leave that up to me! That's not your job and I love them just as much as I do you!

So, in conclusion, I found that this was my mission, no matter what anyone said to me about not posting from my heart. Maybe some things are supposed to be private and maybe I shouldn't share so much. I also have taken a lot and I do mean a lot of criticism about how I worded things, what I said, and what I shouldn't have said. I even had family members who believed I was picking on them. My response was that the Lord knew what was in my heart. He knew what He wanted to say through me, I was just a tool like Dr. Sears that God was using to help people. I prayed and prayed. *Yes* there were times I said I was going to stop just to make everyone shut up because God knows I had enough to deal with without adding the extra frustration from all the negative comments people had to say. I did stop posting for a while and I felt God speaking to me to continue; there was a need for this and I needed to finish this. I sure am glad I listened! It has been so rewarding! And I think it is one of many blessings God gave me.

The way I see it, people need to see what is real, they need to know how it works, especially in today's world. I thought if maybe people could see what our life was like on a day-to-day basis, maybe, just maybe, people would change. Quite possibly, maybe people would drive more carefully and maybe people who had motorcycles like Chad would be more careful. I was praying that people really would wake up and start caring about one another. This I didn't find to be happening too much yet, but I still pray every day for it and I am so thankful that some people have started to change. I always said from the beginning, by going through all this, if it only helped one person, then it was worth it, and that's all I was going for, was to save one person!

I later found that if I spent some time in prayer, my postings would be effective. I learned to have "tough skin". I could listen to someone get on me about something I posted or something I did and let it roll right off my back. I also let God deal with those people and like I mentioned before, it was well worth it if it helped bring one person to Christ! So, there you have it, the lesson? If you walk with the Lord and let Him guide you and pray about it, He will come through for you every time!

~

I am sorry that my family sometimes didn't want me to post, and yes, I am sorry if some people didn't agree with me or see things my way, but sometimes you have to take a stand and stand up for what you believe. I am so thankful though that my family stands behind me and has faith in me even if they don't agree.

Though my father and mother forsake me, the Lord will receive me.

Psalm 27:10

Hard Times and Lonely Times

You know, one would think if you had a loving family that you could get through things faster. It doesn't work that way. I learned that early on in the beginning of this whole ordeal. My feelings got hurt a lot in the beginning. I got sick of people telling me to stop doing everything for Chad. Also, I got sick of people just assuming that Chad was never going to walk because it has already been a couple years since his accident and he was still not walking. My family just assumed I had not faced reality and they were waiting for me to have a melt down. When that didn't happen, they stayed away. Or they just stopped calling and some stopped helping.

When I say lonely times I mean when I needed a break there was no one there for me. I needed just for once to stop running Chad around. I needed to have some time for me. This had become my new life taking care of Chad and all his needs and I had no time for me not even to be allowed to get sick myself. Everything and I do mean everything, revolved around Chad and what Chad needs. This threw me into a deep depression. Although I never sought help for this, mainly because there was no time for me to go and talk to someone, I just prayed through it, I kept repeating to myself, "The Lord never gives us more than we can handle." It got to be that I looked forward to the day just ending and I found when sleeping I didn't have to think or deal with anything.

Another thing that was really hurtful to me is that I really felt that my friends at the time stopped calling me or coming over because they couldn't deal with what I was dealing with and they were thankful it wasn't them. I hate to say this but even my own relatives would shy away. Many of them said this had been Chad's problem because he himself made the choice that day to get on that motorcycle. Many, like I mentioned earlier, were mad at Scott and me for allowing our son to have the motorcycle in the first place. Oh, and there was all those excuses, some of them lived too far away and the price of gas was just too much. It hurt at first but then the Lord laid on my heart if people were using excuses like that and not dropping things to come to my aid and help me even if they were family members then that meant the Lord didn't want them there to help me because it would have added more of a burden on me than it would helped me. And I believe that. Besides, it was true. Like I said earlier, I had a friend from church that had seven (7) adopted foster children that were from elementary age to teens who all had special needs. She had no help at home and she was the one who took my kids to get school supplies and school clothes! Get the picture? It wasn't easy at that time in my life. I had to deal with not knowing if Chad was even going to live and yet at the same time, I still had to deal with people. I vowed to never be one of those people. I even had, and this is no lie, the neighbors down the road who had a baby that was born prematurely before Chad's accident that I had watched since birth. When I came home with Chad to our new life and said I couldn't watch their baby anymore they were mad. Yet, they still kept asking me occasionally if I could sit while they went out. Yes, even a couple times they asked me to keep their baby overnight, knowing I was so busy with Chad and not getting sleep myself! It ruined our relationship.

When this is all thrown at you and you have no help and there are four other children to raise and devote time to; and a husband who is gone working endless hours in our family business with no help, one becomes overwhelmed. My experience includes people coming in and out of our house on a daily basis to do things with Chad and on top of all that, we were losing friendships. People were talking about how bad we were because we did this or that. To tell you the truth, it tends to just make you scream! That's really when I started talking to God. I would say to myself, "Well, I can say things to Him and He will know what I mean and how to take what I say. He will never stop wanting me for a friend. God will understand what I am going through, and I can scream and yell at the top of my lungs and tell Him how VERY angry I am at Him and He will always love me unconditional!

I will not leave you as orphans; I will come to you.

John 14:18

Scott was so busy with work, trying to keep the business going. Our older daughter Kayla had a manager job at one of the family business dry cleaning plants. Kaitlyn was a senior in high school and had a job to go to after school. Besides, this was supposed to be the best years of her life. That left Kaycee and Noah who were also going to school, and they needed time to be kids. I didn't want to bother them with this, it wouldn't be fair.

Scott would try to help when he got home from work but it usually just depressed him more and that in itself was enough to deal with. My Mom would offer to help, but she lived a distance away and she had been burdened with her Mother before she died, I couldn't ask her to do that again, it wouldn't be fair either. So, that left just me. I got through some how and Chad and I had our good days and our bad days. There were times when the rest of the family didn't even want to come home, they knew they would have to listen to Chad and I argue.

And surely I am with you always, to the very end of the age.

Matthew 28:20

Then there were the people who offered to help and when I did ask they made excuses or never showed up when they said they would. That happened a lot, especially with Chad's friends. They said they would come and get him and never showed up either or made excuses. Who could blame these people though? This was all new to us. Why would anyone in their right minds want to break a wheelchair apart in the cold and help someone in and out of the car and into their wheelchair all the time when they didn't have to? So, I just did what I had to do to make it through the day. Every day was a challenge. Those were the hard times.

We have pretty much made it through those days, thank God; Chad does a lot on his own now, but still requires some assistance from time to time. It does get better and like they say, *time does heal*; and, hopefully, those hard times are behind us. Hopefully, we are starting to get used to our new lives like it or not. It still isn't great, but I am thankful because it could have been a lot worse. And Chad has made remarkable progress!

Chapter Twenty-Nine – Three Hips Later

This chapter to me was by far my most frustrating one. The date I wrote this chapter was July 15, 2012; and, 'no' – five years since the accident and Chad is still not walking. Now here we are still going on the forth hip. Let me explain.

In order for Chad to stand or even take additional steps, he needs a hip. Remember in the crash he shattered his own hip and they did surgery on it and all was okay until he started therapy. We believe at the U of M the day he was to come home his hip fell out of the socket; and when he told them that, they just kind of sloughed it off...because...remember at this particular place, they believed he would never walk again! When Chad told the therapists there he felt like the hip had slipped out of the socket, well, they basically said it was impossible. One of the medical staff had said that even if it had, it would be alright and discharged him. And that's just what they did; on October 12th, 2007, the day Chad came home.

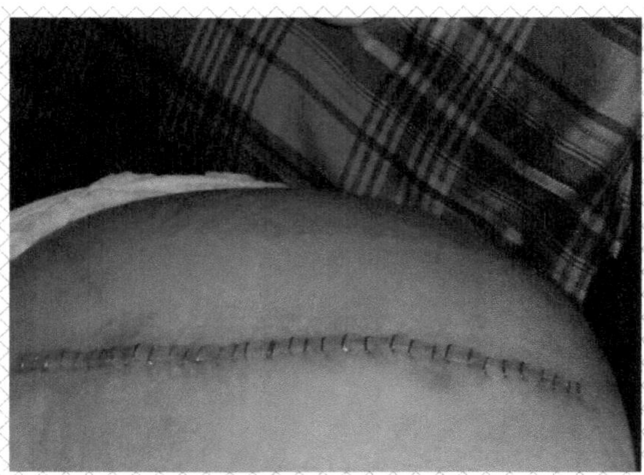

{Infection set in after third hip replacement}

Chad started therapy at home by Dr. Sears' instructions and it wasn't until Chad started sweating really bad and kept complaining of this ache in his right hip that we finally discovered the truth – the hip had indeed really fallen out of place.

When you are a spinal cord patient, your body has a way of sweating to tell you there's a problem because you can't feel that something is wrong. And as far as Chad complaining about the hip aching, it's true that he could not feel, but when he said it ached, we at first thought it was a good sign. So, then we tried to control the pain with mild pain killers. Nevertheless, this went on for several months, which caused us some alarm.

It wasn't until Chad started therapy at Bay Rehab Facility where Kaitlyn was doing her co-oping, that the therapist there said after Chad did walk those 185-feet that our son needed a hip. We knew he couldn't go on like this and the pain was getting to be too much for him. So with the therapist's recommendation to the health insurance company and a referral to the U of M doctor everyone had agreed that Chad should have his hip fixed. So surgery was set for January 24, 2009. Sadly, we did not know that with that surgery and date, yet another nightmare for us would begin.

The doctor first was hesitating to do this surgery because they still believed Chad would not walk. That was until I showed him the video of Chad walking those 185 feet. After seeing the video, the doctor thought that there might be some hope and he agreed to do the surgery. So they took Chad in the OR and gave us a beeper, which would activate when the surgery was completed. Sure enough, the beeper went off.

At 1:00 p.m. they took Chad in and at 1:13 p.m. the beeper went off. As Kayla, Scott and I looked at one another we knew something was up. And of course me, as worried and nervous as I'd been for so long...and being the natural worry wart, I got scared and thought he had passed. However, the doctor came out and took us in this little room and told us that our son was still on the operating table but he had made the decision as Chad's surgeon to just cut the ball off the top of the femur bone to alleviate Chad's pain. Hours earlier, I clearly remember my son saying to the doctor, "Just give me something I can walk on, and if you can't do that, please leave it alone!"

That's all I kept thinking about when the doctor told us about his decision. I mean Chad was still lying on the table not even closed up yet and the doctor comes out and tells us this! My thoughts were why couldn't he just come out and tell us this before he cut off the bone that holds the hip in the socket? This operation by the way was called a *girdle stone* and it was what they were supposed to give Chad. We were shocked! Seriously, we couldn't utter a sound! The damage had been done; this kid needed a hip! How does one walk without a hip? Honestly, I thought this was a sick joke.

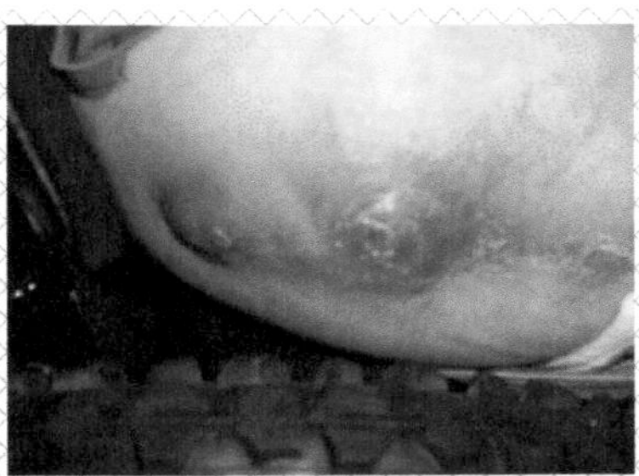

{Infection clearly evident}

The atmosphere changed so much so that I lost all hope at that moment. Sadness covered us all when we learned that Chad would not walk again. It was over as far as I was concerned and once again, I found myself furious with God! Where was God and why could He let this happen?

So after surgery, and while in the recovery room, the doctor came in; they somehow knew we weren't happy with our current status. He explained to us that the pain was his number one priority and that he had old people whose hip replacement hadn't work and they later on walked just fine without a hip. Seriously, I was still so angry I just wanted to slap him! We had just seen our son walk 185 feet when they said he would never do it and now what? It was like they just had to do this to prove they were going to be right.

Even after we arrived at home, honestly we were still in shock and didn't know what to do. To make matters worse, Chad did try therapy again and found he couldn't even stand on what was left of the hip. He had far too much pain and was changing his shirt at least seven times a day because it was soaked with sweat from the pain being unmanageable.

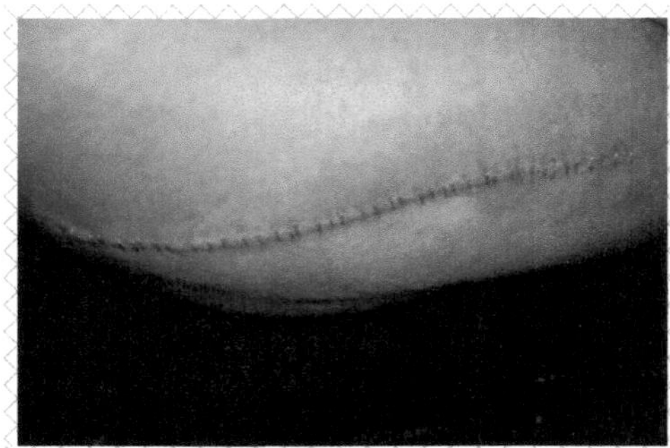

{The incision from third hip replacement – 44 staples}

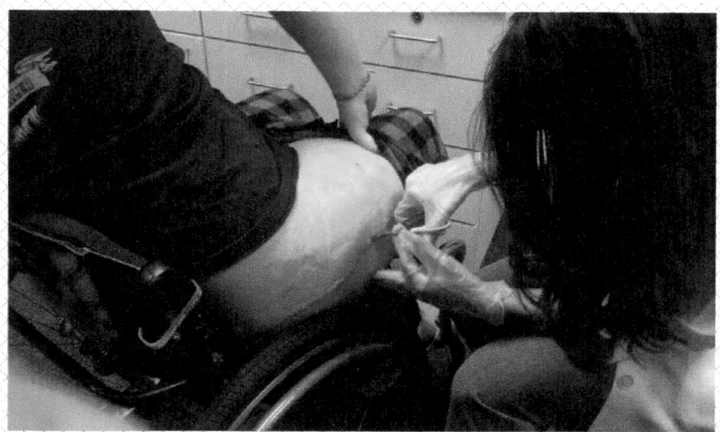

{Getting staples removed}

At this point, the therapists said they would no longer work with him until he had a hip. They gave us a lot of referrals but there were no doctors around where we lived who would touch Chad. They wouldn't touch him because at this point he had had a test done to see if the nerves were working in his legs and they were! The doctors here did not feel qualified to touch Chad in fear that while doing a hip surgery, they would touch the nerves that were waking up and then it was possible that the nerves would stop working.

Hence, I spent days, which turned into months, begging someone to look at my son and give him a total hip replacement! And on top on the nerves thing, the doctors were afraid that the hip replacement would not work because of the muscles not being able to hold the new hip in place.

With each new day I grew madder and angrier because I kept getting the doors slammed in my face. No one would help us and it seemed like God just didn't care to direct me and show me what to do. I finally got mad and fell down on my knees and told God that he had allowed this mess to happen and so I truly wanted him to be the one to fix it...I had had enough!

I told God that I had lost all hope and that I was sick of Him punishing us. I prayed that if this was what we had to keep going through and He wasn't going to step in and help us, then I was through with Him too! And, at the time, I meant it! I opened my mouth and sounded like an idiot to show God's Will to people. I had been kind and nice and above all forgiving! Oh it was not a pretty sight at all. And I am so ashamed of myself to this day for saying such things to God! I mean this was the loving God I talked about whom I knew was there with my son holding him while I wasn't at the accident. This is the same God who gave my son a second chance and gave him back to us. And, yes, He was also the same God who had shown us many miracles time and time again.

Well, after months of being lost and feeling alone and as if God had abandoned me, I poured my heart out on the Care Pages and my newly found friend, Susan Holt wrote and said that her son's fiancée, Lisa, (*yes*, this is the Josh that I told you earlier about who also was paralyzed and came to surprise us and meet us at out church the day we gave our testimony about Chad's accident), works with a orthopedic doctor who loves to tackle special cases like this and he was sure he could do something for Chad and put a hip in for him. So I called and made an appointment in Grand Rapids, Michigan.

Our first meeting I knew was a gift from God. Oh yes, it felt like I was on good terms again with God at this point because once again, He came through and fixed this mess.

The doctor was very confident, as he looked us in the eyes when he talked and said he would try to help Chad and recommended at new total hip replacement. So on October 3, 2010, Chad got his new hip. We had to be very careful; he was on complete bed rest for 90 days. The winter was very long, but we made it. I was praising and thanking God all this time.

It was also in my prayer time because I had a lot of praying to do especially humbling myself for being such an idiot and talking to God the way that I had earlier.

My son and I were both under 'lock and key', as I called it, for 90 days! Once again, I had to do everything for him! Dress him, lift him without lifting and bending 90 degrees with the new hip in place and all was well.

During our next doctor visit, they removed the 44 staples and everything seemed fine. We came home smiling and were talking with Chad on our long ride, as to what was next. Chad couldn't wait to get back to therapy. He also mentioned that he wanted to go to school now seeing as he was almost a year behind now in college. What a great day... well it was at least until that evening after dinner. I had come into my home office to catch up on some work I had missed being so busy with Chad, and after I put Chad into the shower, I put myself right to work. I felt it was okay because in this big ol'e farmhouse we have the bathroom adjacent to my office. So I could see and hear Chad if he needed me.

I was typing away at my computer – deep in thought as to what needed to be taken care of there...when, I looked up and saw my son fall from the shower bench right out on the floor trying to transfer into his wheelchair. Chad fell right on his hip that he had just had the staples removed from only hours earlier.

"Mom, I'm alright," Chad said. However, when I went to lift him up and get him back into his chair I saw a puddle of blood. He had torn open the incision and I never gave it a second thought that he could have knocked his hip out. So I called for Scott who was outside or Noah who was with him to come in the house and try to get Chad up for me as he was just too heavy for me now. They didn't hear me so I had no choice but to get him into his chair myself; which by the grace of God, I did. Next, I butterflyed his flap of skin back together. Later, Scott came in and said I did a good job. He thought everything was going to be okay. He never thought the hip could be out either.

About two weeks later, Chad started sweating and having pain again and *yes*, by then, it was too late for repairs to be made. We got an X-ray, which confirmed our worst fears. The hip had come out. So I called the doctor who told me to take him straight to our local ER and get more X-rays and send them right over to him that night.

They took Chad by ambulance to Grand Rapids and scheduled surgery for the following morning. They first tried to pop the hip back in place but it had been out too long and was too stiff to try to pop back in place.

Surgery for a second hip was scheduled for December 21, 2011. All I kept thinking was that it was a good thing my Christmas tree was up; my baking was done and presents had been purchased and wrapped! But more so than that, we saw another miracle! When the doctor came out and said he had put another hip back into Chad he said that it really was a miracle! He said that the bone had already started to grow around the new device they had put in for a hip and that while he was putting the hip in Chad he saw Chad's legs moving all around! The doctor had no explanation for it other than a gift from God! The best part of this I should tell you is that with a spinal cord patient, things grow really slowly because nothing is working in that area. That's why they call it paralyzed! But this proved to us in that short a period of time, which was 90 days or so, that Chad's bone had grown and accepted the new hip! The doctor said he would have never believed it if anyone were to tell him but because he did the surgery himself and it was his work, he knew it was an act of God! And he said he held high hopes for Chad to walk!

Still, things didn't go as well as we'd like. In the process of this next 90 days recovery for Chad, depression set in. He was frustrated with not having to do anything. Also he missed going to school and knew he was getting farther behind. But for me, this new set of 90 days brought me the ability to be in touch with God again. I asked God what I did for Chad's hip to come out the first time. I asked God why the doctor cut the bone off to begin with and we had to go through all this. And in the still and quiet, I heard Him say to me this, "YOU didn't ask that first doctor that you let work on your son if he were a Christian or not!"

My heart sank; it was true. Right then and there that I realized I had caused this to my son. Up until this point, every single person from the moment that the priest read Chad his last rights at the hospital, on the day of his accident if they were a Christian person or not. And I never once asked this doctor at the U of M if he was a Christian before he did the surgery. You may think I am crazy and have lost it now, but I swear it is the truth! Plus, I had doubts that this man was a man of God because he was the one who had doubt from the very beginning that Chad would ever walk! It all made sense now. So I repented to God and got on my knees to hear a very loud but calm voice say these words to me: "It is over my child. I am with you always; have peace, be still."

So the next 90 days came and went. We had Chad all scheduled for therapy after the next 47 staples came out after surgery. We were on top of the world until...unbelievably, the hip came out again. It wasn't anything Chad did, or didn't do, and it wasn't anyone else's fault. We all think that the muscle tone from being operated on that many times in a row was not strong enough to hold the new hip in. Our worlds crashed and burned that night. We called and made plans to go back to the hospital the next morning and we thought like always they would put Chad under and do surgery and he would be fitted into the surgery schedule. That's what we all expected.

Not knowing what was ahead of us or not, I remember saying to God that I had already made peace with Him. I fell in such a depressed state of mind, that I told God that if He wanted to take Chad, this time I was okay with it. Also Chad was so depressed thinking he would have to wait another 90 days...this kid had been doing nothing since October 3rd and this was now January 24th 2012.

The doctors told us after the second surgery that Chad's body had not had time to fully recover yet from the other surgeries and that this was a huge risk, but we didn't have a choice with the second surgery...so, this third surgery, I knew was going to take him. He looked so frail and white that this frightened me even more. So like I said...I made peace with God.

Every time when Chad was operated on, my son would tell me, 'don't worry, I'll be fine'. However, this time the words that came from his lips were, "Don't worry, Mom. This time if I don't make it I know where I am going, and I don't want to live like this anymore, for the rest of my life."

So what could I say? I fought back tears and I knew, I just knew, this was it. He was tired and had had enough. It was time. I called my friend Carolyn and even she heard it in my voice. And thank God for her wiliness to pray for me; I just couldn't pray. I couldn't do anything. I was sick.

Everyone waited all day for the doctor to get done with the surgeries already planned for his day. We knew Chad would be at the end, and by now it was 4:00 p.m. The doctor finally came in and said he was not doing surgery. He said it was too much of a risk to put Chad under. The doctor said that he had tried three times and failed and that he didn't know what else to do. We were all fighting back tears. Once again, it just got worse. Scott looked at Chad and I and said, "You two have to know that without a hip, Chad doesn't walk."

Chad looked at Scott in his hospital bed and said the most hurtful words of all, "Dad, I know you really want this for me and I do too, but it's just not meant to be." And Scott started to cry. He pleaded with the doctor to do something, to help us. The doctor said we all needed to pray and he would take the time to do some research and ask his colleague to advise him on what to do next. After all, his colleague was the one who told him how to reconstruct Chad's hip to begin with for the very first surgery.

It was a very long and quiet ride home. By the grace of God we got a call for an appointment later in the month on the 26th of July to see this new doctor. I prayed Chad would get a hip! Also on the 27th the very next day after Chad's doctor visit to see what would happen with getting him another hip, he had an appointment at Oakland Orthopedics to get new leg braces to walk. I kept this appointment because my belief was so strong and I was acting on my faith that God would take care of this and that Chad would need these leg braces after all!

There was even talk by the man who had tested Chad's nerves, to get the factory rep into the doctor's office to see this new device called The ReWalk system. The nerve doctor said Chad was a great candidate for this. Chad of course was fighting me on this because he said he didn't want to be a robot.

If you want to learn more, you should Google it on your computers, Google, www.rewalk.com.

Let me leave you all with this. No matter how bad it looks for us right now, I am still clinging to God's promise in His Word. "By Jesus' stripes we ARE healed.

I believe and know with my whole heart one day in God's time Chad will walk again. The lesson I have learned through this is, God is still with us. He has never left us, and has never promised us we would never go through trials here on earth. Even though on the 29th of July, it had been five years since he last walked – we still believe. But God is faithful still.

Chapter Thirty – "Merchant in The Valley" Movie

Little did we know that this movie was something Donta Young was starting before his accident; in fact, we didn't even have a clue that Chad would ever be involved in this movie at all. It was all just part of God's many miracles He had in store for us before this whole accident happened. It all makes sense now. However, if anyone were to tell me all this and that this would all happen one day, I would have never believed them. Anyway, back to this movie.

{Doug Carter (Donta's father) and Chad at the opening night of movie.}

Our youth pastor, Jesse, asked Chad when he first came home from the hospital if Chad would be interested in just holding the camera while they did some scenes and I suppose Jesse was asking Chad at the time to get our son involved in something to help him feel useful. Most likely they also wanted him to know that he was needed in the church still even after the motorcycle accident.

To my surprise, Chad agreed to hold the camera; so I went with his decision. However, I was worried every step of the way. Finally, I got down on my hands and knees and prayed, "Lord, my boy is still in your hands, if you want Chad to do something in this film then you have to watch out for him." And thus the movie began.

"Merchant in the Valley" is about cleaning up the streets here in Saginaw, Michigan, to help free Saginaw of gangs, drugs and crime. The movie also sends out a message to tell the gangs that God loves them. It also was meant to help them learn to rely on God and His love instead of drugs, guns, etc. The scenes were all shot here in Saginaw and Chad filmed the whole thing! He also starred in one scene. The movie was a huge hit here in Saginaw. We had our local Mayor and the police department working with us and all the support they gave us was great. My whole family (except for me) starred in the movie in one way or another.

There are many more miracles involved in this movie, like for example, Doug, Donta's father starred in the movie as well, and we also found out that Doug was also involved in the scholarship Kaitlyn received from FYI- Family Youth Initiative and that was why I wasn't in the movie. I was with Kaitlyn when the last scene was shot for a commercial for FYI and when we got there who do you think was the head of FYI? Yes, Doug. It is so incredible to think that God was using all of us for different things.

Now, one final thing I guess I should mention is that the writer of the movie, Gail Clark, was used by God. She utilized everyone, including Chad and Jesse to all come together to complete this movie project. We found out that Gail knew Donta and stopped working on this film when Donta had his accident. Later, when she was told who we were, and that we met Donta in the hospital...well, you can just imagine her face. We shared our story and she exchanged with us as the movie pieces unfolded. This was all of God and we knew it was going to be big.

The best part of this movie production was that it got finished. It finished big time, playing in our local movie theater for three weeks with 'sold out' performances. The movie was dedicated to Donta Young, and it brought all of us closer together. Hopefully, it did bring some people to Christ. Also the movie gave Chad a sense of accomplishment and pride. And I was amazed that Chad had this in him.

There was one scene in the movie where a drug dealer takes and throws his gun into the river – on a high bank. Just knowing Chad shot this scene from sitting in a wheelchair was incredible! And I say that's God at work! You see, God had a plan by this accident. He needed to use Chad to bring all of this together. It's just is so awesome to me to see and think of this. God knew all of our life and the way that it was to play out – even before Chad's birth.

ॐ-ॐ

You know, looking back on so many different events that have occurred since Chad's accident – the movie was just one of the many things that came from this terrible accident. I think some days why in the world God had to let this accident happen with Chad just to bring people together; just to bring people to Him, maybe to even bring Chad closer to Him. There are a lot of days I am proud that my son could accomplish the things he does. I kind of feel special and important like Mary sacrificing her Son, Jesus Christ, (although I know my son wasn't nearly that important). Nevertheless, I have to be honest also and tell you I get very mad still to this day. I ask myself, *has it been worth it*? *Do I really care that much – to live this life that is now hell just to save someone outside our family...and...maybe give them eternal life*?

Chad's accident has now gone on five long years, and when it all comes down to it, I have to say, *YES*! Even though my son lost his ability to walk, even though it hurts and makes me sick in the pit of my stomach, and even though this is just a living nightmare every single day of our lives; the answer is still *yes*. I have learned through this accident that's this is what it is all about; saving people and bringing them to Christ. That's what our mission was assigned to be here on earth, like it or not. And I think of Jesus hanging onto that cross in order to save me from all my sins so that I may have eternal life, I think this is a small sacrifice of what I could do for my God and Savior!

Chapter Thirty-One – God Provides

I am convinced that God knew what He was doing from the moment of Chad's horrible accident. Like I have stated before, God never left our sides for one second throughout this whole thing and He is still with us every single second of every single day.

From the beginning, God sent us the helicopter pilot who kissed me on the cheek to prove to me God was in control as the pilot said to me when he took Chad away, "he is in God's hands Mom, don't worry". And even before that, when we arrived at the hospital, the Chaplin met us and prayed with us. Afterward, Pastor Mark came from our church to help us be strong and keep our faith, and then God also sent friends and neighbors who had strong faith to pray with us.

I believe as I said earlier that God was preparing me when I said in, "You guys, this is an accident waiting to happen, and when it does, it's going to be bad!"

God was there when Chad was admitted in the ICU wing at U of M, when the doctor said, "He is in God's hands now, and just pray God will see you through."

As Chad remained in the ICU wing for those 7½weeks, God gave us excellent nurses who prayed with us and prayed over Chad. I mean daily. That was a real blessing!

When Scott and I didn't have a place to sleep, we were sleeping on chairs in Chad's room and in the lobby. The two of us slept anywhere we could sleep because we didn't have any money for a hotel. Our Pastor Mark came and said he wanted to pay for us to stay in a hotel at least for one night because we were so tired we couldn't even think anymore, but we told him, there were no rooms available at the hotel that was attached to the hospital and we were not leaving our son's side to go to another hotel. And low and behold, there was one cancellation the night Pastor Mark was there. He got us a room for one night..., that was all God you see, because to be able to have one of these rooms, you had to be on a waiting list, which we were and we told that to Pastor Mark, but he had faith, and still to this day, we don't know why when we were so far down on the waiting list for the next available room, we got a room but we did. It was only for one night, but it was great!

In our darkest hour, we were sitting in the lobby all alone while Chad was in surgery, wondering why God would allow this to happen. We were scared out of our minds, Scott and I just holding each other crying, and that's when I prayed to God for a sign. My husband and I desired something to show us God was in control and

He was there. I was so desperate, God knew it and that's when He sent Nyeesha. I wish I could put this into words, but words just do not do it justice but I will try.

Like I mentioned earlier, Scott and I were just holding each other crying. I was feeling my son was slipping away and worried that this might be the last time I was going to see him...when I kissed what I could see of his face as they took him to the operating room. I looked up just to see the profile of Nyeesha's face and it had a certain glow. I thought right away it has to be an angel! But it was such a peaceful feeling I felt, looking back on it now, one would think if you saw a real angel you would be really excited, get up, run to it, something. But not me, I sat there, just in awe, thinking how beautiful she was. For a minute I forgot about Chad and everything bad, I had this peaceful feeling, a certain calm that came over me and it felt wonderful! And that's when I looked around, everybody was doing their own thing, and I felt calm. Suddenly, Nyeesha came, bent down, put my hand in her hand and told us that she didn't know why, but the Lord had told her to come and tell us, it was going to be okay. She said that our son was going to be okay!

At that point, I remember Nyeesha asking us what had happened and if we did have a son. We told her our story and that's when we became friends and found out she too was from Saginaw! That's another blessing, we were so far away from home and I longed for a friend or something from Saginaw. I remember later on in our long stay in the ICU unit Nyeesha gave me a book called "The Power of a Praying Parent." That was another blessing to show me God's love for me and to reassure us He was still there!

And we can't forget, after our stay was up at that hospital hotel, we were back to sleeping in Chad's room in chairs. As we were having another bad day with Chad, I recall, Chad's lungs filling up with blood and they were collapsed. Our son's health situation didn't look good at all again. We were standing over Chad's bed praying and Scott and I looked up; Scott didn't know who this man was that came through Chad's door, and I of course didn't recognize him and really to be honest...didn't care, I was concerned with Chad and thought it was just a staff member checking Chad's machine or tubes or whatever. But Scott said he recognized this person but he didn't know from where, but as he looked up; this man had a certain glow about him also. Scott later described to me the same way I felt when I first saw Nyeesha before she came over to see us that day. The man turned out to be one of Scott's customer's. He lived in the Ann Arbor area, and he walked over to Scott and hugged him. He had hugged Scott and extended his hand out to Scott and in his hand he gave Scott a key, a key to his house which was only 20 minutes away from the hospital. This man's name was Mark LeChard. He offered us a mother-in-law suite that he had built onto his home that was not being used any longer. He informed us that we could stay there as long as we needed free of charge. And the best part was, when the rest of our family came for the weekend, they could stay there as well. A bonus was that we could spend the weekends with the rest of our family! Once again, God was right there, we needed a place to stay, and didn't have any money, and God provided!

There was just one little catch to this: I was not about to leave Chad alone no matter what, so God sent my father-in-law, Aveary, to spend the nights at the hospital by Chad's side so Scott and I could be together. The two of us needed to get a good night's sleep and we needed not to have to worry about Chad being alone. Another blessing that came out of this was that it gave Grandpa and Chad a chance to be together and actually, there were a few nights that were really rough but Grandpa pulled Chad through. And Chad has told us many times how he felt comforted to have Grandpa there.

Chapter Thirty-Two – My Memories

I try so hard to focus on the good things. Such as the day Chad graduated from high school. After they called his name, he walked away toward us with his diploma in hand. He looked at us in the bleachers and gave us the Rocky Balboa pose and yelled, "Yeah!" Our son looked so handsome! He was so happy! We were so happy.

{Noah proudly standing with his brother, Chad – Graduation Day]

To think that this would be one of the last times I would see my son walk and be so happy, it just kills me to think of it. Now, that's what I call priceless! Chad was so proud of himself and we were so very proud of him also, especially because he hated school so and thought he was never good at it.

~

Another fond memory I have is of Chad when he was three years old and was down in our basement lifting weights with Scott. He said, "Mom, I am going to be stronger than Daddy, when I get bigger!" He was so puny at the time; I thought to myself, *you just think that way, honey*.

ঌ-ঌ

{Dad (Scott) and Chad lifting weights}

When Chad was putting Wainscoting on our living room and dining room just the summer before his accident, he always wrote, *Chad and Dad were here* on the walls before he covered them up. Scott and I would get so frustrated thinking about why would a 17-year-old write such things. Were we wrong? Now I appreciate it and am never going to paint over it. It is a part of our house; well, under the Wainscoting now, but the writing is still there!

ঌ-ঌ

When our youngest daughter, Kaycee was born, Chad took to her right away. He taught her how to line up the little match box cars all over the counters in the kitchen and the bathrooms. He always called her buddy, and he always shared his candy with her, and yes, Chad still eats candy all the time. He even has told Ray at therapy by far Kaycee is his favorite sister! I say she is his partner in crime! And yes, in all honesty, he and Kaycee were my little hellions. Kaycee is not afraid to knock him out of his chair and wrestle with Chad on the floor. But Chad really loves all his sisters! He really does.

{Best buds – Chad and Kaycee}

Just recently Chad tried to tell Kaitlyn who she can and cannot see. As I said, he is very protective! If any of his friends make comments on how cute Kaitlyn is, Chad says, "Back off. She's my sister and you're not dating her!"

~

When Chad was still in that cute stage at three years, I remember us working on this old house constantly. If Scott and I were in a project and couldn't break away, Chad would tell us he was tired. If we failed to go right away and put him to bed, he would go slowly up the stairs dragging his *blankie* with a baseball cap on and tell us he was going to bed. We would go see if he really went to bed and he always piled a bunch of baseball caps on his head and yes, he'd be sleeping. It was the cutest thing ever! When he wanted to go to bed, he did and that was all there was to it.

~

The cutest story I always tell is when I was cutting the grass and Kayla and Chad were playing in our pool. Now, remember I told you Chad was my little daredevil. He was trying to catch bees and Kayla kept telling him not to do it and he wouldn't listen. So she was screaming at me to shut the lawnmower off and to tell him to stop. I warned him, and sure enough he got stung. So his little legs ran all around screaming and crying, "I got stinged, I got stinged!"

~

When the kids were little I would go to these business expos with Scott. Patty and Doug, Scott's sister and brother-in-law would watch the kids for us. It was not uncommon for Chad to fall out of one of their trees every time we were leaving and we would just keep going and Patty and Doug would laugh. They knew he would be fine. If anybody else was a quiet bystander watching this they would have called the authorities on us!

{Chad hanging from trees just for the fun of it!}

Chad always played a game when he was little. The game was he would get one of his sisters to play his partner which was a construction worker and they would go around with his little Fisher Price tools calling each other Jeff and Joe. I should have known right then and there that Chad would do something with his hands for a living, which is why he wants to be a welder, I bet.

One night Chad found a stray dog while working with Scott on one of our cars. He pleaded with us to let him keep this dog, which he later named Jack. This dog was the dog from you know where! Somehow Chad had trained this dog to take my towels while I was in the bathtub and carry them down the hall to his room. Every single time I got into the tub this would happen. And if that wasn't bad enough, he even managed to train his dog to nip me on the shoulder while in the tub.

{Chad and Noah with dog, Brynn}

{The boys in camo – Dad and Chad hunting}

I could go on and on about stories with Chad in them, but I will close this section with one last story...it will make you laugh. Just before Chad's accident, he had this habit of lighting fire crackers and throwing them around me while I was mowing the grass or using the weed whacker. He'd do it just to scare me. Of course, he never was unsafe in doing this; he knows how I feel about guns and big bangs. He loves to scare me or see me jump. And that's my little devil!

{Chad enjoying life before the accident}

Going out in Public

After our world at the hospital, we had to adjust to a whole new way of living. Taking Chad out in public was a whole new game to me. I call it a game because we never really knew what was going to happen, or who would win. Let me explain...

Getting Chad in and out of the car was a challenge, and to this day, it is different each time we do it. And then to lift the wheelchair in and out; wow! And with burned feet that you couldn't get wet in the middle of winter, well that even added more fun to the game! Not to mention, nobody could bump his feet. Chad's lungs were still on the mend and so, we had to be careful how much cold he breathed in, and we were always needing to be careful about those who were sick out in public. And no one told us about in-home therapy at this point!

Now, for the part in the game where I said you never knew who would win? Some people in today's world can be so cruel and stupid at the same time. Yep, believe it or not? I got called a lot of names from people who called me a rotten Mother for not getting my son in the car fast enough in Meijer's parking lot. People have even asked me why I parked in the handicapped spot, even after seeing me load the wheelchair in the back of my van; that's just plain cruel. I guess part of me believed that people would see...that they would notice...and be more careful around us – more sensitive.

Almost every aspect of the things we were all enduring was all new to me. If we actually treated our situations as if they were games, then who won depended on if I was having a bad day that day, or not. It depended on if I could just pray and ask God to forgive them because they knew nothing about this and to forgive me for the thoughts I was having about that person or their behavior! The truth of the matter was, people just really don't know unless they walk in your shoes!

A STORY KAYCEE WROTE FOR GUIDE POSTS ABOUT HER BROTHER:

Kaycee Clark - Age 12 - September 17, 2008

Everybody knows that motorcycle accidents are bad, but who knew that when it affects your family, how shattering it could be.

I remember that heartbreaking day like it was yesterday. I was outside shooting some hoops with my nine-year-old brother, Noah. Being the great basketball player that I am, all my shots were dead on. Well, not all of them I will have to admit. My seventeen-year-old sister, Kaitlyn, was cracking jokes at all of my missed shots. Little did we know this was no time for fun. I then heard the front door of my loving home slam shut, sounding like thunder on a dark rainy night. My mother zipped by me almost in tears. "Kids, I have to go to the hospital with your father," she choked up, us kids barely understanding half of what she said. Noah, Kaitlyn and I all looked puzzled and it seemed like too many questions were racing through my mind. I finally spoke up. "Well are you hurt or something?" I questioned. "No, no... it's your brother, Chad. He was on his motorcycle and a car collided with him. They say it's a hit-and-run accident. Chad is at the hospital right now. Please, ***please*** *pray for him. For goodness sake, he's only eighteen; and the doctors said he is not looking like he is going to make it."*

My mom and dad hopped inside the car and drove off. About a half an hour later my eldest sister, Kayla, came home from work. We told her the horrible news and she immediately drove us to the hospital that Chad was at. When we arrived there, a kind nurse directed us to Chad's emergency waiting room where he was with a Chaplin. He prayed with us non-stop for hours it seemed like. In the middle of our cries to God, a doctor shuffled into the room. He said his name was Dr. Nesbit and that he had been conducting surgeries on Chad for several hours. He then stated that my brother had been beaten up severely by the other car that had struck him. Dr. Nesbit told us that Chad had many injuries, including: loss of lung capacity, a broken shoulder, a shattered wrist, and many other broken bones. But the worst injury that the doctor said Chad had suffered from was a spinal chord injury located at T4 and T5 and that he would be paralyzed forever.

As soon as my parents heard this news she just broke down and started crying. My parents, who were always the strong ones, the people that would never let anything bring them down, and never cried, had just seemed like they had their whole world stripped away from them. The turning point that really hit me with reality was when my dad started to cry. My dad was always tough as nails and stronger than anybody I knew. And to see him weep over my brother, I knew that this was serious, this was real, this was actually happening to my family.

Once my parents had deescalated their hysterical crying, Dr. Nesbit told us that our best bet of Chad surviving this crash was to fly him down to Ann Arbor to stay there for a while. He said that they would know what to do. When we arrived down in Ann Arbor at the University of Michigan Hospital, the doctors there conducted more surgeries on Chad. My brother recovered the lung capacity that he so desperately needed, and they set his wrist back in place. The gifted doctors placed a plate in Chad's knee to set it in place and put his hip back into the socket.

But I don't believe that the doctors themselves healed my brother. I am convinced that God himself touched Chad and healed his injuries. Except for one; his spinal chord injury. But the doctors said that Chad would be a quadriplegic. In other words, he wouldn't be able to use his hands or have any control of his upper body. But God wouldn't let that happen to Chad. Every time you walked into that hospital room and touched Chad's head, you could feel God working in Chad, somehow, some way.

Chad is getting better each day. He is making a complete turnaround of what they said he wasn't going to do. My brother currently has full control of his upper body and is gaining more control over his legs each and every day. And I give all the glory to God.

To come to an end, I believe that the experience I had with Chad's motorcycle crash has drawn my family closer together. I was never really a religious person. I went to church every Sunday, but I was never really into the whole religious thing, but I am so much more religious now than I used to be. And I think that my family and I have gotten a lot closer with God.

MESSAGES LEFT ON CHAD'S CARE PAGES:

The thing that Sam and I remember the most is our dinner with your family the night before. Sam even remembers what we ate. It was a fun time, grace and bantering during dinner hour. At our house, Sam had just begun tearing the shelves down in the study to begin our home improvement project. All was well with the Clarks; all was well with the world. Then the next day our worlds changed. I thank you for your faith in God and I thank Him for His faith in us. God bless all of you. The Clark journey has touched us all.

My biggest memory is praying with everyone in the ICU. It was very powerful!

By: Tina Gutierrez

I will never forget 'the kiss' down in your basement when the kids were little that happened between Kelsey and Chad. They were so little and cute!

By: Patty Anklam

Charee,

I want faith like yours! My son Paul was in an accident and has been left paralyzed. I turned my back on God so many times because I wondered how he could do this. But your faith has made me turn back to Him. Please pray for my son and me, and also my husband Paul, you inspire me! God bless you all!

By: Shelley

No matter what life throws at you Charee, you always just push through it and just trust. How can you do that? I haven't met you but would really love to someday. Your faith is so strong, how do you do it? I continue to follow Chad's Care Page as your faith just inspires us all. We are so honored to pray for you! Please continue to post as you really have brought some of us through tough times by your faith.

By: An Unknown Church

One of my most favorite memories of Chad is how he always held the doors open for you, Charee when he was in grade school. And your kids were always so polite and respectful. And I always remember Chad and his smile! What a beautiful smile he has and it still continues to be contagious!

By: Unknown

My fondest memories of Chad were in Cub Scouts. What an awesome and respectful young man you and Scott were raising back then. Good job, wish more parents were like you! Chad, keep up the good fight. I was so honored to present that award to you when you were in third grade! You make us all proud!

By: Senator Mike Goshka

{Chad, as a Cub Scout]

Chapter Thirty-Three – Today

Chad is making progress more and more today. It's very slow like I said before. There are days when he can make his legs move, or his feet move from time to time. He has regained feeling in different parts of his lower body – some feeling that stays but mostly goes away. He has days when he can stand up himself, but hasn't actually taken any steps yet. His attitude is that he will walk one day and we all agree with him. Chad is a student at Delta College, taking a full semester of classes. He has a strong will, and fits all these things into a schedule. This has definitely changed Chad's life forever; I mean how could it not?

My hope is that I will live to see our son, Chad walk again. He struggles every day of his life. But I can honestly say this was an accident waiting to happen as I said in the beginning of our Story. The family feels like it was supposed to happen, but that at the same time, God had a hand in it and God will be still controlling this to the end.

~

I still have anger issues, but I am working on them. I have the hardest time while sitting in church especially and seeing all the kids Chad used to be in youth group with. I see them walk up in front of the church and get awards for things, or just plain seeing them walk makes me angry. I am only telling you all this from a Mother's point of view. Yes, I am human; and yes, this is all normal, but it doesn't mean I want to see anyone get hurt and not be able to walk. What really angers me is there are so many kids Chad's age that are in trouble with the law, or are on drugs, some of them drink too much alcohol and there are those who never seem to get punished by God. No, NOT that I would want them to suffer like Chad is, I'm just saying Chad was a good kid and wanted to do something with his life – so oftentimes, life seems unfair for him.

Every single day of my life since this accident I have learned to not take for granted each new day God has given me. I feel that I am blessed more in different ways because of all the good things God has given me. If I had not experienced this I would not be the person that I am today. Lately, I feel so much better about me. I learned to really love myself and my kids and husband in a way I truly believe most people will never in their whole time here on earth learn to appreciate. And the good people, I mean the people who would lay down their lives for you and they have your back no matter what, kind of people God brought into my life through this ordeal. I have had friends, and I am thankful for all of them, but the friends I have now are true friends, it's something I cannot put into words to try to explain to you.

❧-❧

Scott and I have a better marriage today. We are so much closer. And our relationship is so honest and pure. Our love really is a gift from God. My kids are closer, which makes me proud to see them together. I am so thankful to God for giving me all five blessings when some people can't even have children – here I have five! And they are all great kids! Scott and I, along with the rest of the family, stuck through this life-changing thing together. I can't tell you the number of professional people who have told me that most families don't come through this much stress and strife; marriages fail and siblings get into trouble with even less happening to them. I give all the credit to God.

> *Do not be anxious about anything, but in everything, by prayer and petition, with thanksgiving present your requests to God. And the peace of God. And the peace of God, which transcends all understanding, will guard your hearts and minds in Christ Jesus.*
>
> Philippians 4:6-7

Another thing today I have learned is if this accident had not happened, our son Chad might not have gone to Heaven. Until these events began, he didn't fully understand that Jesus came to save his sins, so he could go to Heaven.

❧-❧

The following notes are from our daughter, Kaycee and are how she views me today. She wrote this of me for an assignment. Her teacher thought I would like to see this. Wow, tears filled my eyes as I really thought I was not the favorite mother in the world anymore since Chad's accident. This is an example of how I feel God has let me know He approves of my parenting even through it all.

<u>Kaycee's View of Me Today</u>

Influence. The dictionary defines this word as *the action or process of producing effects on another person's actions*. But as for me, I can simplify this definition into one word: Mom. Most students would say their greatest influence would be their favorite teacher, a fellow peer, a best friend, a pastor, or even their sibling. But in my life, my greatest positive influence has been my mother, Charee Clark.

There are many strings of life that get knit together to make my mother the proud and dignified woman she is, despite the fact that she was raised in an abusive and drug-addicted household. One of these strings is being the mother of five children. In a single income home, she stretches our dollars farther than I would even think imaginable, even if that means she has to do without to make sure that I can get a good education. To show her unconditional love for my siblings and me, she has sacrificed more and opened many doors of opportunities to grow as a leader in my community. My mother is absolutely amazing.

Another reason my mother is such a positive influence in my life is her faith in Jesus Christ. As you have read, she was raised in a toxic environment, and has vowed that she will do everything in her power to make sure that her children are raised in a Bible-based home, with a requirement that all five children earn a college degree. She has always said she will take a second mortgage on the house and go into bankruptcy just so we will get a substantial education; never to end up in the position that she was destined for.

As is the way of life, no family is without struggles and difficulties in life. Every family has its story, but our family's story is just starting to see the light at the end of the tunnel. Our fairytale life has been a nightmare since 2007. The second oldest child graduates from high school, is ready to start college in the fall, but is involved in a hit-and-run accident several weeks after receiving his diploma and is left paralyzed from the waist down, fighting for his life. By 2008, my brother returns home to a completely modified, handicap-accessible home and our family begins the difficult journey towards finding a new normal. As much as it crushed my mother to see her child like this, as it would any loving mother, she renewed her strength in the Lord and got her other kids back on track in life and in school.

I could tell you countless accounts of why mother is such a strong influence in my life, but I think you would be reading for what would seem like an eternity. She has overcome so many obstacles in her life and always rises to the occasion to instill good morals and sound values in her children. I aspire to be even a fraction of a good influence on my children as she has been in my life.

My Beliefs on Religion

I believe what I am about to tell you with my whole heart and all that I am. God brings things in your life not to punish you but to bring you closer to Him. He allows things to happen to you but never leaves you. It's just like His word says, 'no matter what'. He brings these things to YOU to use YOU for His glory one day! I can only imagine what He has in store for me! I feel as if I have been tested and passed the test. And that no more bad things will ever happen to me as bad as this in my future.

It is also my belief that God is using Chad in this situation to help others. Without Chad being right down to these people's levels, no good would come out of it. I believe that I was shown through this the real pain others face on a daily basis. I believe that I have walked in some certain people's shoes. And for that I know I am a better person.

I know that God does exist. I saw one miracle after another throughout our journey and all that has resulted from Chad's accident. I have seen angelic beings in my son's room and things such as him moving parts of his body that experts said would never move in his lifetime.

God has placed special people in my life to get me through trial and tribulations. He has stayed with me; and I know that when you have experienced what we have, you also will know there is no other explanation for any of this except that God has been by our side the entire time.

I also believe and have learned this through this whole accident that every day is really a gift like you hear so many people say. Time really is short. And I have learned that when God gives you a blessing like the gift of a child, He means just what He says in His word; you are to bring that child up in Him. That means being willing to sit down and have talks with your child about God. Let the laundry go and allow the house to look dirty for a while. Start reading Bible stories to them when they are toddlers, so they are able to come to know Him. Just as I have said earlier on, we took Chad to church every Sunday. He was involved in the church but admits he never really came to know Christ until the day of his accident. God works in all sorts of ways. Some people may not agree and some people may even refuse to want to believe, but I know what I know, and I say it like it is. If people don't believe me or believe what is written in God's very own words then I feel really sorry for them. This I do not say lightly. My heart really aches for people who live in doubt because they are missing out! I cannot imagine what it would be like to have to go through this horrible mess if I didn't know the love of God. He has brought love and laughter to us in times of sheer panic to make the bad times go away.

Another thing that really makes me wonder is how people can say there is no God? How could everything exist then? I know there are tons of different opinions out there as to who created what, and all the many dinosaurs and ape theories but nobody can actually prove these; there is proof all over in God's word how these things came to be. In fact, both of my girls, Kayla and Kaycee, have done research papers on Creation vs. Evolution. They have even stumped their teachers who could not even explain what they're teaching our children today. Their answers to my girls were something such as, "Well, we don't really know we just have to teach it!" What? Are you kidding me? Teach what? They teach something that they don't even understand and yet they are teaching it to our children?

> *God is our refuge and strength. A very present help in trouble.*
>
> Psalm 46:1

I have become a better parent, wife, daughter, aunt and friend; hopefully a better Christian too! I have learned the need for me to be a disciple for God. Many people think they get to heaven by doing good works and by being nice to people. In my opinion that's not it, my friends. I know that the end of the world is right at hand. I know I will go to heaven with my family, and that I am no longer scared or terrified. Because of my relationship with God, I am no longer unsure of things in this world.

Today, I understand to the fullest extent that those people who have done me wrong have to deal with God. My main job is to forgive them and this I can easily do with God's help, if I rely on Him to guide me and continue being there for us as a family.

All of this is kind of all summed up in one lump sum – the way my understanding is today – as a woman of faith. There is a lot more to it than that. And I know it sounds as if that is just so easy for me to do, it's really hard work, most of the time I fail.

Still, I hold grudges and have to get down on my knees and really seek forgiveness and help to be able to forgive. One day at a time.

Without going through this deal with Chad, I would have in the past held grudges to those who did me wrong, or talked behind my back. My goodness, I get that so much more now! People really think I am a bad parent, setting up Chad with false hope. Some say that I am a religious freak, and that I have gone off the deep end. But I have peace, inner peace and it's something I have never had before.

In all actuality, it doesn't bother me what people say or how they treat me. I have learned to say the word 'no' to those who take advantage of me, and not feel guilty. And it is so true what I have always been told growing up, that is "when God is alive within you, you have peace, real peace!" It feels so great! That is what my wish would be for everyone to have real peace!

Chapter Thirty-Four – My Days

My days as a mom; seeing my son live this new life are still full of extremely hard days and nights...some-times it still feels like hell. I have good days, but there are still a lot of bad ones mixed in there with the rest! I have days when it takes all I have to get out of bed and move around the house. On some days, I cry all day. I struggle with this all and probably will until the day Chad walks again. And yes, there are days when I am so mad that no one can stand to be around me.

We are still a church going family and it shocks me that there are days that I really feel my anger even right there in God's house. Other times, my anger looks more like envy. Such as when I see one of Chad's friends getting an award, or getting engaged, or when someone who used to be in the youth group with Chad goes in front of the church for something; that's when the negative mood really hits me.

This is my favorite all-time Bible verse since Chad's accident. It's the one I cling to for dear life:

Be still and know that I am God...

Psalm 46:10

I do feel and know that even though my days now aren't how I dreamed they would be at my age, I still find many things each day that help me to be able to still praise God. He has shown us nothing but love and mercy.

Today was a good example of my returning anger. I got angry in our Sunday school class. Pastor was talking about how let down he felt when he prayed over Chad this past surgery and no miracles happened. There was a comment made from someone who said that they did pray over Chad's coat when it was being passed around. This was a revelation to me, as I had no clue my church had passed around and prayed over Chad's coat...just learned this today, but I thank God they did! Anyway, one of the ladies said, "There is a reason even though we all prayed and continue to pray even though it looks like God isn't healing Chad, and that may be that we need to just accept it."

Her comment hurt. I looked at Chad and both he and I had tears in our eyes, and yep, I felt anger burning inside me thinking if this was her and she was in our situation and had to watch one of her kids that she has to watch daily going through this, would she have said such a thing? It's like I said, "It's all together different if you are the one in a life-changing traumatic position.

In Closing...

So my friends, I encourage you all to find and to take your closer walk with God. I pray you never have to do it like I did but I pray that you all walk away with something with these words I have written. We never know how much time we have left or where life is going to take us at any moment. But I pray that you know of God's love and mercy and know that He does stick true to His word. He does love you without any end. His love is like no others. There is nothing in this world you could ever do or have done in the past to ever make God turn away from you.

I would like to share that even though I have said some pretty terrible things in this book, I have shared my whole life with you and admitted things from my past and how I grew up; it's all a part of who I am. I told you from the beginning that I would speak, or in this case, write nothing but the truth, and I have.

My thanks go out to my family on both sides, for being in my life. I admire my father who did have an alcohol problem and love my parents even though they did divorce when I was 26. After leaving home, and getting married to Scott, we had children of our own. Thinking back my memories are of my dad who always put food on the table and of my parents who always made sure we had a roof over our heads. Through Chad's accident I was able to forgive them and I have a better relationship with my father now than I ever did and yes, I used to be a daddy's girl in spite of everything.

I hardly see my mother as she has a new life with her new husband. They live 40 minutes away now from me; however, she lives about three minutes from my sister. Mother enjoys helping my sister with her two boys. Still, I know mother prays for us and I pray that our relationship will improve over time. Also I pray that my only sister and sibling, and I will continue growing as sisters, who love each other. I leave that in God's hands. He knows my heart and He knows I love and cherish my entire family.

My prayers have helped me to learn to let go and let God rebuild any relationships that have gone sour, and as I shared with you a lot of them have due to this accident. But I would only flub anything up if I tried to change people's minds or talk them into anything; besides, they are not going to listen to me anyway and I have found if I give it to God I get to see the result and I am convinced of God's great ability to show me miracles. God does answer my prayers! That's really cool!

All of what I've written is my story, and I pray that my readers will realize that this story is my view...only my opinion and my opinion only. It's MY story no one else's and I have written it to inspire others not to cause conflict with anyone. Some of you may not agree. You may believe there is no God, and you may even believe that God really does punish people. I can only pray and share what I have learned through the course of this terrible accident.

Your relationship with God is what you put into it, not just with God but with anyone. We all have trials in life. God never promised us we wouldn't, but what He did promise is He would never leave us. I found this out through Chad's accident. It feels like my son, my family and I went on a long journey and we actually haven't come back yet. In fact, maybe I never will wholly return, but I have learned and experienced things I know I never would have in my whole life had this accident not happened. Has it changed me forever? Absolutely! But if my story inspires people, it will be worth the hurt. Some days I think, *yes, it's been worth it*. On other days, I think *no*. But I have to believe that God must really think I am a strong person in Him to have put me through such a trial.

Do I think I am one of God's favorites? That's the question I always get asked by the way. People say that God did this to make me strong and that He only does that to people He loves because He wants to make sure they can handle hard things. I don't know. I don't like to think of God as having favorites although in His word He does. I just refuse to lie down and waste any time. Life does go on; every day is a gift and like everyone else, I never know when my last day will be.

~

What really inspired me to write this story were three things:

1. I read the book by Steven Curtis Chapman's wife, Mary Beth, "Choosing to SEE". This was a book about the loss of their adopted little girl who their biological son accidentally ran over with the family car. The little girl's life tragically ended in such a sad way. This was a Christian family and Steven is a well known Christian song writer. I'm sure his life is one lived for the Lord. He and his family were I'm positive trying to do everything right. These two parents parented together and they did it by putting the Lord first, and this tragic event happened to them. I started thinking back then if this is how the Lord shows you that you are his favorite then I don't want any part of it...that is, UNTIL I read this book.

2. Watching my son fight every day and knowing all the love we have for each other. Life is awesome when I think of all the joy

and true peace we have and I think back on all the miracles we have been shown. Right now I am about as close to God as I have ever been in my life and had it not been for Chad's accident I don't think I would have ever known any of this.

Another thing to share with my readers is that I can tell you the fact is God talks to me. I hear his voice. It's a voice words cannot explain but it's the same voice and you know it when you hear it. People think I am crazy, but I KNOW what I KNOW! My family is so close and I can honestly say that although I know we weren't the perfect parents and contrary to that, God has really blessed us with all five beautiful children. God gives me His approval every day on how well we have raised those five blessings. Daily we see it and it is such a great feeling to know God is pleased with you. How nice it is to know you don't have to wonder; you just feel it!

3. I want all of you to have what I have. I want you all to experience what I have and the things we have gotten to do! It's so awesome! I have so many people say to me they want what I have. When in fact, I have no clue what they are talking about and laugh sometimes as I think to myself, "really, you want my life, do you really know how my life is?" When I do ask people what they mean, they tell me they want to be happy, and joyful, and feel peace and no worry. They want to experience God the way I do, which is an honor.

Below are a few pictures we felt we would
Close By Helping
You
Remember
The
Clark Family

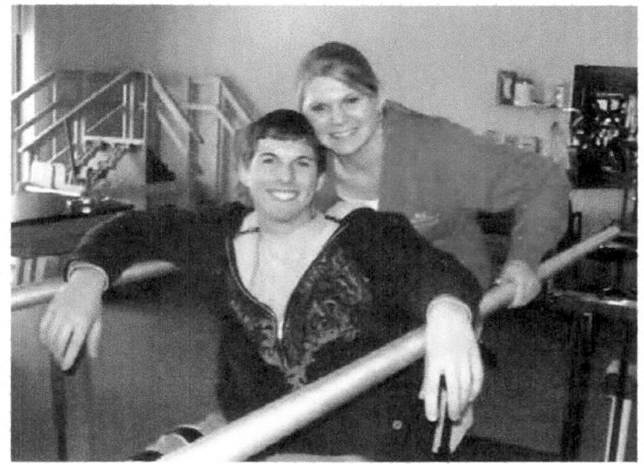

{Kaitlyn helping Chad to enjoy therapy}

{Noah, Kayla and Chad at Kayla's graduation}

{Noah along with his brother Chad and Dad}

{Scott (Dad) proving you can play horsey with 3 kids at once}

{Chad enjoying his many friends}

{Chad using water therapy to stay healthy}

And perhaps – by looking to the future, you too will be instrumental in helping Chad Clark receive an ability to walk again. Or, maybe there will come a day that one of you – one of the readers of our book – will know a physician who will be willing to take a chance and put a 4th hip in him. Quite possibly you know someone who would be willing to go the extra mile and help Chad to walk even without a new hip...

We Believe in Miracles
And we want you to know,
for The Clark Family
this is
Not
The End
For us it is only a beginning!

Please notify our publisher @ editorshepherd@gmail.com or you can email me direct @ theclarks6211@yahoo.com
to communicate with Chad.

Music and Literature that means a great deal to us and helped us all endure these hard times

~

1. Don't Laugh At Me—Mark Wills
2. Anyway—Martina McBride
3. The Impossible—Joe Nichols
4. Jesus Friend Of Sinners—Casting Crowns
5. Heaven Is The Face—Steven Curtis Chapman
6. I Can Only Imagine—MercyMe
7. What Faith Can Do—Kutless
8. Get Back Up—Toby Mack
9. Hero—Abandon
10. The Words I would Say—Sidewalk Prophets
11. Word Of God Speak—Mercy Me
12. My Hope Is In You Lord—Aaron Shust
13. If We've Ever Needed You—Casting Crowns

Music and Literature that means a great deal to us and helped us all endure these hard times

~

14. Learning To Be The Light—Newworldson

15. Carry Me to the Cross—Kutless

16. Blessings—Laura Story

17. Here—Kari Jobe

18. Rise—Shawn McDonald

19. Your Grace Is Enough—Matt Maher

20. Seek Ye First—Praise 2012

21. Better Than a Hallelujah—Amy Grant

22. Hungry Falling On My Knees—Joy Williams

23. Even if the Healing Doesn't Come—Kutless

24. Worn—Tenth Avenue North

Music and Literature that means a great deal to us and helped us all endure these hard times

~

MOVIES:

1. The Blind Side
2. Faith Like Potatoes
3. To Save A Life
4. The Fifth Quarter
5. A Christmas Child
6. Angel Dog
7. The Christmas Shoes
8. The Last Sin Eater
9. A Christmas Snow (a great one on learning to forgive)
10. Live To Forgive
11. Courageous
12. Radio

"Charee Clark would like to thank the following people for all of their support to make this book possible"

~

Carl and Carolyn Maksimowicz

Esther Egbert

Jeanette Taylor

Kathleen, John & Isabel McKinnon

Mary Gomez

Carmen Burrola

Nancy Cardenas

Ann Fowler

Judy Warzecha

Delores Rescigno

Author's Note

"One day, after deciding to write this book, I was on the telephone with VicToria Freudiger, owner/publisher of Entry Way Publishing. We spoke in great detail about the process of how I would go about getting this book published.

After we spoke of the many aspects that are involved, I was looking for a sign as to whether I should use her publishing company or keep researching for a different publisher.

Ms. Freudiger had explained numerous packages to consider that Entry Way has to offer along with the cost of editing, proofreading, formatting, cover design, photo cleanup and printing, etc. in case I would want to hire them on an hourly basis. Once I learned how much money I would need as a down payment to get started, everything began to feel like this was really going to come to fruition. As I was talking to her, I was opening my mail and praying in my head to God for a sign. Just after VicToria gave me the amount of money needed to open the account with Entry Way, I opened a card from a friend only to find a check enclosed for the exact amount VicToria had just quoted. Talk about a quick response from God!"

Though it has been a long process from the day I began writing until now, I want to thank Entry Way Publishing and their staff for doing a professional and top quality job. Also we'd like to thank them for being a company who loves God. A special thanks goes to Linda T. Phillips for our cover design and photo cleanup work.